Broadway Christian Church Fort Wayne
Living Above The Level of Mediocrity:...   CL01 Swi
Swindo'

P9-DDM-323

0000   3531

LIVING ABOVE THE LEVEL OF
MEDIOCRITY

OTHER PUBLICATIONS BY CHARLES R. SWINDOLL

Books:

Come Before Winter
Compassion: Showing Care in a
  Careless World
Dropping Your Guard
Encourage Me
For Those Who Hurt
Growing Deep in the Christian
  Life
Growing Strong in the Seasons
  of Life
Hand Me Another Brick
Improving Your Serve
Killing Giants, Pulling Thorns
Leadership: Influence that
  Inspires

Living on the Ragged Edge
Make Up Your Mind
The Quest for Character
Recovery: When Healing Takes
  Time
Standing Out
Starting Over
Strengthening Your Grip
Strike the Original Match
Three Steps Forward, Two Steps
  Back
Victory: A Winning Game Plan
  for Life
You and Your Child

Booklets:

Anger
Attitudes
Commitment
Dealing with Defiance
Demonism
Destiny
Divorce
Eternal Security
God's Will
Hope
Impossibilities
Integrity
Leisure

The Lonely Whine of the Top
  Dog
Moral Purity
Our Mediator
Peace in Spite of Panic
Prayer
Sensuality
Singleness
Stress
Tongues
When Your Comfort Zone Gets
  the Squeeze
Woman

Films:

People of Refuge
Strengthening Your Grip

Charles R. Swindoll

LIVING ABOVE THE LEVEL OF MEDIOCRITY

A Commitment to
Excellence

WORD BOOKS
PUBLISHER
WACO, TEXAS
A DIVISION OF
WORD, INCORPORATED

PROPERTY OF
BROADWAY CHRISTIAN CHURCH LIBRARY
910 BROADWAY
FORT WAYNE, IN 46802

LIVING ABOVE THE LEVEL OF MEDIOCRITY: A COMMITMENT TO EXCELLENCE

Copyright © 1987 by Charles R. Swindoll.
All rights reserved. No portion of this book may be reproduced in any
form, except for brief quotations in reviews, without written permission
from the publisher.

Unless otherwise indicated, Scripture quotations are from the New American
Standard Bible, © The Lockman Foundation 1960, 1962, 1963, 1968, 1971, 1972,
1973, 1975, 1977.
Other Scripture quotations are from the following sources: The Amplified Bible (AMP).
Copyright © 1965 Zondervan Publishing House. Used by permission. *The Living Bible*
(TLB), copyright 1971 by Tyndale House Publishers, Wheaton, IL. Used by permission.
The Modern Language Bible (MLB), The Berkeley Version in Modern English.
Copyright © 1945, 1959, 1969 by Zondervan Publishing House. Used by permission.
The New Testament in Modern English (*Phillips*) by J. B. Phillips, published by The
Macmillan Company, © 1958, 1960, 1972 by J. B. Phillips. The *Good News Bible*,
Today's English Version (TEV)—Old Testament: Copyright © American Bible Society
1976; New Testament: Copyright © American Bible Society 1966, 1971, 1976.

An effort has been made to locate sources and obtain permission where necessary for
the quotations used in this book. In the event of any unintentional omission,
modifications will be gladly incorporated in future editions.

Library of Congress Cataloging-in-Publication Data:

Swindoll, Charles R.
   Living above the level of mediocrity.

   1. Success.   I. Title
BF637.S8S863   1987   158'.1   87–10537
ISBN 0-8499-0564-8

7 8 9 8 MP 9 8 7 6 5 4 3 2 1

Printed in the United States of America

I know of no one who better models the
message of this book than my wife Cynthia
and those who work on her leadership
team at *Insight for Living*.

With admirable virtue, contagious
enthusiasm, and tireless effort,
each one represents an unconditional
commitment to excellence.

Because *mediocre* is not even a word in
their vocabulary, they have become
a pacesetting group of innovative
thinkers and creative leaders,
encouraging others to live above
the level of mediocrity.

It is with great delight that
I dedicate this volume to those
eagles who soar high . . .
and love every
minute of it.

Contents

Aim So High You'll Never Be Bored!

The
greatest waste
of our
natural resources
is the
number of
people
who never
achieve their
potential.
Get out
of that
slow lane.
Shift
into that
fast lane.
If you think
you can't,
you won't.
If you think
you can,
there's a
good chance
you will.
Even making
the effort
will make
you feel
like a new
person.
Reputations
are made
by searching
for things that
can't be done
and doing them.
Aim low:
boring.
Aim high:
soaring.

Reprinted by permission of United Technologies.

Who's Calling Your Cadence?

. . . it is a wretched taste to be gratified with mediocrity when the excellent lies before us.

—Isaac D'Israeli, 1834

Soaring. That's what this book is about. Not grubbing for worms or scratching for bugs like a pen full of chickens, but soaring like a powerful eagle . . . living above the level of mediocrity, refusing to let the majority shape your standard. Being different on purpose. Aiming high. Soaring isn't something that comes naturally, you understand, nor is it easy. But it can happen, believe me.

Thirty years ago I was a raw recruit in boot camp. Even back then the Marine Corps was "looking for a few good men," so I decided to give it my best shot. What a decision! I'm still a little amazed I lived to tell the story.

The strange world I stepped into was full of bewildering, shocking, and unpredictable activities. The schedule was busy and demanding, one designed to turn undisciplined young civilians into determined fighting men (an objective I heard repeated numerous times during those weeks of basic training). Time and again—especially when our enthusiasm began to flag—we were reminded that the difficulty of the training was *imperative*. Like it or not, we were soft. And in order for us to overcome the odds we were sure to face in battle, we must be prepared. The rigors of warfare would blow us away unless our minds and bodies were tough enough to withstand the demands made upon us.

Looking back, I realize that one of the reasons (no doubt, the major reason) my buddies and I survived was this: We learned to respect our "final voice of authority"—namely, the drill instructor. You will understand how I mean it when I say that for those weeks in boot camp . . . he was "God." Without question, we did precisely what he said to do. Without hesitation, we went precisely where he pointed. We jumped at his command. We marched to his cadence . . . no questions asked.

Matter of fact, we learned to distinguish his voice from the many others on the drill field. Hard as it may be for you to believe, we could follow his directions without difficulty on a field full of a dozen or more other DIs, each one barking out commands and verbal orders. It took time, but within a few weeks each company of young Marines knew the master's voice. When another shouted his instructions, we deliberately ignored the order. But when ours gave the order, we moved instantly. It took weeks to develop that kind of discipline; but finally, after endless hours of constant, painful repetition, it all fell into place.

Three decades have passed since those unforgettable days in boot camp. But some of the lessons learned back then are still with me—lessons like listening to the right voice, like ignoring the movements of the majority, and like being disciplined enough to filter the essential from the incidental. The ramifications of this kind of discipline have been life-changing. They include, for example, committing myself to excellence while many are comfortable with the mediocre, aiming high though most seem to prefer the boredom of aiming low, and marching to the distinct beat of another drummer while surrounded by a cacophony of persuasive sounds pleading for me to join their ranks. Remember Henry David Thoreau's immortal words?

> If a man does not keep pace with his companions, perhaps it is because he hears a different drummer. Let him step to the music which he hears, however, measured or far away.

One of Thoreau's contemporaries, James Russell Lowell, put it another way. He placed great value on aiming high:

> Life is a leaf of paper white
> Whereon each one of us may write
> His word or two, and then comes night.
>
> Greatly begin! though thou have time
> But for a line, be that sublime—
> Not failure, but low aim, is crime.

Long enough has mediocrity called our cadence! Long enough have we taken our cues from those who ask, "Why be different?" or reason, "Let's do just enough to get by." Long enough have we settled for less than our best and convinced ourselves that quality and integrity and authenticity are negotiables. Call me a dreamer, but I'm convinced that achieving one's full potential is still a goal worth striving for—that excellence is still worth pursuing even if most yawn and a few sneer. And, yes, even if I should fail occasionally while reaching. Failure, remember, is not the crime.

Somehow I feel I'm not alone. While there may not be millions out there who think like this, there are some. You are probably among them or you wouldn't have picked up this book in the first place. If I'm talking your language, then stay with me. There's a lot more to be said!

Before doing so, I must express my gratitude to Ernie Owen and Kip Jordon of Word Books. Their mutual encouragement has spurred me on! Beverly Phillips, my editor at Word, deserves high praise for her tireless efforts as she has assisted me through the painstaking process of making my thoughts more readable. I'm also grateful to Michael Standlee for his creative design of both book jacket and division pages. The splendid drawings of eagles throughout the book were done by Dennis Hill, who went far beyond the call of duty in both his careful research and vivid artistry. And, again, I am indebted to Helen Peters, my faithful and diligent secretary, whose own commitment to excellence has never once wavered. Were it not for her remarkable ability to interpret my handwritten sheets, I'm afraid these pages would represent the very thing I stand against—*mediocrity.* I am especially grateful for her assistance with my footnotes—the bane of any author who is not a perfectionist. I could name many others—mentors, friends, colleagues, and family members—whose words and lives have contributed immensely to this volume. I consider myself enriched to have been surrounded by such models of excellence.

And so, my fellow eagle, we're off! And by the time we have completed this flight, we shall be more committed than ever to a life of excellence. We'll be so encouraged that it's doubtful we can ever be satisfied living anywhere near the level of mediocrity again. But then why should we? That's where life gets dull, drab, predictable, and tiring. Or perhaps the most descriptive word is *boring,* a direct result of low aim. Let's lift our sights and aim so high that we start doing the thing God made us for: soaring.

Chuck Swindoll
Fullerton, California

*The mountains are fountains of
men as well as of rivers, of
glaciers, of fertile soil. The great
poets, philosophers, prophets, able
men whose thought and deeds have
moved the world, have come down
from the mountains —
mountain-dwellers who have
grown strong there with the forest
trees in Nature's workshops.*

John Muir
1938

Part One

Confronting Mediocrity Takes Thinking Clearly

It Starts
in Your
Mind

1

Soaring never just happens. It is the result of strong mental effort—thinking clearly, courageously, confidently. No one ever oozed his way out of mediocrity like a lazy slug. Everyone I know who models a high level of excellence has won the battle of the mind and taken the right thoughts captive. The risks notwithstanding, these individuals have chosen to fill the role of an active pen flowing with ink rather than a passive blotter that only sits and soaks up what others do; they've decided to get personally involved with life rather than sit back, frown, and watch life dwindle to a trickle and ultimately stagnate.

In 1947 San Francisco's Potrero Hill was not only a poor South City neighborhood, it was a real ghetto. That year was the year Oren was born. Rickets, a poverty-related disease actually caused by malnutrition, was Oren's major problem. His vitamin-mineral deficient diet caused his bones to soften. His legs began to bow under the weight of his growing body.

Even though the family was too poor to afford braces, Oren's mom refused to sit back, sigh, and resign herself to the inevitable. Being an eagle type, she rolled up her sleeves and took charge. She rigged up a homemade contraption in hopes of correcting her son's pigeon-toed, bowlegged condition. How? By reversing his shoes! Right shoe, left foot; left shoe, right foot; plus an improvised metal bar across the shoe tops to keep his feet pointing straight. It didn't work perfectly, but it was good enough to keep the boy on his feet and ultimately able to play with his buddies.

By the time he was about six years of age, his bones had hardened, his legs were still slightly bowed, his calves were unusually thin, and his head was disproportionately large. Nicknames from other kids followed him around: "Pencil-legs," "Waterhead"; but he refused to let all that hold him back. He compensated by acting tough. Street gangs on Potrero Hill were common: the Gladiators, Sheiks, Roman Gents, Persian Warriors. By age thirteen Oren had fought and won his way to being president of the Gladiators. For all the fighting, he was arrested only three times; that was the crowning achievement of his early youth.

What ultimately happened to Oren? How in the world does a kid with two malformed legs, an oversize head, a juvenile arrest record, and his whole identity connected with a ghetto, *ever* soar? Believe me, he did!

His legs are still a little bowed from the rickets. His head still seems a little large. He still remembers the embarrassment of being bailed out of the slammer at midnight by his mother . . . still recalls those cruel nicknames and each member of the infamous Gladiators. But Oren doesn't have to act tough anymore. He is tough, tough enough to be secure and gentle. Like his brave mother, he's learned to soar.

Those who don't know his background could easily think he got all the breaks. As they look at him today and see this fine and refined gentleman, they would assume he's always been wealthy. He lives in the exclusive Brentwood district of Los Angeles, drives a luxurious car, and has his elegant office (furnished against tones of brown and rust with wood and suede) in an elite bank building. He is now a busy executive with his own production company. He personally handles most of his own financial affairs and business negotiations. He has contracts with the media and various entertainment firms and agencies. In today's terms, Oren has it made. I wouldn't be surprised if he didn't have a statue of an eagle somewhere in his office. What a guy!

But don't think for a minute that he isn't thankful. His memory of the past only heightens his gratitude for all he now enjoys. The home in Brentwood. The many successful careers, including football. That plush office with his name on the door belongs to Orenthal James Simpson. Yes, none other than "the Juice," O. J. Simpson.

The world is full of folks, however, who would quickly give up. They sit back with folded arms, deep frowns, and skeptical stares. Their determination, unlike that of O. J.'s mom, is short-lived. Their favorite words are *"Why try? . . . Give up . . . We can't do that . . . Nobody ever does those things."* And they miss out on most of the action, to say nothing of all the fun! They've got the rules memorized, and their minds are closed to new and creative possibilities. Like rats in a sewer pipe, their whole focus is limited to a tight radius of don'ts, won'ts, can'ts, and quits.

But periodically we bump into a few refreshing souls, who have decided that they aren't going to live in the swamp of the status quo, or run scared of being different, even though others will always say, "It can't be done." Those who aim high are strong-willed eagle types who refuse to be bothered by the negativism and skepticism of the majority. They never even use the words "Let's just quit!" They are the same ones who believe that mediocrity must be confronted. And that confrontation must first take place in the *mind*—the seed plot of endless and limitless possibilities.

We Become What We Think

I'm sure it comes as no surprise to most of us that we act out precisely what we take in. In other words, we become what we think. Long before that familiar line found its way into Psychology 101 and hyped-up sales meetings, the Bible included it in one of its ancient scrolls; it just said it in a little different way: "For as he thinks within himself, so he is" (Prov. 23:7).

The secret of living a life of excellence is merely a matter of thinking thoughts of excellence. Really, it's a matter of programming our minds with the kind of information that will set us free.

Free to be all God meant us to be. Free to soar! It will take awhile, and it may be painful—but what a metamorphosis!

Sid was an ugly caterpillar with orange eyes. He spent his life groveling and squirming in the dirt on God's earth. One day Sid got a terrific idea. He crawled up the stem of a bush, made his way to a branch, and secreted a translucent fluid onto that branch. He made a kind of button out of the fluid, turned himself around, and attached his posterior anatomy to that button. Then he shaped himself into a "J," curled up, and proceeded to build a house around himself. There was a lot of activity for a while, but before long Sid was entirely covered up and you couldn't see him anymore.

Everything became very, very still. You might have concluded that nothing at all was happening. But, as a matter of fact, plenty was happening. Metamorphosis was taking place.

One day Sid began to raise the window shades of his house. He let you look in and see a variety of colors. On another day an eruption took place. Sid's house shook violently. That little cocoon jerked and shook until a large, beautiful wing protruded from one of the windows. Sid stretched it out in all its glory. He continued his work until another gorgeous wing emerged from a window on the other side of the house.

At this stage of Sid's life you might have wanted to help. But you didn't, for if you tried to pull the rest of Sid's house off you would maim him for the rest of his life. So you let Sid convulse and wriggle his way to freedom without any outside intervention.

Eventually Sid got his house off his back, ventured out onto the branch, stretched, and spread his beautiful wings. He was nothing like the old worm he used to be. And do you know what? Sid didn't crawl back down the bush and start groveling and squirming in the dirt again. No indeed! Instead, he took off with a new kind of power—flight power. Now, instead of swallowing dust, Sid flies from flower to flower, enjoying the sweet nectar in God's wonderful creation.[1]

Perhaps you read those words with a sigh: "Well, that may be the way it is for a caterpillar named Sid, but somehow I just don't qualify; flight power *sounds* stimulating, but I'm made for mediocrity, swallowing dust not sniffing flowers."

Hogwash! With that kind of attitude, you've managed to think your way *out* of the very things you long to enjoy. You have become what you've been thinking. No wonder your metamorphosis is on hold!

THE MIND: TARGET OF THE ENEMY

Let me get to the heart of the issue. Since the mind holds the secrets of soaring, the enemy of our souls has made the human mind the bull's-eye of his target. His most insidious and strategic moves are made upon the mind. By affecting the way we think, he is able to keep our lives on a mediocre level.

There are a couple of extremely significant sections in the New Testament that address Satan's scheming nature. Let's look first at Ephesians 6:10–11.

> Finally, be strong in the Lord, and in the strength of His might. Put on the full armor of God, that you may be able to stand firm against the schemes of the devil.

Notice those four final words: "schemes of the devil." The Greek term translated "schemes" is *METHODIA,* from which we get our English word *method.* The Amplified Bible captures the correct idea by rendering it "strategies of the devil." He has a well-thought-through strategy, time-honored and effective—a plan that works like a charm. To understand it we need to remember that the battle is not in the visible realm. "For our struggle is not against flesh and blood . . ." (Eph. 6:12). The struggle (that's a good word for it, isn't it?) is not a flesh-and-blood struggle. It's not tangible; it's mental—it's simply not in the realm of something we can see, touch, or hear.

Remember that as we look next at a similar statement made in another part of the New Testament:

> But whom you forgive anything, I forgive also; for indeed what I have forgiven, if I have forgiven anything, I did it for your sakes in the presence of Christ, in order that no advantage be taken of us by Satan; for we are not ignorant of his schemes (2 Cor. 2:10–11).

Obviously, the larger subject here is forgiveness. Those people in ancient Corinth were being chided because they had half-forgiven a fellow in their church. By failing to forgive fully, they provided Satan with an "advantage," an opportunity to infiltrate and demoralize them. Note that the writer Paul adds a most insightful comment: ". . . we are not ignorant of his schemes." Earlier, the Greek word translated "schemes" was the root word for "method." But here the Greek term comes from a root word meaning "the mind." May I suggest a loose paraphrase? "Our desire is that the enemy not get a grip on us by twisting our thoughts, for we are not unaware of his mind-oriented strategy." Satan plays mind games with us, and unless we're clued in, he will win! Maybe Paul was not ignorant of the Devil's mind-oriented strategy, but most people I meet are. Frankly, for years I was too. Not until I became aware of the things I'm about to share with you in this chapter did I even begin to realize what it meant to soar.

Travel with me a little bit further in this same letter to the Corinthians:

> And even if our gospel is veiled, it is veiled to those who are perishing, in whose case the god of this world has blinded the minds of the unbelieving, that they might not see the light of the gospel of the glory of Christ, who is the image of God (2 Cor. 4:3–4).

Once again we find the enemy (called here "the god of this world") working in his favorite territory, the mind. Those who live in unbelief do so because he has "blinded the minds of the unbelieving." Many—in fact, most—live their lives in spiritual blindness. It's as if a thick, dark veil were draped across their thinking to keep them from seeing the light. Only the power of Christ can penetrate that veil and bring light and hope and happiness. Paul describes this so vividly a couple of verses later:

> For God, who said, "Light shall shine out of darkness," is the One who has shone in our hearts to give the light of the knowledge of the glory of God in the face of Christ (2 Cor. 4:6).

Thankfully, there are those who turn from darkness to light. But don't think for a moment that the enemy relinquishes his long-held territory without a fight, a fight that endures throughout life! Before you challenge that, take a good look at these words:

> For though we walk in the flesh, we do not war according to the flesh, for the weapons of our warfare are not of the flesh, but divinely powerful for the destruction of fortresses. We are destroying speculations and every lofty thing raised up against the knowledge of God, and we are taking every thought captive to the obedience of Christ (2 Cor. 10:3–5).

What descriptive language! Clearly, the scenes of battle are woven through those lines. You can almost smell smoke and hear the reports of massive weapons, except for one problem—it isn't a "war according to the flesh." As we learned earlier, it's a mind-oriented struggle, a "warfare . . . not of the flesh." It all takes place in the invisible, intangible realm of the mind.

THE BATTLE: AN INSIDIOUS STRATEGY

Even though Paul uses military words and ideas that suggest physical combat, it is imperative that we keep the right perspective. Everything being described in 2 Corinthians 10:3–5 occurs in the mind. What we find here is the strategy used against us to keep us ineffective and defeated—in other words, *mediocre.*

In ancient days cities were built within thick, massive walls. The wall provided a formidable barrier that protected the city, holding the enemy at bay. Before any alien force could expect to conquer a city, it first had to overcome that protective shield. Towers were even erected in strategic places within the wall. In times of battle, seasoned men with an understanding of military warfare would position themselves in these stations that towered above the surrounding wall. From these vantage points, they would be able to see the location of the advancing troops and shout their commands in hopes of counteracting the enemy attack.

In order for the enemy to take the city, three objectives had to be accomplished. First, the wall had to be scaled or penetrated. Second, the towers had to be invaded. Third, the men of military strategy had to be captured. (After capturing—or killing—the military leaders, conquering the inhabitants was no big deal.) Such was the strategy of first-century battles. In 2 Corinthians 10, we have this very principle illustrated—not in a city, but in a mind.

Don't forget what we discovered earlier: Our minds were originally enemy-held territories. For years we were blinded by the
power of the enemy. The mind was his "base of operations" until
the light shone within. At that time, the veil was lifted and we
were no longer blinded. It was a supernatural event in which new
life was given, and the enemy was relieved of his command.

But I am increasingly more convinced that Satan doesn't want
to give up his territory. He is a defeated foe who knows his future.
But he fights to the last degree to maintain the hold he has had on
us. His "stronghold" reveals itself in our humanistic, horizontal
nature—in the habits we established back then, and the whole
lifestyle we lived under enemy command. This is one of the reasons that those who become Christians later in life have such
tremendous battles in the realm of the mind. The intensity of the
warfare can hardly be exaggerated!

The verses we've been looking at describe the battle in detail.
Remember the reference to "the destruction of fortresses" and
"destroying speculations"? Let that represent the wall around
the mind. Perhaps the speculations represent the reasonings, the
thought patterns, the traditional habits of thinking built in by
the enemy for many, many years. In order for the truth of God to
win, those speculations that encompassed our mind have to be
penetrated. How does that happen? The Lord brings a divinely
powerful weapon, the Holy Spirit, with His magnificent armory
of truths from Scripture, His remarkable filling, and His dynamic
empowering.

Once the Lord breaks through the wall-like fortress and speculations, He encounters those "lofty things." Remember the verse
". . . destroying . . . every lofty thing raised up against the
knowledge of God . . ."?

Let's call these "lofty things" the mental blocks we've erected
against spiritual viewpoints. You and I are prompted to go back to
carnal habits when under pressure, when under attack, when un-
dergoing a test, when doing without, when persecuted, when ma-
ligned, criticized, or done wrong. Our tendency is to rely on those
traditional "lofty things"—those established thoughts that were
passed on to us by our parents, our friends, and our colleagues.
Such mental blocks are natural and humanistic to the core.

I am indebted to Roger von Oech for his insights regarding

what he calls "mental locks." In his creative book *A Whack on the Side of the Head* (you owe it to yourself to read it!), he lists no less than ten statements that hold us back, keeping us from soaring into new, innovative realms. If you are like me, you will smile by the time you get to the end of the list; we've heard them and said them so much they are cast in mental concrete!

1. "The Right Answer."
2. "That's Not Logical."
3. "Follow The Rules."
4. "Be Practical."
5. "Avoid Ambiguity."
6. "To Err Is Wrong."
7. "Play Is Frivolous."
8. "That's Not My Area."
9. "Don't Be Foolish."
10. "I'm Not Creative."[2]

God is interested in our breaking free from such locks. He realizes each "lofty thing" has dug in its heels and must be dislodged. As we often say, "Old habits are hard to break." For too many years, we have convinced ourselves that *we lack this* or *we cannot do that . . . we should not risk . . . we are sure to fail . . . we ought to accept the status quo as our standard.* But these programmed "lofty things" <u>must</u> be conquered! We occasionally need "a whack on the side of the head"!

And what is God's ultimate goal? Just as we read in 2 Corinthians 10:5—to take "every thought captive." When He invades those lofty areas, His plan is to transform the old thoughts that defeat us into new thoughts that encourage us. He has to repattern our whole way of thinking. And He is engaged in doing that continually because old habits are so hard to break. Can you see now why those reactions you've had for dozens of years are still problem areas? Finally, you have some insight on your battle with lust, or envy, or pride, or jealousy, or extreme perfectionism, or a negative, critical spirit. And, more importantly, now you realize that there is hope beyond such mediocre mindsets. God's offer is nothing short of phenomenal! Remember it? It is "taking every thought captive to the obedience of Christ." Or, as one paraphrase reads:

PROPERTY OF
BROADWAY CHRISTIAN CHURCH LIBRARY
910 BROADWAY
FORT WAYNE, IN 46802

It is true that we live in the world, but we do not fight from worldly motives. The weapons we use in our fight are not the world's weapons but God's powerful weapons, which we use to destroy strongholds. We destroy false arguments; we pull down every proud obstacle that is raised against the knowledge of God; we take every thought captive and make it obey Christ (2 Cor. 10:3–5, TEV).

CONQUERING MEDIOCRITY: A MENTAL METAMORPHOSIS

The essential question isn't difficult to state: *How?* How can I, a person who has absorbed so many years of mediocre thinking, change? How can I, like Sid the caterpillar, move from squirming in the dirt to enjoying the sweet nectar in God's creation? As in Sid's case, a radical metamorphosis must occur. It is a process that will be difficult, demanding, and lengthy—but, oh, how sweet the results! If you are really serious about conquering mediocrity (which, remember, starts in the mind), then I have three words to offer—memorize, personalize, and analyze.

Memorize. In order for old defeating thoughts to be invaded, conquered, and replaced by new, victorious ones, a process of reconstruction must transpire. The best place I know to begin this process of mental cleansing is with the all-important discipline of memorizing Scripture. I realize it doesn't sound very sophisticated or intellectual, but God's Book is full of powerful ammunition! And dislodging negative and demoralizing thoughts requires aggressive action. I sometimes refer to it as a mental assault.

Where to begin? How about setting up a strong strategy of assault with several victorious promises? For example:

But thanks be to God, who gives us the victory through our Lord Jesus Christ. Therefore, my beloved brethren, be steadfast, immovable, always abounding in the work of the Lord, knowing that your toil is not in vain in the Lord (1 Cor. 15:57–58).

The horse is prepared for the day of battle, but victory belongs to the Lord (Prov. 21:31).

But thanks be to God, who always leads us in His triumph in Christ, and manifests through us the sweet aroma of the knowledge of Him in every place (2 Cor. 2:14).

I can do all things through Him who strengthens me (Phil. 4:13).

For whatever is born of God overcomes the world; and this is the victory that has overcome the world—our faith (1 John 5:4).

Yet those who wait for the Lord will gain new strength; they will mount up with wings like eagles, they will run and not get tired, they will walk and not become weary (Isa. 40:31).

How can a young man keep his way pure? By keeping it according to Thy word. With all my heart I have sought Thee; do not let me wander from Thy commandments. Thy word I have treasured in my heart, that I may not sin against Thee (Ps. 119:9–11).

I can also think of a few scriptures that I repeat to myself when I get a little weak-kneed in the daily battle:

But Moses said to the people, "Do not fear! Stand by and see the salvation of the Lord which He will accomplish for you today; for the Egyptians whom you have seen today, you will never see them again forever. The Lord will fight for you while you keep silent" (Exod. 14:13–14).

Be on the alert, stand firm in the faith, act like men, be strong (1 Cor. 16:13).

"Ask, and it shall be given to you; seek, and you shall find; knock, and it shall be opened to you. For every one who asks receives, and he who seeks finds, and to him who knocks it shall be opened" (Matt. 7:7–8).

Thy words were found and I ate them, and Thy words became for me a joy and the delight of my heart (Jer. 15:16).

Therefore, take up the full armor of God, that you may be able to resist in the evil day, and having done everything, to stand firm. Stand firm therefore, having girded your loins with truth, and having put on the breastplate of righteousness (Eph. 6:13–14).

But He gives a greater grace. Therefore it says, "God is opposed to the proud, but gives grace to the humble" (James 4:6–7).

"Do not fear, for I am with you; do not anxiously look about you, for I am your God. I will strengthen you, surely I will help you, surely I will uphold you with My righteous right hand" (Isa. 41:10).

"These things I have spoken to you, that in Me you may have peace. In the world you have tribulation, but take courage; I have overcome the world" (John 16:33).

No need for me to list more. The possibilities are virtually endless. All you have to do is get hold of a Bible, read it thoughtfully, and when you come across a statement that addresses some issue you're struggling with or some area of need in your life, write it down and spend part of your day tucking it away in the folds of your mind. You'll be amazed at the strength it will give you.

Personalize. Here's where the excitement intensifies. As you begin the process of replacing old, negative thoughts with new and encouraging ones, put yourself into the pages of the Bible. Use *I, me, my, mine* as you come across meaningful statements. To show you what I mean, let's go back again to 2 Corinthians 10:3–5:

> For though [I] walk in the flesh, [I] do not war according to the flesh [then I meditate on that thought], for the weapons of [my] warfare are not of the flesh, but divinely powerful for the destruction of fortresses. [I am] destroying speculations and every lofty thing raised up against the knowledge of God, and [I am] taking every thought captive to the obedience of Christ.

Get the idea? That's called personalizing Scripture. Here is another example. First, let's look at how the words appear in the New American Standard Bible:

> Be anxious for nothing, but in everything by prayer and supplication with thanksgiving let your requests be made known to God. And the peace of God, which surpasses all comprehension, shall guard your hearts and your minds in Christ Jesus.
>
> Finally, brethren, whatever is true, whatever is honorable, whatever is right, whatever is pure, whatever is lovely, whatever is of good repute, if there is any excellence and if anything worthy of praise, let your mind dwell on these things (Phil. 4:6–8).

I suggest you personalize them like this:

> [I should not be anxious about anything], but in everything by prayer and supplication with thanksgiving, [I need to] let [my] requests be made known to God. And the peace of God, which [passes] all [my] comprehension, shall guard [my heart and mind] in Christ Jesus.
>
> Finally, [put your name here], whatever is true, whatever is

honorable, whatever is right, whatever is pure, whatever is lovely, whatever is of good repute, if there is any excellence and if anything worthy of praise, [I should let my] mind dwell on these things.

Got the picture? Believe me, if you keep this up, it won't be long before the old "fortresses" will be scaled, the "lofty things" will be invaded, and your thoughts will begin to be transformed.

Analyze. Instead of continuing to tell yourself you are little more than a helpless victim, take charge! As soon as you catch yourself responding negatively or defensively, think—analyze the situation. If you are a student, do a little analysis of your situation at school. If you're in business, working in an office where the turkeys outnumber the eagles (that's usually true!), analyze the circumstances with the understanding that you and they will never be "in step," marching to the same cadence. Then ask yourself a few tough questions. "Why am I getting so hot and bothered by this?" Or "Is there something I'm afraid of?" Or, maybe, "Am I reacting negatively because I have a reason or simply because I've formed some bad habits?" Yes, those are thought questions, but without such analysis, we tend to become like those around us or get even worse. Breaking longstanding mental habits is neither easy nor quick, but those who don't can erode into cranky and crotchety folks who wind up alone and miserable.

Maybe the challenge to memorize, personalize, and analyze seems too simplistic to you. Perhaps you expected something else. You really expected some high-powered "secret" to success.

No, I have no quick 'n' easy secret, no overnight-success pill you can take. Perhaps the best single-word picture is *visualize.* Those who break through the "mediocrity barrier" mentally visualize being on a higher plane. Then once they "see it," they begin to believe it and behave like it! People who soar are those who refuse to sit back, sigh, and wish things would change. They neither complain of their lot nor passively dream of some distant ship coming in. Rather, they visualize in their minds that they are not quitters; they will not allow life's circumstances to push them down and hold them under.

The next time you find yourself tempted to succumb to life's hard knocks, take a mental journey back to an office in Brentwood and remember it is occupied by that bowlegged eagle who soared all the way from a pathetic ghetto in Potrero Hill to the National Football League Hall of Fame . . . and far beyond.

It Involves Another Kingdom

2

Ours is the YUPPIE generation. Yes, YUPPIE—young urban professionals.

What a difference between the hippies of the 1960s and the yuppies of the 1980s! They not only look different, but they ask different questions. Today's upwardly mobile young adult isn't burning draft cards and questioning the establishment. Instead, he's asking, "What's in it for me? How much will I make? What are the benefits, the perks you can promise? How rapidly will I be promoted?" The implications in their questions are bold and brazen: "What's so bad about greed?" And, "Why not look out for number one?" Their three-piece suits are neatly pressed, and their professional intensity reflects strong determination. They not only look trim and proper, they even smell good.

How different from the hippies! Those who bothered to attend classrooms back then wore cut-offs and often no shirt at all, sometimes no shoes. One of the last things they cared about was their appearance. And least important to them was prosperity and success. How times change!

Early in the 1980s *Fortune* magazine published an article that left nobody in doubt regarding today's young entrepreneur. Even the title was revealing—"On a Fast Track to the Good Life." The article gave research findings on the attitudes and the values of twenty-five-year-olds who were taking their places in the current business world. The purpose of the research was to give readers an idea of what to expect from young adults during the next decade. Talk about an accurate crystal ball!

One astute thinker has analyzed the results in six observations:

1.   These young people believe that a successful life means financial independence and that the best way to gain financial independence is to be at the top of a major corporation.

2.   They believe in themselves. They believe that they have the abilities and capacities to be the best. There is no "humble talk" among them.

3.   They believe in the corporate world. They are sure that the corporations they would lead are the most worthwhile institutions in the world.

4.   They view as "a drag on success" any relationship that slows their ascent of the corporate ladder. Marriage is an acceptable option only if it does not interfere with their aspirations for success. Having children, for most of them, is something to which they will have to give a great deal of thought.

5.   Loyalty is not high on their list of values. Unlike "The Organization Man," described by William Whyte, Jr., in his book of the same name during the '50s, the young Turks of this new breed have their resumés ever at hand. They are ready to move from one company to another and believe that loyalty to one company could lead to staying in a system that might not maximize upward mobility.

6.   They are convinced that they are more creative and imaginative than those who now hold top corporate positions, and they believe that there is not much they can learn from these older types before they take their places.[1]

In a hard-hitting book entitled *Money, Sex, and Power,* author Richard Foster exposes the soft underbelly of today's yuppie philosophy. He goes to the heart of the issue when he writes:

The demon in money is greed. Nothing can destroy human beings like the passion to possess. . . .

> The demon in sex is lust. True sexuality leads to humanness, but lust leads to depersonalization. Lust captivates rather than emancipates. . . .
>
> The demon in power is pride. True power has as its aim to set people free, whereas pride is determined to dominate.[2]

Then, toward the end of his book, as he returns to the subject of power, Foster concludes:

> Power destroys relationships. Lifelong friends can turn into mortal enemies the moment the vice-presidency of the company is at stake. Climb, push, shove is the language of power. Nothing cuts us off from each other like power. . . . Power's ability to destroy human relationships is written across the face of humanity.[3]

What does all of this have to do with living above the level of mediocrity? Everything, really. To live on that level requires thinking clearly, thinking beyond today. Frankly, it requires dealing with selfishness and putting the axe to the roots of greed. If we hope to demonstrate the level of excellence modeled by Jesus Christ, then we'll have to come to terms with which kingdom we are going to serve: the eternal kingdom our Lord represented and told us to seek (Matt. 6:33) or the temporal kingdom of today, whose philosophy could best be described in a different version of an old hymn:

> I'll have my own way, Lord, I'll have my own way,
> I'll be the potter, You be the clay;
> I'll mold You and make You after my will,
> While You are waiting, yielded and still.

In a world like ours, it's terribly, terribly difficult to think through the maze, especially since a number of religious groups have climbed on the yuppie bandwagon. They tell us, "If you want anything bad enough, you just claim it and God will give it to you. He's a good God, and He's certainly a prosperous God. He owns the cattle on every hill. He'll sell some and make it possible for you to enjoy whatever you really want in life." Sounds so appealing, so right. But when we examine it closely we find that it is light-years removed from everything Jesus taught and modeled. The kingdom He represented and urged His followers to embrace was a kingdom altogether different from the me-ism world of today.

LET'S UNDERSTAND WHAT "KINGDOM" MEANS

Before we press on in our pursuit of overcoming mediocrity, let's pause long enough to understand what I'm referring to when I mention the *kingdom.* It's one of those terms we like to use but seldom define. Part of our problem is that it is a tough thing to analyze.

For example, while the kingdom is full of righteousness, peace, and joy, it isn't a physical, tangible thing. It isn't something we can touch or see. "For the kingdom of God is not eating and drinking, but righteousness and peace and joy in the Holy Spirit" (Rom. 14:17).

Furthermore, this kingdom isn't verbal, something we can actually hear with our ears, even though it is powerful. "For the kingdom of God does not consist in words, but in power" (1 Cor. 4:20).

If that isn't mysterious enough, I should add that while it is unshakable, it isn't visible either!

> Therefore, since we receive a kingdom which cannot be shaken, let us show gratitude, by which we may offer to God an acceptable service with reverence and awe (Heb. 12:28).

How about that! We're supposed to seek something we cannot see, feel, or hear. And we're expected to embrace something that is intangible, inaudible, and invisible.

Enough tongue-twisting. Generally speaking, *God's kingdom is a synonym for God's rule.* Those who choose to live in His kingdom (though still very much alive on Planet Earth) choose to live under His authority.

Maybe a supersimple outline of the Bible will help us understand the definition of God's kingdom even better. But first let me warn you—it's so basic you'll probably sneer!

I. God creates the heavens and earth and all things in them, including mankind. That's Genesis 1 and 2.
II. Mankind, alone, rebels against God's authority. That's covered in Genesis 3.
III. God moves through history to reestablish His authority over all creation. That's Genesis 4 through Revelation 22.

How's that for a quick summary?

If you're wondering where you and I fit into this oversimplified outline, take a look at category three. For centuries God has been at work reestablishing His rulership. Jesus' words in Matthew 6 describe the problem:

"No one can serve two masters; for either he will hate the one and love the other, or he will hold to one and despise the other. You cannot serve God and mammon. . . .

"For all these things the Gentiles eagerly seek; for your heavenly Father knows that you need all these things. But seek first His kingdom and His righteousness; and all these things shall be added to you" (vv. 24, 32–33).

All this leads me to some helpful news, some bad news, and some good news! The kingdom is the invisible realm where God rules as supreme authority. That's *helpful news*. The *bad news* is that we, by nature, don't want Him to rule over us; we much prefer to please ourselves. We'd much rather serve mammon (the word means "money") than the Master. Illustration: the yuppie lifestyle, materialism. More bad news is this: Most people do serve mammon. Just look around. Who's in charge, God or mammon? What's happening? The mediocre majority have bought into a mammon lifestyle.

Now, the *good news*. We don't have to live that way. God has given us an avenue of escape. It's called a birth from above. Jesus spoke of it when He met with a Jewish leader late one night.

Among the Pharisees there was a man named Nicodemus, a ruler of the Jews, who visited Jesus by night and said to Him, "Rabbi, we know that You are a teacher who has come from God; for no one can work the signs You work unless God is with him."

Jesus answered him, "Truly I assure you, unless a person is born from above, he cannot see the kingdom of God." Nicodemus said to Him, "How can a man be born when he is old? Can he enter his mother's womb a second time to be born?" Jesus replied, "Truly I assure you, unless one's birth is through water and the Spirit, he cannot enter the kingdom of God. What is born of the flesh is flesh, and what is born of the Spirit is spirit" (John 3:1–6, MLB).

Nicodemus struggled back then just as we do today. To put it bluntly, we don't want anybody other than ourselves ruling over us! Much like those people in a story Jesus once told, "We do not want this man to reign over us!" (Luke 19:14). Not until we experience a spiritual rebirth will we submit to God's rule.

So when I write of God's kingdom, I'm referring to His rightful authority over our lives. Only then can we experience true excellence.

OUR MAJOR STRUGGLE WITH GOD'S KINGDOM

God's kingdom authority isn't easily accepted in our yuppie generation. We've got too much pride to submit without a fight. As I mentioned at the beginning of this chapter, we like being in charge. We want our way. We push for the top spot—the place of glory. In doing so, we opt for a lifestyle that has no room for submission. That's nothing new.

In ancient days there lived a king whose middle name could have been Pride. He strutted his stuff all over Babylon. His surroundings were impressive and his lifestyle was opulent. But King Nebuchadnezzar had a dream which troubled him. To make matters worse, he could find no one in his vast kingdom who could interpret that dream. No one, that is, until he heard about a Jewish prophet named Daniel. Once the two men stood face to face, things started to pop. Daniel not only told him the reality of the dream, he also leveled the monarch with a prophecy concerning his future:

> "It is you, O king; for you have become great and grown strong, and your majesty has become great and reached to the sky and your dominion to the end of the earth.
>
> "This is the interpretation, O king, and this is the decree of the Most High, which has come upon my lord the king: that you be driven away from mankind, and your dwelling place be with the beasts of the field, and you be given grass to eat like cattle and be drenched with the dew of heaven; and seven periods of time will pass over you, until you recognize that the Most High is ruler over the realm of mankind, and bestows it on whomever He wishes.
>
> "Therefore, O king, may my advice be pleasing to you: break away now from your sins by doing righteousness, and from your iniquities by showing mercy to the poor, in case there may be a prolonging of your prosperity" (Dan. 4:22, 24–25, 27).

The prophet's counsel was tough but true. In effect, he told Nebuchadnezzar to release his grip on his possessions, to empty himself of all that stubborn self-will—in essence to recognize God's rightful authority over his life. Do you think that proud king would do such a thing? Well, ultimately, yes, but not before he went nuts. Read the next episode of this true story very thoughtfully.

> All this happened to Nebuchadnezzar the king. Twelve months later he was walking on the roof of the royal palace of Babylon. The king reflected and said, "Is this not Babylon the great, which I myself have built as a royal residence by the might of my power and for the glory of my majesty?" While the word was in the king's mouth, a voice came from heaven, saying, "King Nebuchadnezzar, to you it is declared: sovereignty has been removed from you, and you will be driven away from mankind, and your dwelling place will be with the beasts of the field. You will be given grass to eat like cattle, and seven periods of time will pass over you, until you recognize that the Most High is ruler over the realm of mankind, and bestows it on whomever He wishes." Immediately the word concerning Nebuchadnezzar was fulfilled; and he was driven away from mankind and began eating grass like cattle, and his body was drenched with the dew of heaven, until his hair had grown like eagles' feathers and his nails like birds' claws (Dan. 4:28–33).

Nebuchadnezzar remained in that tragic condition for an undetermined period of time. When he finally saw the light, the struggle ended. The once-proud king did a 180-degree turnaround.

> "But at the end of that period I, Nebuchadnezzar, raised my eyes toward heaven, and my reason returned to me, and I blessed the Most High and praised and honored Him who lives forever;
>
>> For His dominion is an everlasting dominion,
>> And His kingdom endures from generation
>> to generation.
>> And all the inhabitants of the earth are
>> accounted as nothing,
>> But He does according to His will in the host
>> of heaven
>> And among the inhabitants of earth;

And no one can ward off His hand
Or say to Him, 'What hast Thou done?'

"At that time my reason returned to me. And my majesty and
splendor were restored to me for the glory of my kingdom, and my
counselors and my nobles began seeking me out; so I was reestab-
lished in my sovereignty, and surpassing greatness was added to
me. Now I Nebuchadnezzar praise, exalt, and honor the King of
heaven, for all His works are true and His ways just, and He is able
to humble those who walk in pride" (Dan. 4:34–37).

Look again at those concluding words of Nebuchadnezzar's
testimony. Pay close attention to his comments about God's do-
minion, God's kingdom, God's authority, God's works, God's
ways. What a change! Here was a broken man who finally surrendered. Only then was he able to fulfill his God-appointed role
and reach his full potential on the earth.

The same is true today. People who live proud, unbroken lives
may become great, gain popularity, and accomplish incredible
feats, but all that power and pride stand against the qualities that
God considers great.

It is extremely difficult to have these thoughts embraced in our
world of high-powered hype. This is the day when people consider it the greatest thrill in life to have their picture in a magazine or to appear in films or on television. Malcolm Muggeridge
made an insightful comment in his penetrating work *Christ in the
Media* (Wm. B. Eerdmans, 1977). He said if Jesus were to return
to earth today and endure a similar wilderness experience with
Satan throwing those three temptations at Him, the adversary
would surely add a fourth: to appear on national television.[4]

What a cunning, driving force is Ambition, twin sister of Pride.
Those who pursue true excellence, those who soar, are people
who've come to terms with pride.

OBSERVATIONS AND APPLICATIONS

Okay, okay, I can hear your thoughts. You're wondering what
all this kingdom stuff has to do with living above the level of
mediocrity. You're thinking you missed a couple of pages in the
transition, right? Well, you didn't. What I have wanted to communicate in this chapter is that a life which soars is one that

doesn't get caught in the trap of the temporal. People of excellence are those who see through the clutching greed of our times—people who have declared their undivided allegiance to Christ's message, a message that (like the restored king of Babylon) praises and exalts and honors the King of heaven, knowing He is able to humble those who walk in pride. Such a commitment represents authentic excellence, leaving no excuse for mediocrity. People who soar, that is, soar like God intended, are people who have humbled themselves to Christ's sovereign authority. They are citizens of His invisible kingdom.

Jesus spoke often of God's kingdom to those who wished to follow Him. In fact, right up to the end He had kingdom authority on His mind. Before His ascension back to the Father, He met with His own. And the topic of discussion? The kingdom.

> To these He also presented Himself alive, after His suffering, by many convincing proofs, appearing to them over a period of forty days, and speaking of the things concerning the kingdom of God (Acts 1:3).

What a revelation! Did you realize that's what Christ talked about between His resurrection and His ascension? It wasn't a lengthy class on theoretical prophecy, not at all. It was practical, relevant teaching about how to live under His authority and for His glory—how to live a life above the mediocre level (that level where you push and shove to get your own way). No doubt, He passed along some insightful techniques, some truths his followers could apply when tempted to live like the majority.

Did these early disciples learn their lesson well? Let's find out by working our way through the balance of the Book of Acts, which traces the history of these followers of Jesus from His ascension to the last half of the first century. In each one of the following vignettes, we'll find something extremely significant about life that is lived above the level of mediocrity, "kingdom living" in action.

Our First Stop-off: Acts 8:12–13

> But when they believed Philip preaching the good news about the kingdom of God and the name of Jesus Christ, they were being

baptized, men and women alike. And even Simon himself believed; and after being baptized, he continued on with Philip; and as he observed signs and great miracles taking place, he was constantly amazed (Acts 8:12–13).

Interesting. "Even Simon himself believed. . . ." Who's Simon? The previous three verses tell us.

Now there was a certain man named Simon, who formerly was practicing magic in the city, and astonishing the people of Samaria, claiming to be someone great; and they all, from smallest to greatest, were giving attention to him, saying, "This man is what is called the Great Power of God." And they were giving him attention because he had for a long time astonished them with his magic arts (vv. 9–11).

Simon was a magician whose reputation had won him the title "the Great Power of God." Talk about a man people today would turn out to see . . . all the television networks would be after this guy! Yet, upon hearing Philip's message, "the good news about the kingdom of God," Simon accepted it, no questions asked. Believing the good news is both simple and quick. Fleshing it out is a different matter. Simon would soon find that out.

Then they began laying their hands on them, and they were receiving the Holy Spirit. Now when Simon saw that the Spirit was bestowed through the laying on of the apostles' hands, he offered them money, saying, "Give this authority to me as well, so that everyone on whom I lay my hands may receive the Holy Spirit" (vv. 17–19).

Why, of course! That's exactly the way yuppies would respond. "This kind of power is worth whatever it costs. . . . I want to buy fifty shares!" So Simon offered them money. "I would love to get into that act. I'll market it. Gimme some of that Holy Spirit power!"

Look at Peter. There are times when he really distinguishes himself, and this is one of those wonderful moments:

. . . "May your silver perish with you, because you thought you could obtain the gift of God with money! You have no part or portion in this matter, for your heart is not right before God. Therefore repent of this wickedness of yours, and pray the Lord that if possible, the intention of your heart may be forgiven you. For I see that you are in the gall of bitterness and in the bondage of iniquity" (vv. 20–23).

Now that's what I'd call a rebuke! No doubt about it, Peter had gotten this guy's attention. I mean, here's Simon, "Okay, okay." But it wasn't a surly kind of okay. Look at his response.

But Simon answered and said, "Pray to the Lord for me yourselves, so that nothing of what you have said may come upon me" (v. 24).

There was someone honest enough to say, "Simon, you're off base. That has nothing to do with the kingdom of God. That's mediocre pizzazz. That's hype. That's carnal merchandising. You're out of line, Simon." And when Simon realized his fault, he acknowledged it.

The observation that we need to remember from this incident is *kingdom authority diminishes the significance of all other powers.* The accompanying application is equally important:

WHEN FACING THE TEMPTATION TO MAKE A NAME FOR YOURSELF, CALL ON KINGDOM POWER.

If you are greatly gifted, you may be able to do marvelous things that would cause the public to be swept up in your skills and in your abilities. In the process of your growing, you will find great temptation to make a name for yourself, to make a big splash, to gain attention, to get the glory, to strut around, to increase your fees, to demand your rights, and to expect kid-glove treatment. You're in authority now! People are talking about you! But instead, remember Simon. Realize, as well, the ministry of small things.

In experiences of hiddenness we learn that the ministry of small things is a necessary prerequisite to the ministry of power. . . .
The ministry of small things is among the most important

ministries we are given. In some ways it is more important than the ministry of power. . . .

Small things are the genuinely big things in the kingdom of God. It is here we truly face the issues of obedience and discipleship. It is not hard to be a model disciple amid camera lights and press releases. But in the small corners of life, in those areas of service that will never be newsworthy or gain us any recognition, we must hammer out the meaning of obedience.[5]

Ruth Harms Calkin does a masterful job on this same subject in her poem "I Wonder":

You know, Lord, how I serve You
with great emotional fervor in the limelight.
You know how eagerly I speak for You at a Women's Club.
You know my genuine enthusiasm at a Bible study.
But how would I react, I wonder,
if You pointed to a basin of water
and asked me to wash the calloused feet
of a bent and wrinkled old woman
day after day, month after month,
in a room where nobody saw and nobody knew?[6]

Still enamored by the lights, Simon continued to look for ways to promote himself, until he learned about kingdom authority. So whenever you're faced with the temptation to claim glory for yourself, call on kingdom power.

Our Second Stop-off: Acts 14:21–22

As we jump ahead, we move from Samaria to the little city of Lystra. Lystra means nothing to most people on the street, but to Bible students it means the place where Paul was a victim of stoning. Literally, he was left for dead. Yet, he came out from under those rocks more determined than ever. It took him awhile, but he brushed himself off, gathered his senses, and pressed on to present the gospel to that area of the world where God had called him. Watch what happened.

And after they had preached the gospel to that city and had made many disciples, they returned to Lystra. . . . (Acts 14:21).

Can you believe it? The very place he was stoned. That's like going back to the job where you were fired. That's like returning to a friendship that the other person has cut off. But they returned to Lystra anyway:

> . . . strengthening the souls of the disciples, encouraging them to continue in the faith, and saying, "Through many tribulations we must enter the kingdom of God" (Acts 14:22).

Once again, allow me to present our yuppie point of view. First of all, yuppies hate the thought of suffering. "I don't wanna suffer, because I want gratification. I don't simply want gratification, I want *instant* gratification. I don't want to wait if I can get it now. And if I can get it now, I want more rather than less." And yet Paul says that through many tribulations we must enter the kingdom of God. It's a rigorous statement and, without question, an unpopular one.

Now the observation is clear: *Kingdom living involves many tribulations.* I think of a related truth found in 2 Timothy 3:12 which says: "And indeed, all who desire to live godly in Christ Jesus will be persecuted." But the accompanying application reveals a source of strength:

WHEN GOING THROUGH TIMES OF TESTING, COUNT ON KINGDOM ENDURANCE.

Now if you're in life only for yourself, you'll have no endurance. On that precarious top of the ladder, you'll always have to maintain your balance by maneuvering and manipulating, lying, deceiving, and scheming. But if you're committed to kingdom-related excellence, when you go through times of testing, you can count on kingdom endurance to get you through.

British theologian John R. W. Stott writes on this unpopular subject of suffering in his book *Christian Counter Culture*:

> Few men of this century have understood better the inevitability of suffering than Dietrich Bonhoeffer. He seems never to have wavered in his Christian antagonism to the Nazi regime, although it meant for him imprisonment, the threat of torture, danger to his own family and finally death. He was executed by the direct order of Heinrich Himmler in April 1945 in the

Flossenburg concentration camp, only a few days before it was liberated. It was the fulfillment of what he had always believed and taught: "Suffering, then, is the badge of true discipleship. The disciple is not above his master. Following Christ means *passio passiva* suffering because we have to suffer. That is why Luther reckoned suffering among the marks of the true Church, and one of the memoranda drawn up in preparation for the Augsburg Confession similarly defines the Church as the community of those 'who are persecuted and martyred for the gospel's sake' . . . Discipleship means allegiance to the suffering Christ, and it is therefore not at all surprising that Christians should be called upon to suffer."[7]

God has great lessons to teach us when we go through painful times. I love the words of the country preacher who said: "When the Lawd sends us tribulation, He 'spects us to tribulate!"

Our Third Stop-off: Acts 19:8

And he entered the synagogue and continued speaking out boldly for three months, reasoning and persuading them about the kingdom of God (Acts 19:8).

The scene changes from Lystra to Corinth. Paul, once he won a hearing in the synagogue, spoke openly for three months, "persuading" those who attended. About what? "The kingdom of God." I'm sure he must have started with the basics, saying "You will not find yourself better off because you believe, that is, more prosperous, more popular, more successful, or in greater demand. You will find that some of this message is going to cut deeply into your life."

I know that must have been hard for the Corinthians to hear because Paul uses the words *speaking out boldly, reasoning,* and *persuading.* The words *speaking out boldly* mean "to declare, as if making a proclamation." You can be sure that caught their attention. The next word (*reasoning*) carries with it the idea of "dialoguing." In fact, it's from the Greek term *dialegomai* from which we get the word *dialogue.* It includes the thought of "pondering" and "disputing." One scholar renders it "debating." So Paul threw out to them thoughts of the kingdom, and then he entertained their disputes. Perhaps this same dialogue continued for three months as Paul tried to *persuade* them. The word *persuading* means "to prevail upon so as to bring about a change." Today we would call it "selling them." And the result? "Some were becoming *hardened.*" See that word *hardened?* Interesting. It means "to dry." And it conveys the idea of being austere, stern, even severe. "They dried up" is the idea. Some were drying up with that message.

They were hardened and disobedient. Remember the line out of Jesus' story, "We will not have that man rule over us"? That's what these people were thinking in their hearts.

> But when some were becoming hardened and disobedient, speaking evil of the Way before the multitude, he withdrew from them and took away the disciples, reasoning daily in the school of Tyrannus (Acts 19:9).

The observation is clear: *Kingdom emphasis thins the ranks.* The accompanying application:

WHEN WONDERING WHY MOST PREFER MEDIOCRITY, REALIZE THE KINGDOM SEPARATES.

I think when the kingdom presses itself into a life, an individual fully embraces it or simply cannot tolerate it. So rather than facing it and releasing the pride, many—maybe most—will run. We should not be surprised to find the majority opting for a mediocre lifestyle, even some who once played roles as religious leaders. Kingdom truth does its own pruning. As Jesus Himself taught, we *cannot* serve two masters at the same time.

Our Fourth Stop-off: Acts 20

Here, we find Paul in the little coastal town of Miletus. He calls for the elders of the church at Ephesus, and then delivers his swan song. In verses 18–35, he pours out his soul to his friends from Ephesus, not knowing what would happen to him in Jerusalem. Note what he says to them in verses 20 and 27:

> ". . . I did not shrink from declaring to you anything that was profitable, and teaching you publicly and from house to house.

"For I did not shrink from declaring to you the whole purpose of God."

The observation is obvious: *Kingdom truth is central to the whole purpose of God.* What I want you to notice by my quoting those two verses is that it's easy to shrink from the message. It's easy for me to shrink from preaching it. When tempted to do so, I need to remember 2 Timothy 4:2:

. . . preach the word; be ready in season and out of season; reprove, rebuke, exhort, with great patience and instruction.

Why? The passage goes on to say:

For the time will come when they will not endure sound doctrine; but wanting to have their ears tickled, they will accumulate for themselves teachers in accordance to their own desires (v. 3).

I ask you, is that relevant for today? Is it possible for you to find a teacher who'll tell you what you want to hear? Sure is. In fact, you don't have to look very far or very long; you'll find someone who will tell you how great you are, how wonderful things are, and how prosperous you can become.

So the accompanying application is obvious:

WHEN COMING TO TERMS
WITH THE WHOLE PURPOSE OF GOD,
REMEMBER KINGDOM COMMITMENT.

If you say that you're the kind of Christian who wants to embrace excellence, who really wants the whole purpose of God, then you dare not leave out *kingdom commitment*. That means your motives must be investigated. For example, every time you make plans to acquire a sizable possession—a car, an expensive boat, a house, and such like—you must deal with it before God and ask: Is this His will? Would this honor Him? Would this glorify Him? Before you hang onto something for a long, long time, you have to ask yourself: Is this worth hanging onto? It may be, but the question should still be asked. Is this the kind of thing that honors His kingdom? . . . that helps me seek His righteousness? This type of self-examination is the outworking of "the whole purpose of God."

When I became convinced of the importance of quality Christians becoming actively involved in "another kingdom," I spoke on the subject at the church I serve as senior pastor in Fullerton, California. Many of the things I've emphasized in this chapter, I openly declared from the pulpit that day. Sitting in the congregation was a man who listened very carefully and came to terms with his relationship with the Lord. Later, he wrote me this letter.

> I have attended the Fullerton Church for about two months. I've reached a pivotal point in my 40-year life. . . . I married at 18, had three sons by age 21 and spent years in drug and alcohol abuse. At age 25 I gave my life to the Lord but slipped back a couple of times.
>
> A year ago I had a beautiful 23-foot sailboat, a beautiful car, a beautiful van, a beautiful home, etc. At that time I was with a new company and my boss said he would get health insurance but lied about that and other things.
>
> Last February my wife had a brain aneurysm and almost died, but with prayer and surgery she lived. I lost everything but my family.
>
> I drive an old car about to break down. I am broke financially and my new boss emotionally destroys me, but I need the job. I said it with my mouth that the Lord giveth and the Lord taketh, blessed is the Lord, but my heart was still bitter. In your message I could relate very much with King Nebuchadnezzar, and you ended with a story that hit me so hard. I walked to my car with tears streaming down my cheeks and a pain in my throat. I came home and my wife and I cried and talked and prayed. At that time I gave it all to our Lord.
>
> I know I will struggle in my life, but I see everything differently now. I am undereducated, but very talented. I will work as unto the Lord. I need a church home for me and my family and believe I have found where we belong.[8]

Am I suggesting that you take a vow of poverty? No, not that. My message is not that you go hungry and give up all nice things. I just say you give up control of them. I'm not saying that because you're a Christian now, every day of your life is supposed to be grim, and you're supposed to carry yourself around like a prophet of doom, wearing only black and looking somber. I'm simply suggesting that those who live—I mean really soar—above the grubby, greedy level of mediocrity, have learned how to live from the perspective of another kingdom. They've learned to give all they have to the Lord God and to trust Him to give back all that they need.

Legend has it that a man was lost in the desert, just dying for a drink of water. He stumbled upon an old shack—a ramshackled, windowless, roofless, weatherbeaten old shack. He looked about this place and found a little shade from the heat of the desert sun. As he glanced around he saw a pump about fifteen feet away—an old, rusty water pump. He stumbled over to it, grabbed the handle, and began to pump up and down, up and down. Nothing came out.

Disappointed, he staggered back. He noticed off to the side an old jug. He looked at it, wiped away the dirt and dust, and read a message that said, "You have to prime the pump with all the water in this jug, my friend. P.S.: Be sure you fill the jug again before you leave."

He popped the cork out of the jug and sure enough, there was water. It was almost full of water! Suddenly, he was faced with a decision. If he drank the water, he could live. Ah, but if he poured all the water in the old rusty pump, maybe it would yield fresh, cool water from down deep in the well, all the water he wanted.

He studied the possibility of both options. What should he do, pour it into the old pump and take a chance on fresh, cool water or drink what was in the old jug and ignore its message? Should he waste all the water on the hopes of those flimsy instructions written, no telling how long ago?

Reluctantly he poured all the water into the pump. Then he grabbed the handle and began to pump . . . squeak, squeak, squeak. Still nothing came out! Squeak, squeak, squeak. A little bit began to dribble out, then a small stream, and finally it gushed! To his relief fresh, cool water poured out of the rusty pump. Eagerly, he filled the jug and drank from it. He filled it another time and once again drank its refreshing contents.

Then he filled the jug for the next traveler. He filled it to the top, popped the cork back on, and added this little note: "Believe me, it really works. You have to give it *all* away before you can get *anything* back."

People who risk living like that really soar.

It Costs
Your
Commitment

3

Even though we're not very far along in this book, you have already noticed several references I have made to soaring. Obviously, my favorite analogy to illustrate that word picture is an eagle.

For thousands of years the eagle has been respected for its grandeur. There is something inspiring about its impressive grace in flight, its great wingspan, its powerful claws. It glides effortlessly at breathtaking altitudes, seemingly unaffected by the turbulent winds that whip across and between mountain crevices. Eagles do not travel in flocks nor do they conduct themselves irresponsibly. Strong of heart and solitary, they represent qualities we admire.

The eagle mates for life and returns to the same nest each year, making necessary repairs and additions. He takes an active role in providing for his family, protecting it from approaching dangers, and teaching little eaglets to fly. Responsibility, liberty, beauty, stability, and a dozen other admirable traits seem woven into the eagle's makeup, and such qualities cause me to agree with Solomon that "the way of an eagle in the sky" is nothing short of "wonderful" (Prov. 30:18–19).

Perhaps because eagle sightings are so rare, we don't easily forget those times when we've seen one soaring. I love the outdoors, and through the years, I've spent time fishing and hunting. During those outings, I've enjoyed many of the indescribable beauties of nature and encountered its harsh realities as well. But in spite of the numerous occasions I have been on streams and lakes, in the wilderness, and high up in the mountains, only twice have I spotted a bald eagle in flight—once while my sons and I were fishing for salmon and hunting caribou in Alaska and once while we were fishing for walleye and northern pike in central Canada. I can recall both moments to this day. All alone, the majestic bird seemed buoyed by the strong wind currents beneath its massive wings, soaring to its destination apparently without the slightest concern for us down below. While enraptured with the sight, each time I envisioned some day writing a book that would use the eagle as an illustration of living above the level of mediocrity—an illustration of the importance of being so committed to a standard of excellence that nothing deters us from our flight plan.

We may not be very far along in this study of excellence, but no doubt you are already aware of the fact that an eaglelike lifestyle doesn't come cheap. Being different is costly, especially when most are satisfied to blend in with the majority. There aren't many magnets on earth stronger than peer pressure. Even though all of us have only a few years to spend on this little planet in space, rare are the ones who decide to ignore the "average" and fight against the pull of the mediocre magnet. Face it—it's tough! As a familiar motto goes, "It's hard to soar like an eagle when I'm surrounded by so many turkeys!"

A PSALM THAT SETS US FREE

Tucked away neatly in the heart of the Hebrews' ancient hymnal is a simple prayer I often repeat to myself. It comes on the heels of several references to the brevity of life. I'm thinking of Psalm 90:

- Our years are "like yesterday" (v. 4).
- Life is "as a watch in the night" (v. 4).
- Our days are swept away "like a flood" (v. 5).
- Looking back over our lives, time seems almost "like grass," flourishing in the morning and fading by dusk (vv. 5–6).
- We finish our journey "like a sigh" (v. 9).

No one has done a better job paraphrasing the opening lines of this grand old hymn than Ken Taylor. Read his words slowly and thoughtfully:

> Lord, through all the generations you have been our home! Before the mountains were created, before the earth was formed, you are God without beginning or end.
>
> You speak, and man turns back to dust. A thousand years are but as yesterday to you! They are like a single hour! We glide along the tides of time as swiftly as a racing river, and vanish as quickly as a dream. We are like grass that is green in the morning but mowed down and withered before the evening shadows fall. We die beneath your anger; we are overwhelmed by your wrath. You spread out our sins before you—our secret sins—and see them all. No wonder the years are long and heavy here beneath your wrath. All our days are filled with sighing.
>
> Seventy years are given us! And some may even live to eighty. But even the best of these years are often emptiness and pain; soon they disappear, and we are gone (Ps. 90:1–10, TLB).

Yes, "we glide along the tides of time as swiftly as a racing river" for seventy, maybe eighty years; then it's curtains! What is it we need so desperately to live differently? The psalmist tells us in the simple prayer that follows these vivid verses:

> Teach us to number our days and recognize how few they are; help us to spend them as we should (v. 12, TLB).

That's it! Gripped by the inescapable reality of life's brevity and death's inevitability, the man prays for all of us ("Teach us") and asks for wisdom for the balance of our days on earth ("help us to spend them as we should").

May I press the point? He doesn't ask "help us to spend them like the majority" but *as we should*—uniquely, fully, triumphantly. Not like a pen full of turkeys preoccupied only with life's mediocre demands, but like an independent-thinking, strong-minded eagle who lives a cut above, soaring freely across the trackless paths of incredible heights. If that's your prayer, be ready to pay a price.

In 1776 Thomas Paine, American Revolution patriot and writer, wrote about the price of freedom:

> What we obtain too cheap, we esteem too lightly; 'tis dearness only that gives everything its value. Heaven knows how to put a proper price upon its goods; and it would be strange indeed, if so celestial an article as *Freedom* should not be highly rated.[1]

I sometimes think that those of us who choose to live like soaring eagles need to sign a mental declaration of independence. Let's put our name on the line, pledging ourselves with firm resolve, much like those brave men did on July 4, 1776, in Philadelphia when they signed the Declaration of Independence.

Did you know that of the fifty-six courageous men who signed that original document in Philadelphia, many did not survive the war that followed? Five were captured by the British and tortured before they died. Nine others died in the Revolutionary War, either from its hardships or its bullets. Twelve had their homes sacked, looted, burned, or occupied by the enemy. Two lost their sons in battle. One had two sons captured. Yes, the price of freedom was high indeed for those men. But deciding to be free, to think and live independently, to soar above the masses is always a costly decision.

As we discovered in the previous chapter, people who consecrate themselves to such a lifestyle must actually think in terms of another kingdom. And we learned that this kind of thinking thins the ranks—literally!

A MESSAGE THAT THINS THE RANKS

Some folks have the mistaken idea that Jesus deliberately tried to draw big crowds. It's true that large gatherings frequently followed Him during His three-plus years of earthly ministry, but never once did He attempt to generate a big audience. On the contrary, more than once He deliberately addressed certain issues that quickly diminished the number of onlookers. On one occasion, for instance, He pressed His points so stringently that many listeners walked away:

> Many therefore of His disciples, when they heard this said, "This is a difficult statement; who can listen to it?" . . .
> As a result of this many of His disciples withdrew, and were not walking with Him any more (John 6:60, 66).

On another occasion, Jesus did a similar thing. Both times it was *commitment* that thinned the ranks. Let's take a closer look at what happened in that second encounter Jesus had with the growing crowds. Dr. Luke sets the stage: "Now great multitudes were going along with Him . . ." (Luke 14:25).

A groundswell of curiosity had created quite an interest among the public regarding Jesus. His popularity had pulled people from villages all around. Many had come merely to gawk, to see a few miracles, and nothing more. Realizing that anything of a sensational nature could easily increase the frenzy of the crowd—something He loathed—Jesus found Himself unable to overlook the situation for one more minute:

> He turned and said to them, "If anyone comes to Me, and does not hate his own father and mother and wife and children and brothers and sisters, yes, and even his own life, he cannot be My disciple. Whoever does not carry his own cross and come after Me cannot be My disciple. For which one of you, when he wants to build a tower, does not first sit down and calculate the cost, to see if he has enough to complete it? Otherwise, when he has laid a foundation, and is not able to finish, all who observe it begin to ridicule him, saying, 'This man began to build and was not able to finish.' Or what king, when he sets out to meet another king in battle, will not first sit down and take counsel whether he is strong enough with ten thousand men to encounter the one coming against him with twenty thousand? Or else, while the other is still far away, he sends a delegation and asks terms of peace. So therefore, no one of you can be My disciple who does not give up all his own possessions" (Luke 14:25–33).

Here was a "great multitude" merely "going along" for the ride —a gigantic crowd of mediocre tirekickers, who were spectators, nothing more. It was a situation which prompted Jesus to look them squarely in the eye and confront their lack of commitment. Who wouldn't be stabbed awake by His thrice-repeated "You cannot be My disciple"? We're talking straight talk here! Jesus touches three nerves as He addresses the cost of commitment—*personal relationships, personal goals and desires,* and *personal possessions.*

Personal Relationships

"If anyone comes to Me, and does not hate his own father and mother and wife and children and brothers and sisters, yes, and even his own life, he cannot be My disciple" (v. 26).

When Jesus mentions that we're to "hate" father and mother, wife, children, and sister or brother, He doesn't suggest that we're to treat them maliciously and be ugly toward them. What He is doing is emphasizing the very real possibility of *competition in our loyalty* between Himself and those we love so dearly. Top-flight, uncompromising commitment to Christ mixed with the quality of life He expects of His followers leaves no room for competition. Outsiders who don't understand a Christian's commitment to put Christ first might observe such devotion to the Lord and misjudge it as hatred toward other relationships. It isn't hatred, but rather a matter of priorities—deciding who or what comes first. I discuss priorities in much greater detail in chapter 7.

Personal Goals and Desires

"Whoever does not carry his own cross and come after Me cannot be My disciple" (v. 27).

Here the penetration of Jesus' words goes a level deeper as He refers to surrendering our personal goals and desires to His authority. Negatively speaking, it means saying a firm *no* to what you and I want and *yes* to what God wants. Already we can understand why many decided not to hang around any longer.

In the first century if anyone was seen "carrying his own cross," it was clear to everyone that he was on his way to die.

Jesus uses that word picture to describe dying to our own personal pursuits and, instead, following Him fully. Such self-denial is rare in our day, as rare as a soaring eagle.

Denying oneself is not to be equated with losing one's uniqueness or becoming of no value. There have been great people in each generation who modeled self-denial as they made significant contributions to humankind. One such man was General Robert E. Lee, commander-in-chief of the Confederate troops during the Civil War. Few eagles soared higher during these darkest days of our nation's history than General Lee. In fact, none of his biographers have overlooked his trait of self-denial when describing the qualities of that Southern gentleman. Douglas Southall Freeman, in fact, concludes his lengthy volume, *Lee,* with these moving words that illustrate the extent of the General's humility:

> Of humility and submission was born a spirit of self-denial that prepared him for the hardships of the war and, still more, for the dark destitution that followed it. This self-denial was, in some sense, the spiritual counterpart of the social self-control his mother had inculcated in his boyhood days, and it grew in power throughout his life. His own misfortunes typified the fate of the Confederacy and of its adherents. Through it all, his spirit of self-denial met every demand upon it, and even after he went to Washington College and had an income on which he could live easily, he continued to deny himself as an example to his people. Had his life been epitomized in one sentence of the Book he read so often, it would have been in the words, "If any man will come after me, let him deny himself, and take up his cross daily, and follow me." And if one, only one, of all the myriad incidents of his stirring life had to be selected to typify his message, as a man, to the young Americans who stood in hushed awe that rainy October morning as their parents wept at the passing of the Southern Arthur, who would hesitate in selecting that incident? It occurred in Northern Virginia, probably on his last visit there. A young mother brought her baby to him to be blessed. He took the infant in his arms and looked at it and then at her and slowly said, "Teach him he must deny himself."[2]

That's good avice for anyone who wants to soar.

Personal Possessions

"So therefore, no one of you can be My disciple who does not give up all his own possessions" (v. 33).

Here again we see the accommodating language used so often by our Lord. He employs dramatic terms to communicate the intensity of His point. In today's vernacular, committed individuals live with shallow tent pegs. They may own things, but nothing owns them. They have come to terms with merchandise that has a price tag and opted for commitment to values that are priceless.

We're back to some of the things I was getting at in chapter 2, aren't we? It is this precise principle (the principle of shallow tent pegs) that disqualifies full-fledged yuppies from being high-flying eagles. They are hanging on to too much stuff!

Now take a look at a few related scriptures. Each of these is so relevant, so self-explanatory, that additional comment from me would be superfluous. Simply read and think about how each applies to you.

And He said to them, "Beware, and be on your guard against every form of greed; for not even when one has an abundance does his life consist of his possessions" (Luke 12:15).

"Sell your possessions and give to charity; make yourselves purses which do not wear out, an unfailing treasure in heaven, where no thief comes near, nor moth destroys. For where your treasure is, there will your heart be also" (Luke 12:33–34).

"He must increase, but I must decrease" (John 3:30).

But godliness actually is a means of great gain, when accompanied by contentment. . . .
Instruct those who are rich in this present world not to be conceited or to fix their hope on the uncertainty of riches, but on God, who richly supplies us with all things to enjoy. Instruct them to do good, to be rich in good works, to be generous and ready to share, storing up for themselves the treasure of a good foundation for the future, so that they may take hold of that which is life indeed" (1 Tim. 6:6, 17–19).

Eagles that soar up where the air is pure and thin aren't weighed down by a lot of excess baggage. For them, materialism is a menace, a terminal disease. If we want to soar like eagles we must free ourselves from the fetters of materialism.

AN EXPLANATION THAT MAKES SENSE

Sandwiched between those last two points Jesus made is some more helpful information. Read what He says carefully and see if you don't agree.

> "For which one of you, when he wants to build a tower, does not first sit down and calculate the cost, to see if he has enough to complete it? Otherwise, when he has laid a foundation, and is not able to finish, all who observe it begin to ridicule him, saying, 'This man began to build and was not able to finish.' Or what king, when he sets out to meet another king in battle, will not first sit down and take counsel whether he is strong enough with ten thousand men to encounter the one coming against him with twenty thousand? Or else, while the other is still far away, he sends a delegation and asks terms of peace" (Luke 14:28–32).

These two stories explain why Christ spoke in such stringent terms to the crowd. The first has to do with *building* and the second, with *fighting*. In each case, Jesus emphasizes the importance of quality. In building a tower that will last, quality builders are essential. And they cost a lot. In fighting a battle, quality soldiers (not the quantity of them, please notice) are all-important. They, too, are costly.

For years I taught that *we* are to "count the cost." It seemed so plausible. But suddenly one day, it dawned on me that Jesus never once told His followers to count the cost. No—*He's* the One who has already done that. He is the "king" (v. 31) who has already determined what it will take to encounter and triumph over life's enemies. And what *will* it take? A few strong, quality-minded champions whose commitment is solid as stone. And the cost will be great.

TOUGH QUESTIONS ONLY YOU CAN ANSWER

I've not pulled any punches in this chapter. But you have hung in there with me, and I commend you. These haven't been easy pages to write, but they are expressions I felt it necessary to make. Instead of wrapping up these thoughts in a traditional manner, I think it would be of greater benefit to ask a few pointed questions. So here they are. Don't hurry through them. Chew on each one, pondering your answer before going on to the next. Since confronting mediocrity takes thinking clearly, be painfully honest with yourself. There is no better time than now to make up your mind about these issues.

- Since life is so brief, what are the things you need to deal with that will enable you to soar during your remaining years? Be specific.
- Has peer pressure paralyzed you? Is that the reason you've not made your own "declaration of independence"? How can you overcome this paralysis?
- Where are you in the Luke 14 account? Among the few close followers or the many spectators? Why?
- Do you have any personal relationships that hinder your commitment to Christ-honoring excellence?
- What about your own goals and desires? Is self-denial your strong suit . . . or your downfall? Are you willing to surrender to Him?
- Does materialism have you in its grip?
- Isn't it about time for you to enlist as a full-fledged, committed follower of Christ? What's holding you back?
- If our country were overtaken by an enemy force that denied us the privilege of living openly for Christ, how would you react? Would your commitment be firm enough to keep you true?

Stories from the underground church in Russia never fail to jolt us awake. I came across another one just this past week. A house church in a city of the Soviet Union received one copy of the Gospel by Luke, the only scripture most of these Christians had ever seen. They tore it into small sections and distributed them among the body of believers. Their plan was to memorize the portion they had been given, then on the next Lord's Day they would meet and redistribute the scriptural sections.

On Sunday these believers arrived inconspicuously in small groups throughout the day so as not to arouse the suspicion of KGB informers. By dusk they were all safely inside, windows closed and doors locked. They began by singing a hymn quietly but with deep emotion. Suddenly, the door was pushed open and in walked two soldiers with loaded automatic weapons at the ready. One shouted, "All right—everybody line up against the wall. If you wish to renounce your commitment to Jesus Christ, leave now!"

Two or three quickly left, then another. After a few more seconds, two more.

"This is your last chance. Either turn against your faith in Christ," he ordered, "or stay and suffer the consequences."

Another left. Finally, two more in embarrassed silence with their faces covered slipped out into the night. No one else moved. Parents with small children trembling beside them looked down reassuringly. They fully expected to be gunned down or, at best, to be imprisoned.

After a few moments of complete silence, the other soldier closed the door, looked back at those who stood against the wall and said, "Keep your hands up—but this time in praise to our Lord Jesus Christ, brothers and sisters. We, too, are Christians. We were sent to another house church several weeks ago to arrest a group of believers—"

The other soldier interrupted, ". . . but, instead, *we were converted!* We have learned by experience, however, that unless people are willing to die for their faith, they cannot be fully trusted."[3]

In segments of the world where Bibles are plentiful and churches are protected, faith can run awfully shallow. Commitment can stay rather lukewarm. Eagles can learn to fly dangerously low. "What we obtain too cheap, we esteem too lightly."

It Calls for Extravagant Love

4

P*lease do not touch.* That brief imperative is seldom ever found scrawled out in a bold manner; instead it's usually neatly printed in elegant places, stating the obvious. Because there are always a few fools who are anxious to rush in where angels would not dare, those four words appear as a warning so people won't try to handle priceless things in a careless manner. The untouchable may be something as small as a fine china cup or as large as a one-of-a-kind classic car. Instead of handling such things, we are encouraged merely to enjoy them from a distance. Look, but keep your hands off.

Many years ago a group of tourists was making its way through the house where the great German composer Ludwig van Beethoven spent his last years. As they arrived at that special conservatory where the man had spent so many hours at the piano, the guide paused and spoke quietly, "And here is the master's instrument." A well-meaning but thoughtless woman in the back of the group pushed her way up front, sat down at the bench, and immediately began to play one of Beethoven's great sonatas as she said, "I suppose a lot of people love to play this piano." The guide placed his hand on hers to stop her as he answered, "Well, Ignace Paderewski was here last summer. Several in the group wanted him to play. But he responded, 'Oh, no . . . I am not worthy to play the same keyboard as the great Beethoven.'"

There are certain scenes in Scripture that seem too sacred, too priceless to touch. Some are majestic psalms of praise; others are intimate prayers and scenes of tragic grief. But I especially feel a sense of reverence when I come to the passages that record the last week of Jesus' life. It's almost as if a small sign should appear before all who enter this section: "Please do not touch." There is something sacred about a place where someone has died, certainly someone as valuable and significant as Jesus. I never arrive at the record of His final hours without a heightened sense of respect. Instead of plunging in without regard for his dignity, like the tourist at Beethoven's piano, I find myself hesitant.

It is almost as though the Holy Spirit has guided us here, then put His hand on ours and said, "Here is where He spent His final days. Here is what He did. Here is the way He died. Just be quiet and experience it. Take time to feel the emotion, to grasp the significance of these words."

In the first three chapters of this book, we traveled rather rapidly from one scene to the next. We found that the mind is of utmost importance, a veritable battleground of mental warfare. We even went a step further and found that there is a choice of kingdoms, which forces us to get off the fence if we hope to confront and conquer mediocrity. In the chapter that followed, we discovered that such a decision is costly. Commitment is essential if we hope to soar like an independent, keen-thinking eagle.

Now it's time to change the pace. Let's slow down and stroll quietly through a scene that will add some needed perspective. Before we get so intensely independent and start operating as if excellence means isolation, let's linger at a place where love was so extravagant it was shocking.

SETTING THE SCENE

Let me see if I can set the scene in such a way that you can appreciate it as it was meant to be appreciated. I'll try to handle it with great care.

> Now the feast of the Passover and Unleavened Bread was two days off; and the chief priests and the scribes were seeking how to seize Him by stealth, and kill Him; for they were saying, "Not during the festival, lest there be a riot of the people" (Mark 14:1–2).

If there were calendars hanging in Jewish kitchens in the first century, for sure, Passover would have been circled in red. What Thanksgiving is to America, Passover was to the ancient Jews, and, oh, so much more. It was a time of hearty celebration, the singing of great Jewish songs, the acting out of a drama dripping with emotion. It was a time in which signal fires were lighted around the city of Jerusalem. Trumpets blared and banners waved as the festivities continued. The festive spirit was contagious. People poured into Jerusalem from Galilee and Peraea and regions beyond. Like a vast family reunion, thousands upon thousands filled the streets for days as they relived their historic deliverance from bondage in Egypt. Ordinary business ceased as everyone in Jerusalem observed the holiday.

But even though a festive spirit was in the air, this year not everyone waved banners and sang songs. A few religious officials in high places were planning an execution. These men were putting the final touches on a plot that would lead to Jesus' death. They're identified as ". . . chief priests and scribes [who] were seeking how to seize Him by stealth." That word *stealth* means "a trick, a surprise tactic." (Who would've ever expected a kiss from one of the disciples? "That's perfect—just perfect.") Today we would say, "A conspiracy was being fine-tuned."

While the city was preoccupied with celebrating, singing, and laughing, those priests and scribes, alone and quiet, were frowning. Within a matter of hours Jesus would be nailed to a cross. Why would they want to kill Him? What was it that drove these men to such extreme rage?

The late British commentator, G. Campbell Morgan, clearly explains:

> . . . He had rebuked their ideals through the whole course of His public ministry. Ideals are always closely related to conduct; consequently the whole tenor of His teaching had been to rebuke their conduct.
>
> During the latter days of His ministry He had rebuked their failures as shepherds of the people. . . . Their hatred of Jesus was consequently of One Who had revealed their failure.[1]

Can't you just hear their whispered murmurings? "Why, the *audacity* to tell us that we are failures!"

The problem was, of course, that more and more people believed Jesus. According to a comment recorded in John 12, "Many of the Jews were . . . believing in Jesus" (v. 11). So the chief priests and scribes had a problem. I can almost hear them plotting, "We want to kill Him, but not during the festival, lest there be a riot. He has a lot of followers. People are believing in this fool, this liar, this troublemaker." And they probably thumped their fingers on the desk and stroked their beards as they waited for just the right moment to strike.

Suddenly, we are lifted from that scene in Jerusalem and transported a few miles away to a modest home in Bethany, where more than a dozen people are reclining around a table, relaxing and enjoying themselves.

> And while He was in Bethany at the home of Simon the leper . . . (Mark 14:3).

The residence is identified as the home of Simon the leper. Obviously, no one would eat with a leper unless the leper had been healed (or, to use the biblical word, "cleansed"), and that is exactly what had happened to Simon. What an irony! Simon owed his entire life to the One who had cleansed him from leprosy—the same One others were planning to kill. Another guest also owed his life to Jesus. That guest was Lazarus—a man recently raised from the dead by Jesus.

What stories Simon and Lazarus could tell! Wouldn't you love to have been invited to that dinner with Lazarus? You could hear him tell how it was three to four days beyond death. Think of it!

You could even ask Simon, "How was it as a leper? How is it now?" And in addition to these two, Jesus would be there. And with Jesus, most of the twelve disciples. And with a group that large, you need to have someone serving. Guess who? Right—that called for Martha. She was there serving. Martha was always serving!

The dinner must have been great, and the conversation even greater. Maybe there was some laughter, maybe not. Whatever, they must have had a memorable time. Don't you love places and times like that? Everyone relaxed. Everybody knowing each other—everyone at ease.

But someone was conspicuous by her absence. She has appeared only twice in Scripture in a significant way. Once (Luke 10) she was sitting at the feet of Jesus listening while her sister Martha was serving. And the other time she was falling on her face before our Lord (John 11) after her brother died. Mary was not one of the more prominent characters, not until this moving, almost-sacred scene we're about to witness. Here, she distinguishes herself as a woman who was unafraid of others' opinions and committed to excellence.

EXTRAVAGANT DEVOTION—EXTREME REACTION

Now you have to understand that things are quite different today in America from what they were in those days in Jerusalem. Back then, a Jewish woman never reclined at a table full of men. And she certainly never let her hair down in public. She would prepare the meal and serve it to the men, but then she would back away to eat in another room, like the kitchen, much like the custom in Arabia to this day. I mention that so you will be properly prepared for the shock of what occurred. Hang on!

> And while He was in Bethany at the home of Simon the leper, and reclining at table, there came a woman with an alabaster vial of costly perfume of pure nard; and she broke the vial and poured it over His head (Mark 14:3).

Genuine nard was made from dried leaves of a rare Himalayan plant. And the particular vase Mary used, if it were like others used in that day to hold expensive contents, was itself a thing of beauty. Commonly, such vases were capable of holding not less than a Roman pound, *twelve full ounces,* of this costly perfume.

Allow me to interrupt the narrative long enough to acquaint you with the cost of certain fragrances today. One authority I spoke to recently informed me that Jean Patou 1000 is perhaps the finest. It sells for $110 a quarter-ounce. The next, in the opinion of this person, is Pheromone, which goes for a cool $150 a half-ounce!

But Mary's vase most likely contained twenty-four times that amount. This woman had a perfume so expensive that if you were to weigh its significance in dollars and cents you could have fed hundreds of families an entire meal. Over a year's wage was contained in that little vase. We're talking superextravagant, top-notch quality stuff!

And without hesitation, Mary broke the vase and poured its entire contents over Jesus' head. (In John's account, we read that she also took her hair and wiped Jesus' feet with this magnificent perfume.) Imagine the fragrance which swept across that room when Mary broke open the vase, and poured its contents down across Jesus' head. Then to the amazement of everyone except Jesus, she poured the last of the perfume across His feet, pulled down her hair, and then wiped His feet with her hair.

> Mary therefore took a pound of very costly, genuine spikenard ointment, and anointed the feet of Jesus, and wiped His feet with her hair; and the house was filled with the fragrance of the ointment (John 12:3).

What an explosive act . . . what extravagance! How *could* she?

> The delicious fragrance ran down over His shining hair and thick beard. It enfolded His body with its delightful aroma. Even His tunic and flowing undergarment were drenched with its enduring pungency. Wherever He moved during the ensuing forty-eight hours, the perfume would go with Him: Into the Passover: into the Garden of Gethsemane: into the high priest's home: into Herod's hall: into Pilate's praetorium: into the crude hands of those who cast lots for His clothing at the foot of the cross.

> The special rite of perfuming the head and body was a rare ritual reserved only for royalty. It was the most lofty honor that could be bestowed by a common person. Jesus recognized this

and so did those around Him. It was a significant moment of momentous meaning.[2]

That helpful insight reminds us that Mary's devotion lingered; it wasn't just for that moment, then quickly forgotten. Since His garments weren't changed, the aroma went with Him everywhere He went until shortly before His death. Even those who later gambled for His garments must have recognized the lingering fragrance. Don't forget, Mary had poured it all over Him. Talk about excellence . . . talk about extravagant love . . . *I love it!*

But not everyone loved it. The magnificence of the moment was marred by the murmur of some small-minded men. Those who watched this act were men who made their bed under the stars and ate figs they picked from trees and fish they caught in the sea. I mean, those guys calculated life by the bits and pieces. And their logical minds, their two-dimensional figuring simply couldn't put this together. They absolutely couldn't believe Mary had broken the whole thing! She didn't just dip her finger in the vase and wipe a little here and there, she broke it and poured it all out. They were indignant. How could she do such a thing? They were in shock. You think I'm imagining that? Read for yourself:

> But some were indignantly remarking to one another, "For what purpose has this perfume been wasted?" (Mark 14:4).

Now wait a minute. Before we get too sophisticated about all this, remember we're observing a scene that happened in the first century. Folks like us have had nineteen centuries to think about it. Extravagant deeds such as this were considered appropriate and even heroic a few hundred years later. One would wonder how many great cathedrals were raised against the wishes of the public, how many fine pieces of art were built in spite of the sneering crowd who calculated by exacting weights and measures. This kind of expense never makes sense at the moment, especially to those of an extremely practical mindset. And if you figure everything on the basis of bare essentials, any expression of art is considered extravagant!

So these men shouted that the perfume had been wasted. "How could she? Do you realize what could have been done with this amount?" They've already got it figured out.

"For this perfume might have been sold for over three hundred denarii, and the money given to the poor." And they were scolding her (Mark 14:5).

There will always be a breakdown in the logic of extreme devotion if the basis of comparison is the poor. Furthermore, there will never be an understanding by those who confine themselves to operating in that tight, rigid radius. You miss that, you miss it all. People to this day operate with that mentality. Function still gets more votes than devotion. Practicality will always win over beauty. "Lighten up on the music so we can serve more food . . . no need for sculpture or fine paintings or lovely structures so long as the poor are present. If black-and-white is cheaper, color is wasteful . . . if a little electronic organ will do the job, a pipe organ is extravagant!" On and on the argument goes.

We shouldn't be too surprised to read that these men "scolded" Mary. We're not told what they said, but you can certainly imagine—especially if you are an eagle who has soared in the heights of "extravagance" on occasion.

JUSTIFICATION AND DEFENSE

Jesus not only defends Mary's action, He justifies the woman on the basis of purity of motive and urgency of the hour. Don't miss that. Jesus said, "Let her alone." (In today's terms, "Shut up, men. Be quiet.")

> . . . why do you bother her? She has done a good deed to Me. For the poor you always have with you, and whenever you wish, you can do them good; but you do not always have Me. She has done what she could; she has anointed My body beforehand for the burial (Mark 14:6–8).

Jesus' death and burial were two of the last things His disciples wanted to think about that day. I can just hear them saying, "This evening meal is a delightful time of celebration together; don't talk about death, talk about life."

But Mary had her focus right. She wasn't enamored by the celebration of the season; she had not forgotten that her Lord's days were numbered. "You don't know when it will happen, men. . . . She's simply giving Me everything she owns. She's broken the vase in honor of My death." It was an "early embalming." How that changed the perspective!

I hope you didn't overlook Jesus' comment, "The poor you always have with you." There has to be some kind of implication in that statement. You and I know, for sure, that it is not, in any sense of the word, a put-down of the poor. We know Jesus better than that. No one has been a more significant instrument for helping the poor than Jesus of Nazareth. No one has demonstrated a greater heart of compassion. Then what could He mean by that comment? He's looking at Mary's act in light of its overall perspective. He sees His death as imminent. He sees her devotion as properly extravagant. And so He says, in effect, "It's all right. Don't criticize or try to stop her. For this moment [allow Me], *forget* the poor! Her 'extravagance,' in this case, is absolutely appropriate. In fact, commendable!"

Jesus accepts Mary's act of praise which she gave for all the right motives. Her commitment of sincere devotion may seem to us to be an overreaction, but He did not consider it so. Not at all.

> "And truly I say to you, wherever the gospel is preached in the whole world, that also which this woman has done shall be spoken of in memory of her" (Mark 14:9).

This follow-up statement by Jesus is one of those often forgotten lines. It tells us that He planned for this whole incident to have a perpetual impact. Unfortunately, this woman's act of devotion has not always been given the prominence it deserves. The truth is that Mary is seldom, if ever, remembered. And when she is mentioned, it is almost with the wave of a hand, "Merely a gush of fanaticism, irresponsible extravagance, little more." Yet Jesus considered her deed worthy of being mentioned throughout time, around the world. How greatly we need the memory of Mary, and yet how seldom we hear of it! She is one of those misunderstood people who chose to live above the level of mediocrity—one who truly soared like the eagles, a model of elegant excellence.

LASTING MEMORIAL—LINGERING LESSONS

As I said in the beginning of this chapter, this episode at Simon's home is one of those accounts that needs to be handled with care. In some ways it is so sacred an event that I hesitate to touch it. But since it contains such important lessons for those who want to soar through life, living above mediocrity, I will risk returning to the story and reflecting on it from the viewpoint of excellence.

In a nutshell, I believe this event has been preserved to teach one major message: *There are certain times when extravagance is appropriate.* I will go further. In our day of emphasis on high-tech calculations and finely tuned budgets with persistent reminders of cost, restraint, and propriety (that is, never being "guilty" of doing anything outside the bounds of the ordinary), *anything* beyond the basics can be misconstrued as excessive. If you buy into that ever-present Spartan philosophy, then everything you build will be functional, ordinary, and basic. Everything you purchase will be at the lowest cost. Everything you do will be average.

We used to laugh at a comment one of the American astronauts made years ago, but the laughter has hushed since the *Challenger* tragedy. The way the story goes, someone stuck his head inside the nose capsule before the team of astronauts had launched and asked, "Well, how does it feel?" With a grin, one of them replied, "It really makes you think twice in here when you realize everything in this whole project was constructed according to the lowest bid!" Many—dare I say, most—conduct their entire lives "according to the lowest bid." This is never more obvious than in the evangelical community today. Let anything appear the least bit expensive and you can expect a critical response.

Not only is abundance suspected as being inappropriately extravagant, it is openly criticized. The majority will never understand. They will always make the ordinary their standard. I challenge that! On the basis of this magnificent story, I feel there are times when "extravagant" gifts are not only appropriate, they are occasionally essential! So are "extravagant" purchases and "extravagant" expressions of love, especially if we are determined to live above the level of mediocrity. "Extravagant" memorials need to be erected. "Extravagant" art needs to be appreciated. Yes, even "extravagant" displays of our devotion to the living Lord. I believe there are times when God, as it were, shouts with a smile, "Break a vase!"

Think back. Do you know what God did when He built that magnificent tabernacle in the wilderness? He broke a vase. Of all things, He instructed those wilderness wanderers to construct a fabulous, albeit temporary, place of worship—a tabernacle. And they followed His design to the nth degree. Lots of gold. Beautiful tapestry. Lovely wood craftsmanship. Impressive creativity. And throughout those years in the wilderness God's glory resided in that so-called "extravagant" worship center.

As the years passed, God's people settled down in a land they could call their own. By and by, their king, Solomon—a man of peace—heard God's voice again: "Break a vase, Solomon!" And the result? An incredible temple, which became one of the ageless "wonders of the world." Study the details for yourself. You won't believe its beauty. You talk about extravagance! You talk about quality and creative craftsmanship! So perfectly shaped and polished were those stones that comprised the walls in that awesome building, not a sound was heard as each stone was slipped into place by the stonemasons. And what about those veils, the colorful curtains, the ornate windows, the elegant steps, the mercy seat! Gold—some of it solid, much of it beaten, other sections overlaid—it was everywhere! God broke a vase. Yes, it was an exception all right, but it was also a call to excellence—a call to live above the level of mediocrity. Likewise, there are times today when extravagance is appropriate, especially if we are to soar like an eagle.

Paul himself said, "I have learned how to be abased and how to abound." So we see that occasionally God broke a vase in Paul's journeys, too. There were times He let Paul stay in the penthouse. Some of us would have great difficulty staying in a penthouse. Our reasoning might go something like this: "It just isn't right. It's too extravagant. But I'd sure like to try it a time or two." (Just now I can picture a wife saying to her husband, "Honey, listen to something Swindoll wrote . . . and listen closely.")

Have you ever taken a close look at the "new Jerusalem" in Revelation? Ever done an intelligent study of the heavenly city where God has designed for His people to spend eternity? We're talking *wall-to-wall broken vases!* If that thought makes you nervous, you'll be nervous throughout eternity.

I'm told that Harry Ironside, a fine pastor and conference speaker of yesteryear, once checked into a hotel where a church had made reservations for him. Without a word, one of the bell-boys led the pastor to the designated accommodations and unlocked the door. One look and Ironside realized he was in the penthouse. It was like nothing he had ever seen. At first he just stood in the doorway staring in disbelief at the plush furnishings—among them a silver service sitting on a carved table and lots of highly polished brass. On further investigation he discovered multiple rooms, including several bathrooms with thick, luxurious towels and marble finishings. Immediately, Pastor Ironside went to the phone and called the desk attendant downstairs, "I think there's been a mistake," he said.

The receptionist asked, "Are you Harry A. Ironside?"

"Yes."

"Are you ministering at such and such a church tomorrow?"

"Yes."

"Well, I have a note here that I don't understand, but it says, 'If Dr. Ironside calls you and has any concerns, just say, "We want you to learn how to *abound,* Dr. Ironside."'"

Before you get your hopes up, remember, that's not what we can expect . . . nor should we. Like the account of Mary's anointing Jesus, such rare moments need to be handled with care, not flaunted. Vases were not broken over the Savior every day. He didn't smell of luxurious perfume throughout His life. But how perfectly fitting it was at this moment.

Now for a few pointed questions:

- Must all the places where God is represented look mediocre?
- Must all the furnishings be of lowest quality or just moderate?
- Must every semblance of art be omitted?
- Must we live all our lives under constant restraint and self-imposed guilt, for fear of being told that we are overlooking the poor?
- Must *everything* be just "adequate"? Why not occasionally use something of the highest quality?

Let me give you a new thought: *If you can explain it, it may not be extravagant enough!* Did you notice that Mary never once said a word here or in any other passage of Scripture explaining herself? She never said one word, not even when they rebuked her. How could she even begin to explain such extravagance? A better question: Why should she? Even if she tried, they were the type who would never have understood. So Mary simply did what her heart told her to do—without explanation.

It takes pure motive and a strong inner confidence to be that secure. Such extravagant love cannot be explained nor can it be justified to calculating, rigid, narrow minds. And because the majority will always be driven by what is practical, the majority will never understand.

There's an old theatrical expression actors sometimes use in jest when a person is about to go out on the stage: "Hey, break a leg." I've got a new one for quality-minded, high-flying eagles. When we greet one another: "Hey, break a vase!" When's the last time you broke a vase? When's the last time you did it and you were so secure you didn't even feel the need to explain it, though you were questioned and criticized? Believe me, those who soar will understand. Those who don't, I repeat, won't.

One who understands writes:

> In Mary we see the gaiety of abandoned praise. With glorious imprudence she broke the container and with loving care used the whole contents. She was liberated out of herself in a dramatic devotion. Her unimpaired impulses moved her to give a great gift. The serendipity of love had a free agent. It was not smothered with caution and prejudice. She was lifted out of arithmetic calculation to abandoned compassion.
>
> She did not allow reserve to keep her from the moment which would never come again. . . . There is a time . . . when people should be careful, but there is also a time when they ought not to be cautious. There is something to be said for careful saving of our resources in order to make possible a great moment of unrestrained thanksgiving. . . . The Christian is not a tight-fisted, clenched-teeth, grim-faced person. Rather, he is one who loves and laughs and gives himself to Christ lavishly. In Mary we are challenged by extravagant love. . . . "A certain excessiveness is an important ingredient of greatness."[3]

Do you at times act upon that impulse to abandon restraint? Do you ever have the courage to risk an extravagant expression of love? Then you're on your way to living above the level of mediocrity. Extravagance is an exception, I remind you, but there are times when it is appropriate.

Not long ago one of my staff members told me he had made a

decision that was most unusual for him. He had decided he would take his wife to Hawaii. And they were going to take the trip without the kids. They had wanted to go for years, but were never able to afford it. When they sold their home, they had made a little extra, so he decided to splurge. I distinctly remember grabbing him by the shoulders and saying, "Good for you. That's great! It's about time you soared like an eagle." He smiled, "You sound like my wife."

I know of a school that has raised a memorial to a couple of very significant people in their history. The school decided to place a lovely (and I might add, expensive) set of chimes in the center of the campus in honor of this husband-wife team, alumni who have contributed so much to the life of that school. I openly applaud the school for the "extravagance" of that memorial. It fits. It's beautiful. It's right! When the president of that fine institution risked that decision, he "broke a vase!" What a refreshing, delightful thing to do!

I don't know how many times I have enjoyed reading Anne Ortlund's insightful words on this very subject. She approaches this story from a slightly different angle, but because her thoughts fit so beautifully, I draw this chapter and the first section of my book to a close with her comments.

A while back, Ray preached on Mark 14:3. "Here came Mary, . . . with her alabaster vase of nard to the dinner where Jesus was. She broke the bottle and poured it on Him."

An alabaster vase—milky white, veined, smooth, precious.

And pure nard inside! Gone forever. According to John 12:3, the whole house became filled with the fragrance.

Some story.

———

Christians file into church on a Sunday morning. One by one by one they march in—like separate alabaster vases.

Contained.

Self-sufficient.

Encased.

Individually complete.

Contents undisclosed.

No perfume emitting at all.

Their vases aren't bad looking. In fact, some of them are the Beautiful People, and they become Vase-Conscious: conscious of their own vase and of one another's. They're aware of clothes, of personalities, of position in this world—of exteriors.

So before and after church (maybe during) they're apt to talk Vase talk.

Mary broke her vase.

Broke it?! How shocking. How controversial. Was everybody doing it? Was it a vase-breaking party? No, she just did it all by herself. What happened then? The obvious: all the contents were forever released. She could never hug her precious nard to herself again.

Many bodies who file into church, no doubt, do so because they have Jesus inside of them. Jesus!—precious, exciting, life giving. But most of them keep Him shut up, contained, enclosed all their lives. And the air is full of NOTHING. They come to church and sit—these long rows of cold, beautiful, alabaster vases! Then the cold, beautiful, alabaster vases get up and march out again, silently—or maybe talking their cold alabaster talk—to repeat the ritual week after week, year after year.

Unless they just get too bored and quit.

The need for Christians everywhere (nobody is exempt) is to be broken. The vase has to be smashed! Christians have to let the life out! It will fill the room with sweetness. And the congregation will all be broken shards, mingling together for the first time.

Of course it's awkward and scary to be broken! Of course it's easier to keep up that cold alabaster front.

It was costly for Mary too.[4]

You talk about something too beautiful for words, something so valuable, it's priceless. It is a living vase, broken before others. But don't worry, the "do not touch" sign no longer applies. When the vase is broken, its contents fill a room. And interestingly, it says to everyone, "Please *do* touch."

For some of you, the broken vase is long overdue. I'm talking about an extravagant gift to the work of Christ, the kind Mary gave. And what was that? Herself. For some of you it would be the first time ever that you gave yourself to anyone. Christ invites you to give yourself to Him, completely, extravagantly—a living vase broken before others. Do it now and discover what soaring is all about—become a Christian.

*D*eath and sorrow will be the
companions of our journey;
hardship our garment; constancy
and valor our only shield. We must
be united, we must be undaunted,
we must be inflexible.

Sir Winston Churchill
1940

Part Two

Overcoming Mediocrity Means Living Differently

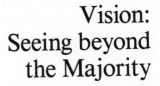

Vision:
Seeing beyond
the Majority

5

For four chapters we have underscored the fact that confronting mediocrity takes thinking clearly. Everything we deal with in life begins in the mind, so we began there. We discovered the intensity of the battle that rages in our minds. We also learned that those who confront mediocrity must do so through the perspective of another kingdom, ruled not by ourselves but by our Lord Himself—a surrender which costs dearly. It costs our commitment. And when that commitment expresses itself (as in Mary's case in the days of Jesus), it is revealed periodically in expressions of extravagant love.

Having come to terms with the importance of thinking clearly, we are ready to tackle the second challenge: *living differently.* Whoever clears away the mental fog is no longer satisfied drifting along with the masses. *Vision* replaces mental resistance. *Determination* marches in, overstepping laziness and indifference. And it's then that we begin to realize the value of *priorities,* a step which dictates the need for personal *accountability.* I will define each of these four terms a little later. But for now, consider them as one domino bumping the next. Each one of these stages precedes the next, forming a unit that spells out the basics of living differently—with excellence—in a world of sameness, boredom, and futility.

Throughout this book I continue to refer to our "world." That may throw you a curve, since I'm usually not referring to the planet we live on when I use the term. By "world" I mean the invisible yet surrounding atmosphere in which we live that "erodes faith, dissipates hope, and corrupts love," as Eugene Peterson puts it.[1] It may be a system of thought that includes human intelligence, persuasive winsomeness, clever and appealing logic, competition, creativity, and resourcefulness, but it lacks the essential ingredients that enable us to soar like an eagle. The most treacherous part of all is the way we become brainwashed by the system, thus blocked from reaching our full potential. The end result is predictable: internal anxiety and external mediocrity.

THREE INDISPUTABLE FACTS ABOUT THE WORLD SYSTEM

Let's go a little deeper into an understanding of the world system. To give ourselves a point of reference, let's look again at Jesus' words. Pay close attention to His repeated remarks about being anxious.

"No one can serve two masters; for either he will hate the one and love the other, or he will hold to one and despise the other. You cannot serve God and mammon. For this reason I say to you, do not be anxious for your life, as to what you shall eat, or what you shall drink; nor for your body, as to what you shall put on. Is not life more than food, and the body than clothing? Look at the birds of the air, that they do not sow, neither do they reap, nor gather into barns, and yet your heavenly Father feeds them. Are you not worth much more than they? And which of you by being anxious can add a single cubit to his life's span? And why are you anxious about clothing? Observe how the lilies of the field grow; they do not toil nor do they spin, yet I say to you that even Solomon in all his glory did not clothe himself like one of these. But if God so arrays the grass of the field, which is alive today and tomorrow is thrown into the furnace, will He not much more do so for you, O men of little faith? Do not be anxious then, saying, 'What shall we eat?' or 'What shall we drink?' or 'With what shall we clothe ourselves?' For all these things the Gentiles eagerly seek; for your heavenly Father knows that you need all these things. But seek first His kingdom and His righteousness; and all these things shall be added to you. Therefore do not be anxious for tomorrow; for tomorrow will care for itself. Each day has enough trouble of its own" (Matt. 6:24–34).

I never read those familiar words without becoming aware of the difference between the way people *naturally* live (full of worry and anxiety) and the way our Lord planned for us to live (free of all that excess baggage). Then why? Why do we opt for a lifestyle that is the very antithesis of what He designed for us? Because the "system" sucks us in! We yield to a lesser lifestyle because "all those things the Gentiles eagerly seek" (v. 32) occupy our attention and ultimately dominate our lives. As I see it, there are three interrelated factors.

1. We live in a negative, hostile world. Face it, my friend, the system that surrounds us focuses on the negatives: what is wrong, not what is right; what is missing, not what is present; what is ugly, not what is beautiful; what is destructive, not what is constructive; what cannot be done, not what can be done; what hurts, not what helps; what we lack, not what we have. You question that? Pick up your local newspaper and read it through. See if the majority of the news doesn't concern itself (and the reader) with the negatives. It's contagious!

This negative mindset leads to incredible feelings of anxiety. Surround most people with enough negatives and I can guarantee the result: fear, resentment, and anger. Negative information plus hostile thinking equals anxiety. And yet Jesus said again and again, "Don't be anxious." The world system, I repeat, works directly against the life God planned for His people. The realization of this led Isaac Watts, over 250 years ago, to write:

> Are there no foes for me to face?
> Must I not stem the flood?
> Is this vile world a friend to grace
> To help me on to God?[2]

2. We are engulfed in mediocrity and cynicism (a direct result of living in a negative world). Without the motivation of divinely

empowered insight and enthusiasm, people tend toward the "average," doing just enough to get by. Thus, the fallout from the system is mediocrity. The majority dictates the rules, and excitement is replaced with a shrug of the shoulders. Excellence is not only lost in the shuffle, whenever it rears its head, it is considered a threat.

3.   <u>Most choose not to live differently.</u> Those who take their cues from the system blend into the drab backdrop of the majority. Words like "Just go with the flow" and "Don't make waves" and "Who cares?" begin to gain a hearing.

Stop and think. In a world where all that cynicism is present, what is absent? Courage! That strong muscle of character that gives a nation its pride and gives a home its purpose and gives a person the will to excel is gone. I'm certainly not the first to point out the danger of a lack of courage. Aleksandr Solzhenitsyn's speeches frequently include such warnings:

> Must one point out that from ancient times a decline in courage has been considered the beginning of the end?[3]

What, then, does it take to live differently? In chapters 5–8 I will be concentrating on four specifics: vision, determination, priorities, and accountability. When I think of *vision,* I have in mind the ability to see above and beyond the majority. Again I am reminded of the eagle, which has eight times as many visual cells per cubic centimeter than does a human. This translates into rather astounding abilities. For example, flying at 600 feet elevation, an eagle can spot an object the size of a dime moving through six-inch grass. The same creature can see three-inch fish jumping in a lake five miles away. Eaglelike people can envision what most would miss.

By *determination,* I think of inner fortitude, strength of character—being disciplined to remain consistent, strong, and diligent regardless of the odds or the demands. Again, the eagle represents this trait. Bald eagles are adamant in the defense of their territory and their young. The strength in the eagle's claws is nothing short of phenomenal—sufficient to grasp and break large bones in a man's forearm. Eagle types possess tenacity.

The other two are virtually self-explanatory. *Priorities* have to do with choosing first things first—doing essential things in the order of importance, bypassing the incidentals. And *accountability* relates to answering the hard questions, being closely in touch with a few individuals rather than living like an isolated Lone Ranger. Eaglelike folks may be rare, but they possess an incredible loyalty when they do link up.

For the remainder of this chapter, let's concentrate on the value of vision.

TWO COURAGEOUS MEN
WHO DISAGREED WITH THE MAJORITY

The best way I know to stimulate you toward a renewed commitment to excellence is to return to Scripture for an inspired account. The one I have in mind is tucked away in the fourth book of the Old Testament, the Book of Numbers, chapter 13.

Some Background

Five things should be remembered in order for us to be brought up to speed here in Numbers 13.

First, there has been an exodus. The Israelites have been set free from Egyptian bondage. Pharaoh has let the people go. They have departed from Egypt with all their belongings and with all their family members.

Second, under Moses' leadership God's chosen people have arrived at the edge of the Promised Land. According to the last verse of chapter 12, "the people . . . camped in the wilderness of Paran," right at the edge of Canaan (the Promised Land). In the exodus God showed Himself strong. He displayed His miraculous power when the Israelites went through the Red Sea and when He directed them safely across the wilderness to the land of Canaan. When they arrived at the border, the Israelites could see smoke rising from the cities in the misty distance. Perhaps from that vantage point they could even see some of the walls that surrounded the larger cities. I'm sure their hearts beat faster as they expressed their relief and excitement: "Finally . . . we made it!"

Third, the new territory was theirs to claim. God promised it to them.

"Send out for yourself men so that they may spy out the land of Canaan, which I am going to give to the sons of Israel; you shall send a man from each of their fathers' tribes, every one a leader among them" (v. 2).

God clearly promised His people the land. "You'll have to invade it and fight, but I promise you that victory is *guaranteed.*" Nobody on this earth ever had a better deal in battle than those people!

When General Dwight Eisenhower and his brain trust were about to lead our troops through the Normandy Invasion back in World War II, they were filled with anxiety brought on by uncertainty. And anxiety increased when the weather worsened. "Shall we proceed? Shall we wait? Shall we abort the mission entirely?" We can hardly imagine the churning uneasiness. And even though Eisenhower had this massive assault ready to move into operation, he wasn't sure that the troops could make a safe landing, to say nothing of what they might encounter from the enemy forces. Finally, with anxious uncertainty, the general signaled thumbs up.

The Israelites faced nothing like that. They had the sure promise of God. "You will have the land." No troops ever had greater reason to fight with assurance.

Fourth, God commanded Moses to spy out the land. In order to plan an intelligent battle strategy, he was to send in a few selected scouts to spy out the land. So Moses cooperated. Remember this: Not once were the spies asked to give their opinion about whether they could take the land. No need for that since God had already promised. Instead they were told precisely what to do.

So Moses sent them from the wilderness of Paran at the command of the Lord, all of them men who were heads of the sons of Israel. These then were their names: from the tribe of Reuben, Shammua the son of Zaccur; from the tribe of Simeon, Shaphat the son of Hori; from the tribe of Judah, Caleb the son of Jephunneh; from the tribe of Issachar, Igal the son of Joseph; from the tribe of Ephraim, Hoshea the son of Nun; from the tribe of Benjamin, Palti the son of Raphu; from the tribe of Zebulun, Gaddiel the son of Sodi; from the tribe of Joseph, from the tribe of Manasseh, Gaddi the son of Susi; from the tribe of Dan, Ammiel the son of Gemalli; from the tribe of Asher, Sethur the son of

Michael; from the tribe of Gad, Geuel the son of Machi. These are the names of the men whom Moses sent to spy out the land; but Moses called Hoshea the son of Nun, Joshua (vv. 3–16).

Back in those days each one of those names was familiar. They were like twelve famous mayors in America today, or twelve of our more prominent governors or senators. They were famous men among the Israelites. I emphasize that point because I don't want you to think for a moment that some of those men were over-the-hill-type guys, lacking good sense. All twelve were leader types, but only two soared above the restrictive mindset so common in the system.

Fifth, their assignment was clear. Painfully, explicitly clear.

When Moses sent them to spy out the land of Canaan, he said to them, "Go up there into the Negev; then go up into the hill country. And see what the land is like, and whether the people who live in it are strong or weak, whether they are few or many. And how is the land in which they live, is it good or bad? And how are the cities in which they live, are they like open camps or with fortifications? And how is the land, is it fat or lean? Are there trees in it or not? Make an effort then to get some of the fruit of the land . . ." (vv. 17–20).

End of assignment. Once they found out those things, mission accomplished! Never once does Moses say, "And when you return, advise us on whether we ought to invade the land." No, that wasn't their mandate. They were told to scope out the land, to do a quick, secret reconnaissance, and to come back with a report about what they had observed.

The spies left and stayed gone for forty days.

So they went up and spied out the land from the wilderness of Zin as far as Rehob, at Lebo-hamath. When they had gone up into the Negev, they came to Hebron where Ahiman, Sheshai and Talmai, the descendants of Anak were. (Now Hebron was built seven years before Zoan in Egypt.)

Then they came to the valley of Eshcol and from there cut down a branch with a single cluster of grapes; and they carried it on a pole between two men, with some of the pomegranates and the figs. That place was called the valley of Eshcol, because of the cluster which the sons of Israel cut down from there.

When they returned from spying out the land, at the end of forty days, they proceeded to come to Moses and Aaron and to all the congregation of the sons of Israel in the wilderness of Paran, at Kadesh; and they brought back word to them and to all the congregation and showed them the fruit of the land. Thus they told him, and said, "We went in to the land where you sent us; and it certainly does flow with milk and honey, and this is its fruit" (vv. 21–27).

While these twelve men were in the land of Canaan, they took samples of the fruit and brought them back. Once they returned to the Israelite camp, they displayed the grapes and showed them the fruit of the land.

And all the people gathered around and listened as the report was given. So far so good. Beautiful fruit. Delicious. Impressive report. I'm sure there were a few oohs and aahs.

Negative Report

But while everyone was getting excited, ten of the spies went on:

"Nevertheless, the people who live in the land are strong, and the cities are fortified and very large; and moreover, we saw the descendants of Anak there. Amalek is living in the land of the Negev and the Hittites and the Jebusites and the Amorites are living in the hill country, and the Canaanites are living by the sea and by the side of the Jordan."

. . . "We are not able to go up against the people, for they are too strong for us" (vv. 28–29, 31).

I find myself wanting to shout back, "Hey, wait a minute! Who asked you? Nobody wants to know if we're able to go up or not. That wasn't your assignment, men. God has already promised us that it is our land. We just want to know what the land is like."
Notice that these ten men went far beyond their assignment.

So they gave out to the sons of Israel a bad report of the land which they had spied out, saying, "The land through which we have gone, in spying it out, is a land that devours its inhabitants; and all the people whom we saw in it are men of great size. There also we saw the Nephilim (the sons of Anak are part of the Nephilim); and we became like grasshoppers in our own sight, and so we were in their sight" (vv. 32–33).

"Wow! You people cannot believe the size of those giants!" Today I suppose we would say, "They looked like professional athletes!"

Ever been at courtside at a professional basketball game? If you have, then you know what it is like to be around people who make you feel like a grasshopper. I distinctly recall standing alongside the Los Angeles Lakers center, Kareem Abdul-Jabbar. We're talking, "Chuck, the grasshopper."

I have spoken at several professional football pre-game chapel services. And invariably, I feel as if I am surrounded by giants! One time, most of the men were sitting on one side of the room. I asked if some would mind moving to the other side, since the room was beginning to sink on that side. When they began to move about, I definitely felt like an insect. I just hoped one of them wouldn't step on me as they lumbered out the door after the service. That's bound to be how those spies felt back in Moses' day.

Now what kind of impact did this narrow vision have on the people? Just in case you wonder if negativism and restrictive vision are contagious, keep reading:

> Then all the congregation lifted up their voices and cried, and the people wept that night. And all the sons of Israel grumbled against Moses and Aaron; and the whole congregation said to them, "Would that we had died in the land of Egypt! Or would that we had died in this wilderness!" (Num. 14:1–2).

You say, "How could they ever say such a thing? God *promised* they would have the land!" Because negativism is infectious. Because lack of vision from the world system engulfs us. Human reasoning overrules faith! Natural thinking says you can't whip people that big. You can't win if you invade that land. I mean, look at how many there are! Count them: There are the Jebusites and the Hittites and the Amorites and the Canaanites—probably even "the termites." *Everybody* in the land is against this wandering band of Hebrews! And add to that list the sons of Anak, the giants! Can't you just hear those Israelites, "We've got to face the giants!" When you think like that, it's retreat city!

> So they said to one another, "Let us appoint a leader and return to Egypt" (v. 4).

There's always some guy who has a creative idea like "Let's retreat! Let's go back. Too formidable!" You wonder what impact it had on Moses and Aaron?

> Then Moses and Aaron fell on their faces in the presence of all the assembly of the congregation of the sons of Israel (v. 5).

When the majority lack vision, their short-sightedness tends to take a severe toll on those trying to lead.

Positive Report . . . Unlimited Vision

Now the good news is that those ten spies were not the only ones who gave a report. I have purposely left out two courageous men until now. One is named *Caleb*.

> Then Caleb quieted the people before Moses, and said, "We should by all means go up and take possession of it, for we shall surely overcome it" (13:30).

The other is named *Joshua*.

> And Joshua the son of Nun and Caleb the son of Jephunneh, of those who had spied out the land, tore their clothes (14:6).

Both men ripped their garments when they saw Moses and Aaron on their faces and said, "Wait a minute! There's another side to all this. In fact, there is an issue at stake. It's time for us to be courageous. Let's start seeing this challenge through eyes of faith!"

> And they spoke to all the congregation of the sons of Israel, saying, "The land which we passed through to spy out is an exceedingly good land. If the Lord is pleased with us, then He will bring us into this land, and give it to us—a land which flows with milk and honey. Only do not rebel against the Lord; and do not fear the people of the land, for they shall be our prey. Their protection has been removed from them, and the Lord is with us; do not fear them" (vv. 7–9).

I love those courageous words. They always remind me of the opening lines of Psalm 27:

The Lord is my light and my salvation;
Whom shall I fear?
The Lord is the defense of my life;
Whom shall I dread?
When evildoers came upon me to devour my flesh,
My adversaries and my enemies, they stumbled and fell.
Though a host encamp against me,
My heart will not fear;
Though war arise against me,
In spite of this I shall be confident (vv. 1–3).

With vision there is no room to be frightened. No reason for intimidation. It's time to march forward! Let's be confident and positive! And after a Caleb-Joshua speech, people are ready to applaud and say, "Good job. Let's go!" Right?

Wrong—look for yourself. "But all the congregation said to stone them with stones" (Num. 14:10). Which tells you what people think of positive thinking. Here are two men God smiled upon. Two men Solzhenitsyn would have been proud of. Two men you and I admire, men of rare vision. But the majority said, "They're out to lunch. They're wrong. We can't possibly stand against such obstacles." This kind of majority attitude reminds me of a quote by Arnold Toynbee that goes something like this: "It is doubtful if the majority has *ever* been right." Those words always make me smile.

ONE QUALITY ESSENTIAL FOR UNIQUENESS

Now, we are not studying ancient history. We're thinking about living today. My interest isn't in writing a book that traces the Hebrews from Paran into Canaan. I'm far more interested in helping people like us to cope with and conquer today's obstacles. And they are nonetheless formidable. If you told a group of people that giants stand against you, without hesitation most folks would say, "Give up now, surrender, quit." Enter: anxiety. Exit: peace. But since when do people of faith conduct their lives on the basis of sight?

Did you observe something conspicuously absent from that story? The first thing that goes when you imbibe the system is courageous vision. Vision—the one essential ingredient for being an original in a day of copies gets lost, overwhelmed by the odds. Too bad! We start focusing on the trouble. We start numbering the people. We start measuring their height and weighing them in. Then we start comparing the odds. The result is predictable: We become intimidated and wind up *defeated.*

What is your Canaan? What is your challenge? Which giants make you feel like a grasshopper when you face them? What does your future resemble when you measure it on the basis of facts and figures? You'd like not to surrender, right? You'd like to be courageous, wouldn't you? There is a way through, but you'll need one essential quality—vision.

Vision is the ability to see God's presence, to perceive God's power, to focus on God's plan in spite of the obstacles.

I sometimes like to spell out things in A-B-C fashion. So let's close this chapter with an "alphabet" of vision—A-B-C-D-E.

A.   *Attitude.* When you have vision it affects your attitude. Your attitude is optimistic rather than pessimistic. Your attitude stays positive rather than negative. Not foolishly positive, as though in fantasy, for you are reading God into your circumstances. So when a situation comes that cuts your feet out from under you, you don't throw up your arms and panic. You don't give up. Instead, you say, "Lord, this is Your moment. This is where You take charge. You're in this." Caleb and Joshua came back, having seen the same obstacles the other ten spies saw, but they had a different attitude. Remember their words? "We are well able to handle it." So are you, my friend.

B.   *Belief.* This is nothing more than having a strong belief in the power of God; having confidence in others around you who are in similar battles with you; and, yes, having confidence in yourself, by the grace of God. Refusing to give in to temptation, cynicism, and doubt. Not allowing yourself to become a jaded individual. Belief in oneself is terribly important.

> People need an atmosphere in which they can specialize, hone their skills, and discover their distinctiveness. The biographies of the great are sprinkled with accounts of how some teacher or some kindly employer looked closely enough to see a spark no one else saw and for periods, at least, believed in their ability to perfect that gift when no one else did. The Taft family . . . was evidently good at pushing their children to cut their own swath

and to find a specialty of which to be proud. When Martha Taft was in elementary school in Cincinnati she was asked to introduce herself. She said, "My name is Martha Bowers Taft. My great-grandfather was President of the United States. My grandfather was United States senator. My daddy is ambassador to Ireland. And I am a Brownie."[4]

C. *Capacity.* What I have in mind here is a willingness to be stretched. When God has you look at your Canaan with all its formidable foes, He says, in effect, "You must be willing to be stretched. You have to allow your capacity to be invaded by My power."

I like what William James wrote:

> Everyone knows on any given day that there are energies slumbering in him which the incitements of that day do not call forth. . . . Compared with what we ought to be, we are only half awake. Our fires are damped, our drafts are checked. We are making use of only a small part of our possible mental and physical resources. . . . Stating the thing broadly, the human individual thus lives far within his limits; he possesses powers of various sorts he habitually fails to use.[5]

Isn't that the truth! Alleged "impossibilities" are opportunities for our capacities to be stretched.

D. *Determination.* I'm going to save most of my comments on this until the next chapter. Suffice it to say, determination is hanging tough when the going gets rough. I have no magic wand to wave over your future and say, "All of a sudden everything is going to fall into place." Vision requires determination, a constant focus on God who is watching and smiling.

E. *Enthusiasm.* Great word, *enthusiasm.* Its Greek origin is *éntheos,* "God in." It is the ability to see God in a situation, which makes the event exciting. And, by the way, do you know that He *is* watching? Do you realize that? Something happens to our vision that is almost magical when we become convinced that God our heavenly Father is involved in our activities and is applauding them.

Bob Richards, the Olympic pole vaulter of years ago, loved to tell the story of the goof-off who played around with football. He was somewhere between the bench and off the team. If there was mischief to be done, this kid was doing it. Everything was casual, no big deal. And he added very little to the team. He practiced, but he wasn't committed. He had a uniform and would show up to play, but never with enthusiasm.

He liked to hear the cheers, but not to charge the line. He liked to wear the suit, but not to practice. He did not like to put himself out. One day the players were doing fifty laps, and this showpiece was doing his usual five. The coach came over and said, "Hey kid, here is a telegram for you." The kid said, "Read it for me, Coach." He was so lazy he did not even like to read. The coach opened it up and read, "Dear son, your father is dead. Come home immediately." The coach swallowed hard. He said, "Take the rest of the week off." He didn't care if he took the rest of the year off.

Well, funny thing, game time came on Friday and here came the teams rushing out on the field, and lo and behold, the last kid out was the goof-off. No sooner did the gun sound than the kid said, "Coach, can I play today? Can I play?" The coach thought, "Kid, you're not playing today. This is homecoming. This is the big game. We need every real guy we have, and you are not one of them." Every time the coach turned around, the kid badgered him: "Coach, please let me play. Coach, I have got to play."

The first quarter ended with the score lopsided against the coach and his team. At half time, they were still further behind. The second half started, and things got progressively worse. The coach, mumbling to himself, began writing out his resignation, and up came the kid. "Coach, Coach, let me play, please!" The coach looked at the scoreboard. "All right," he said, "get in there, kid. You can't hurt anything now."

No sooner did the kid hit the field than his team exploded. He ran, blocked, and tackled like a star. The electricity leaped to the team. The score evened up. In the closing seconds of the game, this kid intercepted a pass and ran all the way for the winning touchdown!

The stands broke loose. The kid was everybody's hero. Such cheering you never heard. Finally the excitement subsided and the coach got over to the kid and said, "I never saw anything like that. What in the world happened to you out there?" He said, "Coach, you know my dad died last week." "Yes," he said, "I read you the telegram." "Well, Coach," he said, "my dad was blind. And today was the first day he ever saw me play."[6]

Today may be the first day you realized that your heavenly Father is watching you in life. He really is not absent, unconcerned, blind, or dead. He is alive. He is watching. He cares. That can make all the difference in the world.

Even in a world that is negative and hostile. Even in a world where the majority says, "We can't," you can. Trust God today. With eyes of faith, get back in the game. Play it with great enthusiasm. It's time to start soaring . . . which is another way of saying it's time to live differently, which starts with seeing beyond the majority.

The word is *vision.*

Determination:
Deciding to
Hang Tough

6

A disclaimer is probably in order. I would feel a little better if I could set the record straight, lest anyone have an expectation that is unrealistic. The disclaimer? There is no rabbit's foot hidden on some page in this book, so don't look for one.

In a volume that emphasizes the things I have been writing about, it would be easy for some to think that I know a magical secret, some hocus-pocus, cure-all miracle thought that is guaranteed to result in soaring. Sorry, I have no such offer. Living above the level of mediocrity is not going to happen by our taking a pill or repeating a mantra or learning and applying a quick-fix formula. The quality of life I have in mind is definitely possible, but it is definitely *not* a utopia softly and easily entered through the gates of Fantasyland.

When Jesus tells us to "*seek* first the kingdom of God," the very word *seek* implies a strong-minded pursuit. J. B. Phillips paraphrases the idea with "set your heart on." The Amplified Bible says, "Aim at and strive after." The Greek text of Matthew's

Gospel states a continual command: "Keep on continually seeking. . . ." The thought is determination, which I define as "deciding to hang tough, *regardless.*"

There is a well-known local coach in Fullerton, California, whose thirty-five-plus years in athletics have been eminently successful. Hal Sherbeck grew up in big-sky country and became a winning coach at Missoula High School. This led to a coaching career at the University of Montana, where he distinguished himself with an enviable win-loss record. Ultimately, Hal came to our city where he has been coaching at Fullerton Community College faithfully for many years. His incredible career in Southern California speaks for itself. When he was interviewed by the *Los Angeles Times,* the sportswriter wanted to know his secret. What was it that made him so successful? Without hesitation Coach Sherbeck said that his credo could best be stated in words written by an anonymous author. Ever since he was a boy growing up in Big Sandy, Montana, he has lived by these words:

> Press on.
> Nothing in the world
> Can take the place of persistence.
> Talent will not;
> Nothing is more common
> Than unsuccessful men
> With talent.
> Genius will not;
> Unrewarded genius
> Is almost a proverb.
> Education will not;
> The world is full of
> Educated derelicts.
> Persistence and determination
> Alone are important.[1]

Coach Sherbeck had no quick and easy formula for success; he lives by his strong commitment to persistence and determination.

Don't misunderstand. I have in mind being determined to accomplish what is right. I realize that criminal types could just as easily take this credo and commit themselves to a life of crime or some other irresponsible pursuit. But when the objective is good and the motive is pure, there is nothing more valuable in the pathway leading to genuine success than persistence and determination. Following one's dream requires these disciplines.

Almost every week I come in contact with people who have been misled, thinking that success depends solely upon talent or brilliance or education. But the list doesn't end there. For some it's getting the breaks, pulling the right strings, having the right personality, being in the right place at the right time, knowing the right people, playing their cards right, or (I smile every time I hear this) waiting for their ship to come in. Motivational speaker Charlie "Tremendous" Jones says it best: "A lot of people are waiting for their ship to come in even though they never sent one out!"

No, the thing that makes for greatness is determination, persisting in the right direction over the long haul, following your dream, staying at the task. Just as there is no such thing as instant failure, neither is there automatic or instant success. But success is the direct result of a process that is long, arduous, and often unappreciated by others. It also includes a willingness to sacrifice. But it pays off if you stay at the task. In our world of instant everything, these thoughts are not very popular. That's why I emphasized the word *seek* at the beginning of this chapter. If we really want to soar like an eagle, we must keep on continually pursuing—we must keep on seeking.

DEFINING THE KEY TERMS

In the previous chapter our thoughts centered on *vision*. In this chapter the focus is on *determination* and *following one's dream*. Because these three terms are significant in the lives of people who set their hearts on living differently, we need to define each one a little more specifically.

Vision

Vision is the ability to see above and beyond the majority. Vision is perception—reading the presence and power of God into one's circumstances. I sometimes think of vision as looking at life through the lens of God's eyes, seeing situations as He sees them. Too often we see things not as they are, but as *we* are.

Think about that. Vision has to do with looking at life with a divine perspective, reading the scene with God in clear focus.

Whoever wants to live differently in "the system" must correct his or her vision. And, trust me, this kind of vision correction won't come naturally. How can I say that? Let me show you a couple of scriptures that verify the fact that vision is not a natural trait.

The first verse I want to look at is 1 Samuel 16:7. Samuel thinks he has found the Lord's anointed. The former king (Saul) has failed. So God sends Samuel to find a new king. He comes to the home of Jesse where the oldest son, Eliab, is marched in front of Samuel. The old man is so impressed with Eliab's size and his handsome physique that he immediately thinks this must be the man! But the Lord stops Samuel short and tells him Eliab's *not* the one.

> But the Lord said to Samuel, "Do not look at his appearance or at the height of his stature, because I have rejected him; for God sees not as man sees, for man looks at the outward appearance, but the Lord looks at the heart."

You see, it is our natural tendency to focus on the external, to be overly impressed with that which is seen. Wouldn't it be wonderful to develop the ability to look at a heart? Wouldn't it be great to be free of the limitations of strictly physical sight so that we could read hidden character traits? Frankly, I think those who are physically blind often see more than those of us who are sighted. They often perceive much more than we can in the tone of a voice or in the sound of approaching footsteps or in the grip of a handshake. But we who have sight usually lack this insightful depth perception; we lack the kind of vision that can detect the deeper things, the unspoken, the character, the hidden condition of the unspoken. And although God is able (and willing) to give us such vision, it isn't something we're born with.

The second scripture I want to consider is a similar thought written by the prophet Isaiah.

> "For My thoughts are not your thoughts, neither are your ways My ways," declares the Lord. "For as the heavens are higher than the earth, so are My ways higher than your ways, and My thoughts than your thoughts" (Isa. 55:8–9).

Once again we are made aware of the difference between natural sight and supernatural vision. When we look at life with vision, we perceive events and circumstances with God's thoughts. And because His thoughts are higher and more profound than mere horizontal thinking, they have a way of softening the blows of calamity and giving us hope through tragedy and loss. It also enables us to handle times of prosperity and popularity with wisdom.

Following a worship service in the church I serve as senior pastor, I met a couple from Mexico City who had endured that awful earthquake back in 1986. They spoke quietly and even reverently of what they had learned through it. There was something unique about their handshake and embrace as well as a gracious compassion in their voices. They had lost family members. They had been brought back to the very basics of what life is all about. They had seen God's ways; they had sensed His presence. In that tumultuous event they had come to terms with some of the trappings that had become superficial hang-ups for the majority. Clearly, so many things were now much different to them—much different. What was it that pervaded their lives? Vision.

Determination

This is a major step beyond vision. It involves applying the discipline to remain consistent regardless of the obstacles or the odds. I often think of it as faith in the long haul.

One man writes:

> Many people fail in life because they believe in the adage: If you don't succeed, try something else. But success eludes those who follow such advice. Virtually everyone has had dreams at one time or another, specially in youth. The dreams that have come true did so because people stuck to their ambitions. They refused to be discouraged. They never let disappointment get the upper hand. Challenges only spurred them on to greater effort.[2]

I'll be frank with you. I know of no more valuable technique in the pursuit of successful living than sheer, dogged determination. Nothing works in ministry better than persistence— persistence in godliness, determination to stay diligent in study, persistence in commitment to the priorities of ministry, determination in working with people. I often remind myself of those familiar words in 2 Timothy 4:1, "Preach the word; be ready in season and out of season." That's a nice way of saying, "Hang tough! Do it when it comes naturally and when it is hard to come by. Do it when you're up, do it when you're down. Do it when you feel like it, do it when you don't feel like it. Do it when it's hot, do it when it's cold. Keep on doing it. Don't give up."

I once heard W. A. Criswell, long-time beloved pastor of the famous First Baptist Church in Dallas, Texas, tell a story about an evangelist who loved to hunt. As best I recall, the man bought two pups that were topnotch bird dogs, two setters, I believe. He kept them in his large backyard, where he trained them. One morning, an ornery little vicious-looking bulldog came shuffling and snorting down the alley. He crawled under the fence into the backyard where the setters spent their days. It was easy to see he meant business. The evangelist's first impulse was to take his setters and lock them in the basement so they wouldn't tear up that little bulldog. But he decided he would just let the creature learn a lesson he would never forget. Naturally, they got into a scuffle in the backyard, and those two setters and that bulldog went round and round and round! There were growls and yipes as bulldog hair flew everywhere. The little critter finally had enough, so he squeezed under the fence and took off. All the rest of that day he whined and licked his sores. Interestingly, the next day at about the same time, here came that same ornery little bulldog . . . back under the fence and after those setters. Once again those two bird dogs beat the stuffing out of that bowlegged animal and would have chewed him up if he hadn't retreated down the alley. Would you believe, the very next day he was back! Same time, same station, same results. Once again after the bulldog had had all he could take, he crawled back under the fence and found his way home to lick his wounds.

"Well," the evangelist said, "I had to leave for a revival meeting. I was gone several weeks. And when I came back, I asked my wife what had happened. She said, 'Honey, you just won't believe what has happened. Every day, at the same time every morning, that little bulldog came back in the backyard and fought with our two setters. He never missed a day! And I want you to know it has come to the point that when our setters simply hear that bulldog snorting down the alley and spot him squeezing under the fence, they immediately start whining and run down into our basement. That little, old bulldog struts around our backyard now just like he owns it.'"

That is persistence and determination. Staying at it. Hanging tough with dogged discipline. When you get whipped or when you win, the secret is staying at it.

Dream

There is another dimension to hanging tough we dare not miss. It is the thing that keeps you going with vision, the reason behind the determination. I call it a dream. I don't mean those things we experience at night while we're asleep. When the prophet Joel writes of dreaming dreams and seeing visions, he doesn't have in mind some nocturnal images stemming from the subconscious. No, by dream, I mean a God-given idea, plan, agenda, or goal that leads to God-honoring results. People who soar like eagles, people who live above the drag of the mediocre, are people of dreams. They have God-given drive because they have received God-given dreams.

Most of us don't dream enough. If someone were to ask you, "What are your dreams for this year? What are your hopes, your agenda? What are you trusting God for?" could you give a specific answer? I don't have in mind just occupational objectives or goals for your family, although there's nothing wrong with those. But what about the kind of dreaming that results in character building, the kind that cultivates God's righteousness and God's rulership in your life?

Here are a few more ideas about dreams. Dreams are specific, not general. Dreams are personal, not public. God doesn't give anyone else my dreams on a public computer screen for others to read. He gives them to me personally. They're intimate images and ideas. Dreams can easily appear to others as extreme and illogical. If you share your dreams with the crowd, they'll probably laugh at you because you can't make logical sense out of them. Dreams are often accompanied by a strong desire to fulfill them. And they are always outside the realm of the expected. Sometimes they're downright shocking. They cause people to suck in their breath, to stand staring at you with their mouth open. A common response when you share a dream is, "You've gotta be kidding! Are you serious?"

One more thought on dreams: This is the stuff of which leaders are made. If you don't dream, your leadership is seriously limited. I have a close friend who leads an organization that is admired and appreciated by many. He sets aside one day every month to do nothing but pray and dream. I am not surprised that his organization is considered a pacesetter.

This isn't mental voodoo, but simply thinking outside the realm of the seen. It becomes a natural part of one's life. I love the way Henry David Thoreau once put it:

> If one advances confidently in the direction of his dreams, and
> endeavors to live the life which he has imagined, he will meet with
> a success unexpected in common hours.

Mental dreams assist us in determining our flight plan as eagles who soar. The wonderful added benefit is that we "meet with a success unexpected" in a most natural manner—no manipulation, no big-time hype, not even the need for pushing our own selves or promoting our own image.

TWO DREAMERS WITH DETERMINATION

In the previous chapter we met two men who were men of vision: Caleb and Joshua. Let's go back to their story now and travel even further with them.

You will remember that Caleb and Joshua were among the twelve spies who went into the Promised Land on a reconnaissance mission. Forty days later the group returned with a divided opinion. Unlike the majority who panicked, these two brought back a good report. Ten said, "No way!" But these two disagreed. "We are well able. By all means, we should go up and possess the land." Now don't forget, Joshua and Caleb were surrounded by a majority of peers who were convinced the Israelite army could not do it. They were also facing a huge congregation of Hebrews who agreed, "It's impossible. Let's go back to Egypt." Yet in the midst of all those negative voices, these two men calmly stood their ground, "We can do it."

Now, I ask you, how can intelligent men look at the same scene so differently? The answer is not difficult: two have vision, determination, and dreams; the other ten do not. It's that simple. That story is an illustration of life. We spend our years facing the very same dichotomy. To make things even more complicated, those who don't have vision or determination, and refuse to dream the impossible, are *always* in the majority. Therefore, they will always take the vote. They will always outshout and outnumber those who walk by faith and not by sight, those who are seeking the kingdom of God and His righteousness. Those who choose to live by sight will always outnumber those who live by faith.

Ten saw the problem; two saw the solution. Ten saw the obstacles; two saw the answers. Ten were impressed with the size of the men; two were impressed with the size of their God. Ten focused on what could not be accomplished; two focused on what could easily be accomplished by the power of God. Again, the persistence demonstrated by Caleb and Joshua is nothing short of remarkable. Neither was more intelligent than the other ten, nor more talented. They simply possessed bulldog determination.

> Napoleon Hill, who studied the lives of many successful people, stated, "I had the happy privilege of analyzing both Mr. Edison and Mr. Ford, year by year, over a long period of years, and therefore the opportunity to study them at close range, so I speak from actual knowledge when I say that I found no quality save persistence, in either of them, that even remotely suggested the major source of their stupendous achievements."[3]

Do you recall these words from the heart of Caleb's and Joshua's speech?

> "If the Lord is pleased with us, then He will bring us into this land, and give it to us—a land which flows with milk and honey. Only do not rebel against the Lord; and do not fear the people of the land, for they shall be our prey . . ." (Num. 14:8–9).

These men are reminding the Hebrews that the Egyptians had already been killed at the Red Sea and that the people they are about to confront in Canaan have no protection either. It's been removed from them. ". . . Their protection has been removed from them, and the Lord is with us; do not fear them" (Num. 14:9).

Talk about courage! Caleb and Joshua had the audacity to stand alone and challenge the people to trust God. And God honored their courage. I didn't mention it earlier, but something amazing occurred before tragedy struck.

> But all the congregation said to stone them with stones. Then the glory of the Lord appeared in the tent of meeting to all the sons of Israel (Num. 14:10).

Whoa! It's time to seal the lips, to be quiet and listen. Somehow the shining brilliance of God's presence broke on that camp, and God spoke audibly.

> And the Lord said to Moses, "How long will this people spurn Me? And how long will they not believe in Me, despite all the signs which I have performed in their midst? I will smite them with pestilence and dispossess them, and I will make you into a nation greater and mightier than they." But Moses said to the Lord, "Then the Egyptians will hear of it, for by Thy strength Thou didst bring up this people from their midst, and they will tell it to the inhabitants of this land. They have heard that Thou, O Lord, art in the midst of this people, for Thou, O Lord, art seen eye to eye, while Thy cloud stands over them; and Thou dost go before them in a pillar of cloud by day and in a pillar of fire by night. Now if Thou dost slay this people as one man, then the nations who have heard of Thy fame will say, 'Because the Lord could not bring this people into the land which He promised them by oath, therefore He slaughtered them in the wilderness.' But now, I pray, let the power of the Lord be great, just as Thou hast declared, 'The Lord is slow to anger and abundant in lovingkindness, forgiving iniquity and transgression; but He will by no means clear the guilty, visiting the iniquity of the fathers on the children to the third and the fourth generations.' Pardon, I pray, the iniquity of this people according to the greatness of Thy lovingkindness, just as Thou also hast forgiven this people, from Egypt even until now" (Num. 14:11–19).

"Lord, what will we say to the Egyptians? That's the reason they let the people go, in the first place . . . because You're their God. And if You annihilate everyone, then the Egyptians will have the last laugh. You'll be a mockery to them."

Great speech, Moses. And was it effective! Observe the impact:

So the Lord said, "I have pardoned them according to your word; but indeed, as I live, all the earth will be filled with the glory of the Lord. Surely all the men who have seen My glory and My signs, which I performed in Egypt and in the wilderness, yet have put Me to the test these ten times and have not listened to My voice, shall by no means see the land which I swore to their fathers, nor shall any of those who spurned Me see it. But My servant Caleb, because he has had a different spirit and has followed Me fully, I will bring into the land which he entered, and his descendants shall take possession of it" (Num. 14:20–24).

Don't miss that! Caleb had "a different spirit." Was he some kind of superman? Or genius? No, we never read such a thing here or elsewhere. He was simply a man with vision who dreamed great dreams and stuck by them. No wonder he soared!

And as a result, God protected him and Joshua from death in the wilderness.

"'Surely you shall not come into the land in which I swore to settle you, except Caleb the son of Jephunneh and Joshua the son of Nun. Your children, however, whom you said would become a prey—I will bring them in, and they shall know the land which you have rejected. But as for you, your corpses shall fall in this wilderness. And your sons shall be shepherds for forty years in the wilderness, and they shall suffer for your unfaithfulness, until your corpses lie in the wilderness. According to the number of days which you spied out the land, forty days, for every day you shall bear your guilt a year, even forty years, and you shall know My opposition. I the Lord have spoken, surely this I will do to all this evil congregation who are gathered together against Me. In this wilderness they shall be destroyed, and there they shall die'" (Num. 14:30–35).

I call that a serious judgment. God took all the people who had been a part of the original group that had voted to stone the leaders, and He said, "You'll die in the wilderness. It'll take forty years of wandering." Can you imagine the disappointment? They were right on the edge of the land of promise, yet they retreated and wandered, virtually in a circle, for the next forty years while the old generation of negative thinkers died off. Their corpses literally littered that region. And every tombstone was a reminder that God means what He says.

Why weren't Caleb and Joshua numbered among the doomed? They had a different spirit. There was something about those two men that marked them as distinct.

Did Caleb End Well?

Caleb and Joshua began well, but the real question is, Did those two eagles keep on soaring? We find our answer in the Book of Joshua. We'll see if Caleb ended well (Joshua 14) and then we'll look briefly at Joshua's ending (Joshua 24).

By now the old generation has died off. Those who lived on invaded the land and fought their way to victory. Just as He had promised, God gave them the land. And now they're about to parcel it out to the tribes of the nation. When Caleb's turn comes, he stands tall and delivers one of the greatest speeches recorded in all the Bible:

> "I was forty years old when Moses the servant of the Lord sent me from Kadesh-barnea to spy out the land, and I brought word back to him as it was in my heart. Nevertheless my brethren who went up with me made the heart of the people melt with fear; but I followed the Lord my God fully. And now behold, the Lord has let me live, just as He spoke, these forty-five years, from the time that the Lord spoke this word to Moses, when Israel walked in the wilderness; and now behold, I am eighty-five years old today. I am still as strong today as I was in the day Moses sent me; as my strength was then, so my strength is now, for war and for going out and coming in. Now then, give me this hill country about which the Lord spoke on that day, for you heard on that day that Anakim were there, with great fortified cities; perhaps the Lord will be with me, and I shall drive them out as the Lord has spoken" (Josh. 14:7–12).

I love it! Caleb, though eighty-five years old, did not say, "Give me this rocking chair." No, not Caleb. He said, "Give me that mountain—up there where those giants live!" He is *still* unafraid of the giants. The last thing we see of Caleb is his trudging up that mountain at eighty-five years old, rolling up his sleeves to take on the giants. Don't you love people like that—people who live above mediocrity? The majority thinks they are half nuts, but that's okay. Since when do we worry about the majority opinion?

By now we understand the reason Caleb could do it, don't we? He had a dream. He had vision. He had determination. And age had nothing whatever to do with it.

Some time ago the United Technologies Corporation published in the *Wall Street Journal* a full-page message entitled, "It's What You Do, Not When You Do It." The message contained a listing of many eaglelike people who soared at various ages in their lives.

IT'S WHAT YOU DO—NOT WHEN YOU DO IT

Ted Williams, at age 42, slammed a home run in his last official time at bat.

Mickey Mantle, age 20, hit 23 home runs his first full year in the major leagues.

Golda Meir was 71 when she became Prime Minister of Israel.

William Pitt II was 24 when he became Prime Minister of Great Britain.

George Bernard Shaw was 94 when one of his plays was first produced.

Mozart was just seven when his first composition was published.

Now, how about this? *Benjamin Franklin* was a newspaper columnist at 16 and a framer of the United States Constitution when he was 81.

You're never too young or too old if you've got talent. Let's recognize that age has little to do with ability.[4]

You remember that the next time you're tempted to use age as an excuse, okay? You keep telling yourself that age has NOTHING to do with dreams and determination and vision.

Did Joshua End Well?

So much for Caleb. What about his sidekick? Did Joshua end as well as Caleb? Was his determination still intact? Like Caleb, he, too, delivered a great speech. After reviewing God's hand on their lives as a nation, Joshua warns the people to:

"Be very firm, then, to keep and do all that is written in the book of the law of Moses, so that you may not turn aside from it to the right hand or to the left, in order that you may not associate with these nations, these which remain among you, or mention the name of their gods, or make anyone swear by them, or serve them, or bow down to them (Josh. 23:6–7).

His point? Drive out the enemy! How about that! Here is an older man telling a younger generation, "Finish the job. Stay at it . . . get it done."

Finally, Joshua refers to his own family.

> "Now, therefore, fear the Lord and serve Him in sincerity and truth; and put away the gods which your fathers served beyond the River and in Egypt, and serve the Lord. And if it is disagreeable in your sight to serve the Lord, choose for yourselves today whom you will serve: whether the gods which your fathers served which were beyond the River, or the gods of the Amorites in whose land you are living; but as for me and my house, we will serve the Lord" (Josh. 24:14–15).

Yes, there is no doubt in anyone's mind that Joshua finished well. He is as strong in his convictions as he was in his earlier life. But he isn't "cranky." Since there is no way you can force righteousness out of anyone, Joshua chose rather to model it, to communicate it. He realized that a pursuit of godliness is something you have to leave with the will of each individual to make his or her own choice. Far too many of us have tried to force people into righteousness!

I remember when I wasn't the least bit interested in spiritual things, and my mother (for all the right reasons) dragged me from one church to another. And each time I couldn't wait to get seated so I could go to sleep. I wanted to prove to her that I wasn't interested in the stuff she was interested in. Thankfully, over a period of time, my interest in eternal things began to change. My whole perspective on the Lord was altered, and then you couldn't keep me away from the things of God. But, you see, I couldn't be forced. I had to make a choice. Joshua states that fact beautifully. But in doing so he leaves no doubt in anyone's mind where he stood personally.

OBSERVATIONS WORTH REMEMBERING

Three significant observations stand out as we come to the end of this account. First: <u>Age has little to do with achievement and nothing to do with commitment.</u>

Both Joshua and Caleb were young men when they stood alone before their peers. Yet when they grew older they were still standing strong. Both men persisted in their convictions regardless of the passing years. Both men remained true even when they grew old. The ranks of humanity are full of those who *start* well. With determination and persistence, we can also end well. These days in my life I look for people who are finishing well. I love to meet folks in their sixties, seventies, and eighties who are still visionaries, who are still dreaming, still excited about going on with their life, still positive about the future—men and women who are useful in their spheres of influence.

That brings us to the second observation: <u>A godly walk is basic to a positive life.</u> Joshua and Caleb kept repeating their full and firm commitment to the Lord their God. I believe that's a major reason they stayed so positive. Without a proper divine perspective, it is easy for negativism and cynicism to creep in. So if you want to maintain a positive, fulfilling life, you have to keep the Lord in the nucleus of your motivation.

Now for the third observation: <u>Convictions are a matter of choice, not force.</u> Parents of growing, learning children keep this in mind. Remember there is nothing like the magnet of a model. You can shout and scream. You can discipline and punish and threaten. But there's nothing those kids will remember like the model you leave them. That will be cemented in their memory. You just live it, keep living it, and persist in your walk. That alone will be a magnet that will draw them. They will want to know, especially as they reach the older years, how you do it. If they don't know by then, that's your moment to tell them. That's your time. Our kids have a way of signaling when they're ready to be taught—even when they reach adulthood.

APPLICATIONS WORTH DUPLICATING

Let me suggest four "nevers." That may seem a little strange since my emphasis has been so positive, but I think each "never" will be more easily remembered.

- Never use age as an excuse.
- Never take your cues from the crowd.

- Never think your choices obligate anyone else. (If you do, you'll become a self-appointed martyr.)
- Never quit because someone disagrees with you.

If you're so insecure that you must have everybody agreeing with you before you can go on, you are in for an extremely uncertain future. Leadership will elude you, I fear. May our Lord give you fresh courage to stand firm even when others disagree.

Several years ago I met a gentleman who served on one of Walt Disney's original advisory boards. What amazing stories he told! Those early days were tough; but that remarkable, creative visionary refused to give up. I especially appreciated the man's sharing with me how Disney responded to disagreement. He said that Walt would occasionally present some unbelievable, extensive dream he was entertaining. Almost without exception, the members of his board would gulp, blink, and stare back at him in disbelief, resisting even the thought of such a thing. But unless *every member resisted the idea,* Disney usually didn't pursue it. Yes, you read that correctly. The challenge wasn't big enough to merit his time and creative energy unless they were unanimously in disagreement! (I suppose when you're a Disney, you're free to press on when the board says "shut 'er down!") Is it any wonder that Disneyland and Disney World are now realities?

THE WORLD NEEDS MEN . . . [and I might add *women*]

who cannot be bought;
whose word is their bond;
who put character above wealth;
who possess opinions and a will;
who are larger than their vocations;
who do not hesitate to take chances;
who will not lose their individuality in a crowd;
who will be as honest in small things as in great things;
who will make no compromise with wrong;
whose ambitions are not confined to their own selfish desires;
who will not say they do it "because everybody else does it";
who are true to their friends through good report and evil report,
    in adversity as well as in prosperity;
who do not believe that shrewdness, cunning, and
    hardheadedness are the best qualities for winning success;

who are not ashamed or afraid to stand for the truth when it is
   unpopular;
who can say "no" with emphasis, although all the rest of the
   world says "yes."[5]

Once you've decided to live differently, let God be your guide
and hang tough—follow your dreams with determination. Before
you know it you'll be soaring like an eagle.

Priorities: Determining What Comes First

7

L ife is a lot like a coin; you can spend it any way you wish, but you can spend it only once. Choosing one thing over all the rest throughout life is a difficult thing to do. This is especially true when the choices are so many and the possibilities are so close.

At Christmastime I was given the book *A Sense of History* by one of my close friends. Knowing my love for history, he selected one of those volumes you need to read slowly with a lot of thinking time to muse things over. Interestingly, the first thirty-seven pages form a section entitled, "I Wish I'd Been There." Numerous historians, scholars, authors, and editors were asked to choose the one event in American history they would most like to have witnessed. Each was asked to respond to the same intriguing question: "What is the one scene or incident in American history you would most like to have witnessed—and why?"

I found myself glued to those thirty-seven pages, fascinated by the answers. Here is a sampling:

- One historian said he would like to have been among that small company of sailors in the moonlit predawn moment, October 12, 1492, when a lookout aboard a small vessel hailed the sand cliffs of an island never before seen by the eyes of Europeans.

- Another commented he would like to have had an extra long life, enabling him to sit on a pier between A.D. 1200 and 1500 to see who *besides Columbus and Sebastian Cabot* showed up.

- Another said he would like to have been with Lewis and Clark in November of 1805 when they first glimpsed the object of their labors, the Pacific Ocean. He wished he could have looked over the shoulder of William Clark as he scribbled in his log book, "Ocean in view—oh, the joy!"

- A rather interesting selection came from one who wished he could have witnessed that intimate, nostalgic moment when Abraham Lincoln, the President-elect, said farewell to his neighbors in Springfield.

- A history professor at Yale selected for his fantasy the opportunity to look inside the mind of Col. Robert E. Lee on the occasion when Lee was being offered the command of the *Union* forces in 1861.

- Another moved ahead in history to the Emancipation Proclamation. He didn't choose to be by President Lincoln's side, but rather in a little community in South Carolina where a number of people had gathered, including a large number of slaves, to hear the report of that decision that black people were now free. He wished he could have seen the flag as it waved in the sky and could have heard the spontaneous singing of the slaves who were at that moment free. First, a strong, male voice, rather cracked and elderly, began to sing . . . into which two women's voices instantly blended, singing as if by an impulse that could not be repressed, "My country 'tis of thee, sweet land of liberty, of thee I sing."

- Another wanted to be by Franklin Delano Roosevelt's side on December 7, 1941, when he received the news of the Japanese attack. He said he would like to have seen the one who brought the Pearl Harbor dispatch and then to find out whom Roosevelt contacted first . . . and to have known when he first began his "Day of Infamy" speech.

- One said, there was a time when he would like to have been a fly on the wall of the bunker watching the last days and hours of the Third Reich. "But no longer. For the last decade I have yielded entirely to the wish that I could have been there in the White House on that day when Richard Nixon decided to resign his Presidency and knelt with my old friend Henry Kissinger to pray."[1]

What makes the opening section of that history book so interesting is that it is all based on priorities. These scholarly historians were asked to point out one plant from the vast field of history that covers hundreds of years; out of an entire meadow, they were asked to choose one flower they would like to have seen bloom— the one moment in time they would like to have experienced.

OUR TOP PRIORITY

The task those historians had is somewhat like that of those who wish to live above the level of mediocrity. We are forced to choose on the basis of first things first. We will never fly like an eagle until we are willing to determine who and what comes first. Life places before us hundreds of possibilities. Some are bad. Many are good. A few, the best. But each of us must decide, "What is my choice? What is my reason for living?" In other words, "What priority takes first place in my life?"

To be completely truthful with you, however, we aren't left with numerous possibilities. Jesus Himself gave us the top priority. We have looked at it several times already.

"But seek first His kingdom and His righteousness; and all these things shall be added to you" (Matt. 6:33).

He said, in effect, "This is your priority; this comes first." He even uses the words "But seek *first,*" meaning above and beyond everything else, pursue this *first.*

Before going any further, let's take a closer look at this command. The Greek word translated "seek" means "to search, to strive for, to desire strongly." The action is continuous—"keep on striving for, keep on searching after, keep on desiring." Today, we would say, "Go for this *first*. . . ."

Now look even closer and notice the objectives: The kingdom of God and the righteousness of God. Frankly, we don't even have to pray about our top priority. We just have to know what it is, then do it. If I am to seek first in my life God's kingdom and God's righteousness, then whatever else I do ought to relate to that goal: where I work, with whom I spend my time, the one I marry, or the decision to remain single. Every decision I make ought to be filtered through the Matthew 6:33 filter: where I put my money, where and how I spend my time, what I buy, what I sell, what I give away. That means a two-pronged question needs to be asked each time: Is it for His kingdom? Does it relate to His righteousness?

A REMINDER OF UNSEEN VALUES

God's kingdom and His righteousness are unseen, you understand. We will never find His kingdom in tangible form on this earth in our lifetime. We will never hear the sounds of His kingdom or see Him ruling or hear the gavel in the hands of the Lord Jesus coming down in a court room where He sits as Judge. No, as we learned earlier, for the present time His kingdom is invisible, it is inaudible, it is eternal. So those of us who wish to soar above mediocrity have a commitment to His kingdom that forces us to press the whole of life through the filter of something invisible, inaudible, and eternal.

This filter (Matthew 6:33) helps me to conduct myself in terms of this top priority. Should I do this? Is it for God's kingdom? Is it for His righteousness? Should I respond this way? Will my decision uphold His righteousness? Believe me, that can get pretty exacting. Priorities are always tough things to determine. Furthermore, there are times we *think* we are on target, but we're not. If our hearts are right, God will graciously yet firmly overrule even the things we ask Him for.

Our lives can turn out like the unknown Confederate soldier who admitted:

I asked God for strength that I might achieve.
I was made weak that I might learn humbly to obey.

I asked God for health that I might do greater things.
I was given infirmity that I might do better things.

I asked for riches that I might be happy.
I was given poverty that I might be wise.

I asked for power that I might have the praise of men.
I was given weakness that I might feel the need of God.

I asked for all things that I might enjoy life.
I was given life that I might enjoy all things.

I got nothing that I asked for—
but everything I had hoped for. . . .

Almost despite myself, my unspoken prayers were answered.
I am among all men most richly blessed.[2]

As I ponder Jesus' command, I notice that it begins with a contrast, "*But* seek first," the implication being that others are *not* seeking those things. But who are they? The preceding verse identifies them for us. They're called the Gentiles.

In fact, look at what that verse says:

"For all these things the Gentiles eagerly seek; for your heavenly Father knows that you need all these things" (Matt. 6:32).

To identify "these things" we need to go all the way back to verse 24:

"No one can serve two masters; for either he will hate the one and love the other, or he will hold to one and despise the other. You cannot serve God and mammon."

This helps us understand that "the Gentiles" are those who are trying to serve two masters. But Jesus makes no bones about it—"You cannot possibly serve both God and money." Be careful, now. He isn't saying it is impossible to soar and make money.

The key word is *serve.* We cannot be a servant of both. Living out the kingdom life means that everything must remain before the throne and under the authority of the ruler. Everything must be held loosely.

I'll never forget a conversation I had with the late Corrie ten Boom. She said to me, in her broken English, "Chuck, I've learned that we must hold everything loosely, because when I grip it tightly, it hurts when the Father pries my fingers loose and takes it from me!" Things of significant value are the unseen things, aren't they? But that is easy to forget.

I have a friend who, in mid-career, was called into the ministry. In fact, God ultimately led him overseas. At that point he found it necessary to move all his family and as many of their possessions as possible beyond these shores, all the way to the island of Okinawa. He told me, "We packed everything we could in barrels and shipped them on ahead. And then we put all of our possessions that were a part of our trip into our station wagon. We packed that car all the way to the top of the windows."

While driving to the place where they would meet the ship that would take them to the Orient, they stopped for a rest and a bite to eat. While they were inside the restaurant, a thief broke into their station wagon and took *everything* except the car. Nice of him to leave the car, wasn't it? "The only thing we had," he said, "were the articles of clothing on our backs. Our hearts sank to the bottom!" When asked about it later, he said, "Well, I had to face the fact that I was holding real tight to the things in that car. And the Lord simply turned my hands over and gave them a slap . . . and out came everything that was in that car. And it all became a part of the Father's possession."

What tangibles are you holding onto? What are you gripping tightly? Have they become your security? Are you a slave to some image? Some name you're trying to live up to? Some job? Some possession? Some person? Some goal or objective? (Nothing wrong with having goals and objectives; but something is wrong when they have you in their grip.) Now let me give you a tip. If you cannot let it go, it's a priority to you. It is impossible to be a slave to things or people and at the same time be a faithful servant of God.

Now before we let this idea of "letting go" appear too stark, look again at the wonderful promise in verse 33. The latter half of it says, "all these things shall be added to you." How interesting! Remember verse 32—"these things the Gentiles eagerly seek"? Well, now Jesus is saying "these things shall be added unto you." Those who seek them are off target. But those who seek Him are provided with whatever they need. When you think all that through, it just depends on where your priorities are. Isn't that a relief? Once you have given them to the Lord, who knows, He may turn right around and let you enjoy an abundance. Or He may keep them from you at a safe distance and just every once in a while let you enjoy a few. But they'll all be added to you from His hand rather than from your own. God never runs out of ways to bring this into perspective.

You may be able to identify with the man who wrote these words:

I am 42 years old. I work for a large corporation. But I'm no longer moving "up."

I know that working for a large corporation is not exactly *au courant,* but my father owned a small retail store, and after 30 years of his standing behind the counter, neither of us saw the magic of doing "your own thing."

But a big corporation—something plucked right off the Fortune 500; a company with interlocking, multinational profit centers; with well-defined vertical and horizontal reporting relationships— that was just what the doctor ordered, and that was exactly what I got.

Going in, I knew there would be a price to pay. Too much structure can be confining. But for me, the organizational chart was like a children's playground—a place to climb, swing and scramble all the way to the top.

And that was where I was headed. After all, isn't that what it's all about?

Year by year, level by level, I made my way up; and if I wasn't laughing all the way, only rarely did I doubt choosing the corporate life.

Never being one for team sports, never having served in the Army, I enjoyed the camaraderie that comes from being "one of the boys."

I also enjoyed the competition.

Whatever the reason . . . I was immediately perceived to be "a star." And though my corporation was too conservative to have a "fast track," I did burn a few cinders as a steady procession of blue memos charted my upward progress. Over the years I gained titles, windows, salary and perks. These incentives fueled a fire that was burning very bright indeed. I knew in my bones that I would someday reach the top. Some men might stumble. Others might even fall by the wayside. But not me; never me.

Or so I believed, right up to the day, right up to the instant, when I learned the fire was out, the star was extinguished, the climb was over. . . .

. . . I could expect the average salary increases due the average employee. But there would be no more leapfrog advancements. No more seductive little perks. No more blue memos.

I was no longer climbing. I had plateaued out. . . .[3]

No doubt, this man felt the same sense of loss that my missionary friend experienced when he said, "The Lord simply turned my hands over . . . gave them a good slap . . . and out came everything!"

Now I wouldn't wish that jolt on anyone, but it happens to many. If some corporate position is the god of your life, then something terrible occurs within when it is no longer a future possibility. If your career, however, is simply a part of God's plan and you keep it in proper perspective, you can handle a demotion just as well as you can handle a promotion. It all depends on who's first and what's first.

WHO'S ON FIRST?

In searching out what it takes to live differently in our world, we have considered vision, determination, and now priorities. But as I address priorities, I feel the pinch a little tighter, don't you? So it goes for those who are determined to live their lives above the mediocre level. Breaking the magnet which draws things ahead of God is a lengthy and sometimes painful process. There is a line found in the Jewish Talmud that puts it well: "Man is born with his hands clenched; he dies with them wide open. Entering life, he desires to grasp everything; leaving the world, all he possessed has slipped away."

A few words from Colossians 1 never fail to encourage me when things begin to slip away. Since life is like a coin and it can be spent only once, these words are good reminders of the one deserving of our investment. They begin with a reference to God the Father:

> For He delivered us from the domain of darkness, and trans-ferred us to the kingdom of His beloved Son, in whom we have redemption, the forgiveness of sins (vv. 13–14).

That is a wonderful statement of God's eternal rescue. He deliv-ered us from darkness to light. And He transferred us, notice, to a new kingdom—the unseen kingdom—where there are values worth investing in, where we live beyond the entrapment of things and people and events and human ideas. It is called "the kingdom of His beloved Son [Jesus Christ]." He has transferred us to a new realm of existence where we are enveloped in the Son's perfect righteousness and forgiveness.

And what a statement follows!

> And He is the image of the invisible God, the first-born of all creation. For in Him all things were created, both in the heavens and on earth, visible and invisible, whether thrones or dominions or rulers or authorities—all things have been created through Him and for Him (vv. 15–16).

Everything created was through Christ and His power, and furthermore, it was created for His honor. That includes every-day things today. You have a good job? It's to be enjoyed for Him. You have a nice salary? It's to be enjoyed and invested for Him. You have good health? It is for Him. You have a family? The family members are for Him. You're planning a move? It's to be for Him. You're thinking about a career change? It needs to be for Him. That is true because He's the ruler of our kingdom. He is Lord. And that's not simply the title of a chorus Christians sing; it's a statement of faith. He has the right to take charge of our decisions so that He might be honored through them. Every day I live I must address that. Again, it is a matter of priorities.

> And He is before all things, and in Him all things hold together (v. 17).

Isn't this a wonderful section of Scripture? In all these things, Christ is the center. He is in things, He's through things, He's holding things together. He's the glue that makes stuff stick together. He put the stars in space, and their movement is exactly according to His sovereign chronometer, precisely as He arranged it. And everything out there hangs in space exactly as He set it up. His problem is not with planets in space, however. His wrestling match is with people on earth who have been put here but want to go their own way. Note the next verse:

> He is also head of the body, the church; and He is the beginning, the first-born from the dead; so that He Himself might come to have first place in everything (v. 18).

Take your time with those final four words. Read them aloud. Think them through. You're dating a young man. You think you're falling in love with this man. Does Christ have *first place* in that relationship? Or have you decided that a moral compromise really feels better? Maybe you have chosen not to maintain such a strict standard of purity as before. If you've made that priority decision, then face it—Christ really isn't in first place in that romance.

Are you struggling right now between a decision that requires doing what is exactly right and losing closeness with an individual or giving in a little and keeping that friendship? You know the rest of the story. If Christ is going to have top priority, it must be according to the standard of His righteousness. There has to be credibility in what we do or it doesn't fall into the category of seeking His kingdom and His righteousness, does it? Why am I coming on so strong? Because He is to have *first place* in everything. Those who are really committed to excellence give Him top priority.

A RESPONSE OF INCREDIBLE RELEVANCE

On one occasion Jesus was having a meal with a group of people. When the other guests began picking out places of honor at the table, Jesus told them a story about humility. And to the host he said:

> " . . . when you give a reception, invite the poor, the crippled, the lame, the blind and you will be blessed, since they do not have the means to repay you. . . ."

And when one of those who were reclining at table with Him heard this, he said to Him, "Blessed is everyone who shall eat bread in the kingdom of God!" (Luke 14:15).

How interesting! Someone else says this to Jesus. The light finally dawned. He's gotten the message! "Lord, I've heard what You have said and it's clear that the one who is really fulfilled, deeply satisfied, genuinely joyful, is the one who enjoys Your food, who takes Your provisions, and lives in light of them while he's on this earth. I believe that, Lord. Count me in!" That's the general idea.

Jesus heard his response and told another story that illustrates everything I have been trying to say in this chapter.

But He said to him, "A certain man was giving a big dinner, and he invited many; and at the dinner hour he sent his slave to say to those who had been invited, 'Come; for everything is ready now'" (Luke 14:16–17).

"Ding-a-ling-a-ling-a-ling, supper is ready! Come on in, the meal is served." But wait. This isn't a literal meal He's talking about. This is a parable, remember? He is talking about a spiritual meal—that which satisfies one's life in the kingdom realm. He's saying, "I've served a meal, and it will satisfy you. Come and eat." You'd think everybody would have jumped up and joined in. Not so.

"But they all alike began to make excuses. The first one said to him, 'I have bought a piece of land and I need to go out and look at it; please consider me excused'" (Luke 14:18).

I would say this man's decision is amazingly relevant. Here is a guy who has made an investment. Like many, he has bought a piece of land. If you've ever bought a piece of land, you know there's nothing quite as encouraging as walking across the dirt. You want to sort of dig your toes in it and walk rather hard and wriggle your toes, and face it—you feel like Nebuchadnezzar. "It's mine! . . . My land! My piece of property! I own this! I've invested in this!" You see, he was preoccupied with his purchase. He planned to accept the master's invitation, but he thought he would come later. "Right now I want to look over my investment. Please consider me excused. My purchase comes first."

Jon Johnston pulled no punches when he wrote:

> Self-denial is the perennial challenge of humanity. A rampant selfishness is omnipresent in every generation, and the church of the eighties is not immune to me-ism. In fact, many declare our Zion has opted for a double dose. Clergy and parishioner alike calculate every move to maximize personal benefit. . . .
>
> Today, our bonfires of selfishness are fueled by the gasoline of affluence. . . .
>
> Today's self-centered churchgoer asks the same question of God, coupled with another one: "What will you do for me soon?" God is pictured as the dispenser (and withholder) of life's prizes—a television game-show host.
>
> . . . We conclude that such things as good health, fortune, and success are sure indicators of his approval for our lives. This is the Protestant ethic gone to seed. . . .[4]

But let's get back to Jesus' story and see how others responded to the dinner invitation.

> "And another one said, 'I have bought five yoke of oxen, and I am going to try them out; please consider me excused'" (Luke 14:19).

Most of us don't buy oxen today. Nor do we try out oxen. We buy a lot of other things, though. Whatever we buy, we love to try out. We like to take care of it. We like to shine it. We like to look at it. If the truth could be told, deep down inside we tend to make a little shrine out of it, because we worked so hard for it and it means so much. This guest is doing that. He's saying, "I've got this possession and I . . . I want to try it out. Please consider me excused."

I am especially intrigued at the third person's excuse. Look at what this guy has to say:

> "And another one said, 'I have married a wife, and for that reason I cannot come'" (Luke 14:20).

Now there's a creative excuse! "Lord, come on. Gimme a break. At least wait till after the honeymoon. You know, give me a little time. I'll be there later, I promise; but right now there is a relationship that keeps me from coming to Your meal."

Not one of these things is wrong in and of itself. There is nothing wrong with land. Nothing wrong with oxen. Nothing wrong with marriage. So what's wrong then? Well, as good as they are, they prevented these three individuals from being satisfied with the priority of eating a kingdom meal. They took first place, that's all. But that's EVERYTHING . . . really, that's EVERYTHING! And that is precisely Jesus' point.

You wonder how the Lord felt?

> "And the slave came back and reported this to his master. Then the head of the household became angry and said to his slave, 'Go out at once into the streets and lanes of the city and bring in here the poor and crippled and blind and lame'" (Luke 14:21).

If you look at this strictly through first-century eyes, you know Jesus is referring to Jews and Gentiles. "I've given this message to My own people; My own people have rejected it. I came to My own people and My own people did not receive Me. Open it up to the Gentiles. Let the cripples in. Let the lame in. Let the people who get it by grace take advantage of it. It's for all of them." But the application is broader than that.

You see, kingdom life doesn't have to be enjoyed only by those in good health. Sometimes the cripples have things in clearer perspective, sometimes the lame, sometimes the sick, sometimes the blind.

> "And the slave said, 'Master, what you commanded has been done, and still there is room'" (Luke 14:22).

"We still have a lot of room in this place, Master. There are a lot of plates full of food that won't be eaten, still a lot of room in this kingdom."

Look at the next command:

> "And the master said to the slave, 'Go out into the highways and along the hedges, and compel them to come in, that my house may be filled. For I tell you, none of those men who were invited shall taste of my dinner'" (Luke 14:23–24).

William Barclay writes,

> It's possible to be a follower of Jesus without being a disciple; to be a camp-follower without being a soldier of the king; to be a hanger-on in some great work without pulling one's weight. Once someone was talking to a great scholar about a younger man. He said, "So and so tells me that he was one of your students." The teacher answered devastatingly, "He may have attended my lectures, but he was not one of my students." There is a world of difference between attending lectures and being a student. It is one of the supreme handicaps of the Church that in the Church there are so many distant followers of Jesus and so few real disciples.[5]

I think the ranks were thinned. I think He purposely said, "I don't want a big crowd following Me if it means that all these people want to do is feed their bellies and watch miracles and listen to My stories and passively respond to lectures. I want those who give me top priority."

If I stated to you in one succinct sentence the message of this chapter, it would be: Our choice of priorities determines at which level we soar. Stated another way: Whatever is in first place, if it isn't Christ alone, it is in the wrong place. Life is a lot like a coin; you can spend it any way you wish, but you can spend it only once. What are you spending it on?

No need to linger any longer. The point has been made. This final question puts the ball squarely in your court: What is really first in your life?

Accountability:
Answering the
Hard Questions

8

We need heroes. I mean *genuine* heroes, authentic men and women who are admired for their achievements, noble qualities, and courage. Such people aren't afraid to be different. They risk. They stand a cut above. Yet they are real human beings with flaws and failures like anyone else. But these soaring eagles inspire us to do better. We feel warm inside when we think about this rare breed of humanity. The kind we can look up to without the slightest suspicion of deception or hypocrisy. The kind who model excellence when no one is looking or for that matter when half the world *is* looking.

When Aleksandr Solzhenitsyn concluded his Nobel lecture on literature, he closed by quoting a Russian proverb: "One word of truth outweighs the whole world." By changing only two words I think that proverb would say what I believe about heroes: "One person of truth impacts the whole world."

I'm concerned that we seem to be running shy of folks like that. Certainly, there are some, but not nearly as many, it seems, as when I was a small boy. Back then I distinctly recall looking up to numerous people in various segments of society—politics, athletics, education, science, the military, music, religion, aviation—all of whom not only stood tall during their heyday, but they *finished* well. Society mourned their passing. This was no childhood fantasy, you understand; these were not make-believe matinee idols. I can still remember my dad being just as impressed as I was with certain folks—maybe more so. Some of our father-son conversations are still logged in my memory bank. And because he was inspired, so was I.

Perhaps that explains why author Bruce Larson's moving words grabbed my attention. I could easily identify with his experience as a little lad many years ago.

> When I was a small boy, I attended church every Sunday at a big Gothic Presbyterian bastion in Chicago. The preaching was powerful and the music was great. But for me, the most awesome moment in the morning service was the offertory, when twelve solemn, frock-coated ushers marched in lock-step down the main aisle to receive the brass plates for collecting the offering. These men, so serious about their business of serving the Lord in this magnificent house of worship, were the business and professional leaders of Chicago.
>
> One of the twelve ushers was a man named Frank Loesch. He was not a very imposing-looking man, but in Chicago he was a living legend, for he was the man who had stood up to Al Capone. In the prohibition years, Capone's rule was absolute. The local and state police and even the Federal Bureau of Investigation were afraid to oppose him. But singlehandedly, Frank Loesch, as a Christian layman and without any government support, organized the Chicago Crime Commission, a group of citizens who were determined to take Mr. Capone to court and put him away. During the months that the Crime Commission met, Frank Loesch's life was in constant danger. There were threats on the lives of his family and friends. But he never wavered. Ultimately he won the case against Capone and was the instrument for removing this blight from the city of Chicago. Frank Loesch had risked his life to live out his faith.
>
> Each Sunday at this point of the service, my father, a Chicago businessman himself, never failed to poke me and silently point to Frank Loesch with pride. Sometime I'd catch a tear in my father's

eye. For my dad and for all of us this was and is what authentic living is all about.[1]

I love that story. Written between the lines are strong, spine-tingling feelings of respect, the right kind of pride, and an inner compulsion to be all that one ought to be. Wonderful feelings! Essential, in fact, if we hope to soar high, far above mediocrity's drag.

Tell me, who needs to walk by for you to poke your son, daughter, or friend and whisper, "Now, that's a person worth following. Pattern your life after him (or her) and you'll never be sorry"? If you can think of some, I would call them your heroes. Not too many, are there?

You may be surprised to know that for any number of other people, *you* are the person others point to. It may be in the place where you work, and no one has even told you. It may happen in your neighborhood, and no neighbor has been brave enough to encourage you by saying, "You're the one everybody watches. You're very unique. We all respect you." It may be in your profession where you are admired by colleagues and peers. If you knew how many felt that way, I'm convinced you would be all the more careful with the way you practice your profession or the way you conduct your business.

I am certain of this—if you *are* one of those people, then you're not like the majority. You're living differently, and I commend you for it. We are learning in these chapters that it takes unusual people to make a difference in our world. Mediocre people impact no one, at least not for good. But one person of truth can impact the whole world.

For several chapters I have been writing about being that person. If I were asked to make a list of what is involved in such a person's life, I would include at least four qualities.

ESSENTIAL CHARACTERISTICS THAT MAKE AN IMPACT

First, people who live differently are people of *vision*. Vision is the ability to see above and beyond the majority, to be unenamored by statistics, unintimidated by the odds, unmoved by

obstacles like so-called impossibilities, restrictions, and diffi-
culties. They are people like Frank Loesch who don't hold back
even though their lives are threatened, who don't churn through
life, worried over whether a few glass panes in their home will be
broken or whether their children may suffer a little because their
dad or mother is different. They have vision.

Second, people who impact others model *determination.* Determination is nothing more than deciding to stay at it, even
though it's tough. Determination is hanging in there, not giving
up, not lessening one's convictions when the road gets long or
rough. I cannot think of a hero who failed to have determination.

Third, those who soar above mediocrity are people of *priorities.* They think in terms of who and what are first in the home, at
work, in possessions, and in relationships as well. People who
have priorities keep that in perspective. They work hard, but
work doesn't become their god; it is a responsibility not a shrine.
It is a way by which money is earned. And with the money they
buy possessions; but again, their priorities determine which possessions they hang onto and why.

Now, there is a fourth essential characteristic when it comes to
living differently, and I warn you; it is the least popular of the
four. After vision and determination and priorities, I should also
mention *accountability.* People who really make an impact model
this rare quality as well as the first three I have named.

What do I mean by accountability? In the simplest terms, it is
answering the hard questions. Accountability includes opening
one's life to a few carefully selected, trusted, loyal confidants who
speak the truth—who have the right to examine, to question, to
appraise, and to give counsel.

Not much has been said or written about accountability. Practically every time I've spoken on the subject, I've had people say
afterwards, "I never hear this addressed. I don't read much about
it. In fact, I have seldom even used the word!" Because this concept has not been hammered out openly and often, the term itself
seems strange. It can also be misused, since it is so easily misunderstood.

I do not have in mind some legalistic tribunal where victims
are ripped apart with little concern for their feelings. There is too
much of that going on already! Such savagery helps no one. It
doesn't build up others nor encourage them to do better. And

because many fear that accountability means only criticism, they resent even the mention of the word. I realize it is possible to clip people's wings so severely they will never soar. But trust me, that's the farthest thought from my mind when I write of accountability.

FOUR QUALITIES IN ACCOUNTABILITY

People who are accountable usually have four qualities:

- *Vulnerability*—capable of being wounded, shown to be wrong, even admitting it before being confronted.
- *Teachability*—a willingness to learn, being quick to hear and respond to reproof, being open to counsel.
- *Availability*—accessible, touchable, able to be interrupted.
- *Honesty*—committed to the truth regardless of how much it hurts, a willingness to admit the truth no matter how difficult or humiliating the admission may be. Hating all that is phony or false.

That's a tough list! As I look back over those four qualities, I am more than ever aware of why accountability is resisted by the majority. Those with fragile egos can't handle it. And prima donna types won't tolerate it. They have a greater desire to look good and make a stunning impression than anything else. I mean, "the very idea of someone probing into my life!"

Again, don't misunderstand. I'm not suggesting for a moment that accountability gives the general public carte blanche access to any and all areas of one's private life. If you will glance back a few lines you will notice I referred to "a few carefully selected, trusted, loyal confidants." They are the ones who have earned the right to come alongside and, when it seems appropriate and necessary, ask the hard questions. The purpose of the relationship is not to make someone squirm or to pull rank and devastate an individual; no, not at all. Rather, it is to be a helpful sounding board, to guard someone from potential peril, to identify the possibility of a "blind spot," to serve in an advisory capacity, bringing perspective and wisdom where such may be lacking.

"watch over your souls." And not only that, but we are told it is profitable for us to be accountable to them.

Let me try to spell that out so no one misunderstands. There are times when the minister of a church or perhaps an elected official in the church may find it necessary to pull up alongside and ask questions regarding your life. When this happens, it isn't idle or needless probing. And it certainly isn't for the purpose of gossip. This individual has your good at heart because he or she is accountable to God for your life. According to what we read in Hebrews 13, you are to answer the questions graciously, and listen to the counsel gratefully. That is precisely what accountability means; answering the hard questions.

I have been a pastor for some twenty-five years and have encountered the full spectrum of responses from people when it has been my duty to carry out this hard job. There have been times when I have had to get close to an individual and ask hard questions or reprove an individual (always in private, of course) for something that is hurting the testimony of the church. On the one hand, I have had people grateful for the reproof and even *thank* me for it and later tell me how much it has helped them. And even though it was difficult for both of us, even though it hurt, they knew it helped in the long run. People who really want to soar above mediocrity appreciate periodic reproof—and say so!

On the other hand (though I made every effort to handle the situation in a sensitive manner), I have had others resent my remarks and become so offended that I could hardly finish my conversation before they literally walked away. I have even had a few argue with me. Some have said to me later that it was none of my business or I was harsh or too strong a leader, or if I had known them better, I wouldn't have even mentioned the matter.

Allow me this one further comment. Not one of us is an island. We need one another. Sometimes we need to hear another's reproof. Believe me, if you think it is tough to *hear* such reproof, try giving it! Few assignments are more difficult for a spiritual leader. If one has the courage to call you into account and does it in the right way, with the right motive, be humble enough to accept the confrontation. Understand that it was terribly difficult to work up the courage to say anything in the first place. And know that that person has the good of the church at heart, not some private vendetta. In the long run, your commitment to excellence will be enhanced, and you will be able to fly higher.

3. *Accountability to one another is helpful and healthy.* This process is not limited to spiritual leaders, however. We need it on a personal level as well.

Take the time to digest the following scriptures. Read each word. Linger long enough to absorb the truth. And try hard not to be defensive.

> Let love be without hypocrisy. Abhor what is evil; cling to what is good. Be devoted to one another in brotherly love; give preference to one another in honor; not lagging behind in diligence, fervent in spirit, serving the Lord; rejoicing in hope, persevering in tribulation, devoted to prayer, contributing to the needs of the saints, practicing hospitality. Bless those who persecute you; bless and curse not. Rejoice with those who rejoice, and weep with those who weep. Be of the same mind toward one another; do not be haughty in mind, but associate with the lowly. Do not be wise in your own estimation (Rom. 12:9–16).

> Now we who are strong ought to bear the weaknesses of those without strength and not just please ourselves. Let each of us please his neighbor for his good, to his edification. . . .

> And concerning you, my brethren, I myself also am convinced that you yourselves are full of goodness, filled with all knowledge, and able also to admonish one another (Rom. 15:1–2, 14).

> If we live by the Spirit, let us also walk by the Spirit. Let us not become boastful, challenging one another, envying one another.

> Brethren, even if a man is caught in any trespass, you who are spiritual, restore such a one in a spirit of gentleness; looking to yourselves, lest you too be tempted. Bear one another's burdens, and thus fulfill the law of Christ (Gal. 5:25–6:2).

So far everything is theoretical and safe, because I haven't gotten painfully specific. But now I want to risk getting *that* specific. Please know that I write these things with your good in mind. And that is my sole motive. All of us go through stressful times. If we have no one near during an extended period of high-level stress, chances are good we may lose our perspective. If the stress gets great enough, we could crack. The solution? We need to be accountable!

Now let's go a step further. Say you are a high-powered person with a great deal of responsibility and authority. Left to yourself, you could begin to abuse this power without even realizing it. You will be a better steward of your responsibility if there is someone who knows you well enough to tell you the truth. Solution? You need to be accountable!

Perhaps you have begun to make a lot of money, more than ever in your life. Thanks to this burst of prosperity, there are unseen, beneath-the-surface, mines in the harbor of your future. If you have no one who will give you counsel on how to handle yourself or your money, you will likely blow it if you try to handle it alone. Solution? You need to be accountable!

If you are a husband or a wife, accountability needs to be built into that relationship. Marriages that flourish have this safeguard built in. But if there is a breakdown in accountability, it is only a matter of time before there will be a breakdown in the marriage relationship.

There also has to be accountability in a home between children and parents. Without it there is poor communication—ultimately anarchy, which leads to delinquency. I repeat, there must be accountability! We have it with our teachers at school, our bosses at work, our coaches on the team, the bank that holds the mortgage on our home, and the cop on the corner. Strangely, somehow we don't feel the need to cultivate it on a personal level. The home is an ideal place to learn how to be accountable.

I have a theory that might help explain why there is so little voluntary accountability among adults. In the process of growing up and leaving home, we step away from possibly one of the healthiest situations we've ever had, especially if the home was a balanced, stable one. The healthy relationship we step away from includes the accountability we developed with our parents. About the time we reach eighteen or twenty, we move into a dormitory or join the military or move into our own apartment or we marry and establish our own home with our mate. Often at that point, the relationship of accountability that had been consistently in motion for so long suddenly stops. And an unhealthy independence gets set in concrete. Too much privacy replaces previous days of openness. We adopt a lifestyle that includes too much time strictly on our own. Before long, we're living like isolated islands. No one feels the freedom to step in, not even parents, lest they appear to be meddling. And unless we invite a few close friends to come alongside, most will continue leaving us alone.

Moms and dads don't want to say much. They see things, but they are hesitant to comment. Young adults on their own don't want to ask for much advice, lest it appear as if they are still dependent. A chasm, a void of communication, is created. After all, one of the perks of being on one's own is privacy, right? One of the prerogatives of leadership is independence, right? But the hidden part of the equation is seldom addressed. Too much privacy is unhealthy. Too many hours of independence easily leads to a fall—ethically or morally, financially or spiritually. Stop and think. Those you know who have slipped spiritually or fallen into extra-marital affairs or gotten caught in some financial fiasco were not accountable on a regular basis to anyone, were they? Without the safety net of checks and balances, a fall can be not only far but fatal.

I have formed the habit of asking about accountability when stories of someone's spiritual defection or moral fall comes to my attention. Without fail, I ask something like, "Was _____ accountable to anyone on a regular basis? Did he (or she) meet with one, two, or three folks for the purpose of giving and receiving counsel, prayer, and planning?" Without exception—*hear me, now*—without a single exception, the answer has been the same: *NO!* There is no safe place to be in a world system like ours, where anyone can find immunity from the dangers of too much privacy.

Frankly, the ministry is more perilous than most other vocations. Why? The answer isn't that complicated. There are few roles in life where one is granted greater independence, more privacy, and higher respect. Without personal, regular accountability—not forced but invited—few are strong enough to handle the battles alone. To me, that fact best explains the epidemic in the 1970s and 1980s of moral defection and marital failures among those in vocational Christian service. It is one thing to soar high and alone as an eagle, above the level of mediocrity. But it is another thing entirely, to be so alone that we encounter winds we cannot handle. At such times, flying with a few fellow eagles is essential.

HISTORICAL EXAMPLES FROM BIBLICAL DAYS

Not long ago I went on a quick safari through both Old and New Testaments looking for examples of strong-minded, eagle-like people who lived busy, responsible lives, but took the time to cultivate an accountable relationship with at least one (often more than one) other person. Here is what I found.

Lot was accountable to his Uncle Abraham. When that relationship ceased, Lot sank into the mire at Sodom (Gen. 13, 19).

While he was in the home of Potiphar, *Joseph was accountable to Potiphar.* And even when Potiphar's wife repeatedly made those seductive advances toward Joseph, which Joseph refused, he remained accountable to Potiphar (Gen. 39).

When Saul became Israel's first king, he got in a hurry for Samuel the prophet to arrive so an offering could be made. When Samuel was late, Saul got antsy and ran ahead and gathered together the offering, and offered it. He disobeyed, for kings had no business doing that. When Samuel finally did arrive, if you can believe it, he—a prophet—rebuked the king of Israel! And Saul took it on the chin without an argument. Why? Because *Saul the king was accountable to Samuel the prophet* (1 Sam. 13).

When David fell with Bathsheba and the entire nation was scandalized because of his adultery, Nathan the prophet stood before the king of the nation and said to David, "You are the man." King David didn't fight him or try to have him killed. Instead, David confessed, "I have sinned." Why? Because *David was accountable to Nathan the prophet* (2 Sam. 12).

When Nehemiah became convinced he should go to Jerusalem and lead the project of building the wall around the city, he first had to get a green light from Artaxerxes. He refused to leave without it. Even though God had spoken to him and was leading him on that future mission, *Nehemiah was accountable to the king* for whom he worked as a cupbearer (Neh. 1–2).

When Daniel lived as a man of God through several generations of kings, *Daniel made himself accountable to each king* — some great, some not so great. On one occasion his colleagues called the officials of the land and made accusations against Daniel. With search warrants they personally moved in and checked on him. They left no stone unturned! But even after a thorough search, they couldn't find a solitary thing against him. He was clean! But Daniel didn't fight them. The fact is, when he found out about it later, he was very much at ease. There was nothing to hide. *Daniel lived accountable to his peers* (Dan. 1–6). Accountability has a way of keeping one's private life squeaky clean.

Let's now move into the New Testament. When Jesus came to this earth, one of the things that marked his life was submission to the Father's will. John tells us on more than one occasion that Jesus always did the things that pleased the Father. *The Son of God was accountable to His heavenly Father.*

When Christ selected twelve men to work with Him, men to whom He would pass the torch of the work of ministry, there is no question that *the disciples were accountable to Jesus.* Ultimately, *they became accountable to one another.*

When John Mark went on a journey with Paul and Barnabas, *John Mark was accountable to those older men.* In fact, the two older men traveled together for the same reason. *Paul and Barnabas, in turn, were accountable to the church at Antioch,* as were Paul and Silas later on. *Timothy was accountable to Paul,* his father in the faith.

Onesimus the slave was accountable to Philemon. And Paul, when writing the letter to Philemon, said, in effect, "He is willing to come back. Please accept him. Onesimus is accountable to you."

When John the apostle wrote the little letter of Third John, he mentioned Diotrephes. He said, "When I come, I will set the record straight." Why? *Diotrephes was accountable to John as an elder.* A major battle John had with that man was his unwillingness to be accountable to anyone.

I have just hit the high points like a rock skipping across a lake.

But that's sufficient for you to get the picture. The Bible is *full* of examples of accountability. Again and again, people in biblical days benefited from others' presence, counsel, warnings, and encouragement.

Today, we, too, need others to hold us accountable. Sometimes an objective opinion will reveal a blind spot. Sometimes a straight-from-the-shoulder piece of advice will preserve a friend from a fall. Other times a strong reproof will get the wayward back on track. On another occasion, we may simply need a sounding board to help keep us on target. One man hails the benefits of accountability like this:

> . . . Behavioral sciences in recent years have expounded the simple truth that "behavior that is observed changes." People who are accountable by their own choice to a group of friends, to a therapy group, to a psychiatrist or a pastoral counselor, to a study group or prayer group, are people who are serious about changing their behavior, and they are finding that change is possible.
>
> Studies done in factories have proven that both quality and quantity of work increase when the employees know that they are being observed. If only God knows what I am doing, since I know He won't tell, I tend to make all kinds of excuses for myself. But if I must report to another or a group of others, I begin to monitor my behavior. If someone is keeping an eye on me, my behavior improves.[2]

An unaccountable leader is dancing too close to the edge of risk. Unaccountable radio personalities and/or television evangelists live with too much authority and too much privacy. They need others! An unaccountable counselor has too much responsibility and needs too much self-control to handle everything alone. An unaccountable physician can easily stumble. An unaccountable banker, CPA, or attorney can fall as well. Unaccountable entrepreneurs are especially vulnerable. It's simply too great a chance to take without someone or a small group of confidential, objective friends alongside who have your good at heart, those whom you have invited into your private world.

Sometimes blind spots result in notorious disasters. Jonestown is a classic example of an unaccountable leader who went wild with authority. He simply went too far too fast—he was too isolated. No one, finally, was allowed to be honest with Jim Jones.

Some of you are probably wondering about me. You need to know that I am definitely, willingly, and regularly accountable to a carefully chosen, small group of men. Not all of them are part of the church I serve. They are men of wisdom and integrity. They love me too much not to tell me the truth. Just recently Cynthia and I both spent several hours with these trusted, objective, honest men as they hammered away at particular facets of our lives. It was painful at times, but, oh, so beneficial!

Are you accountable to someone outside your family? Someone who can ask you straight questions, hard questions, and make honest observations? Do you spend some time with this person on a regular basis, looking at each other's life? Are you committed to mutual encouragement? Do you think together? Pray together? Play together? I hope so.

PRACTICAL ADVANTAGES OF PERSONAL APPRAISAL

Chances are good that someone will read this chapter and misunderstand me. "Sounds like a torture chamber you're suggesting, Chuck. Who needs to face a gestapo group every other week?" Hold it. Just in case my words have given you that false impression, allow me to set the record straight. To be sure, accountability can degenerate into a dreadful, threatening scene if it is handled the wrong way or if you have the wrong people involved. (By the way, some people would love to make the world accountable to them. They are the frowning ones who wear hair shirts and feel "called of God" to be your personal Nathan who will point out all your wrongs. They have the unique "gift of criticism." They'll be happy to exercise it on your behalf—*often!* My advice? Avoid those folks like the plague! They hurt much more than they help.) That's not what I have in mind.

I'm talking about people who love you too much to let you play in dangerous traffic. They also love you too much to let you start believing in your own stuff. When they spot conceit rearing its head, they say so. But they also love you too much to let you be too hard on yourself. Like Jonathan with David, they are messengers of great encouragemen That's the bright side, and it needs to be emphasized. Soaring eagles need wind beneath their wings!

I can think of at least three practical advantages of account-ability—all based on statements found in the ancient Books of Proverbs and Psalms.

First advantage: *When we are regularly accountable, we're less likely to stumble into a trap.* Other eyes, more perceptive and objective than ours, can see traps that we may fail to detect.

Through presumption comes nothing but strife,
But with those who receive counsel is wisdom. . . .
The teaching of the wise is a fountain of life,
To turn aside from the snares of death. . . .
Poverty and shame will come to him who neglects discipline,
But he who regards reproof will be honored. . . .
He who walks with wise men will be wise,
But the companion of fools will suffer harm (Prov. 13:10, 14, 18, 20).

The last statement is not a verse written to teenagers in high school, though it certainly would apply. I clearly remember my high school years, don't you? Many of us ran around with others who were tougher than we, so we could cover up our own feelings of inadequacy. My mother kept saying to me, "Charles, every time you run with the wrong crowd, you do wrong. When you are with the right crowd, you do right." That was objective, accurate counsel that I didn't want to hear, but she said it often enough to drill truth into my head. Her counsel is still true. If I were to run with the wrong crowd, I would be tempted to do wrong.

And it doesn't stop when we turn twenty. It goes on into adult years as well. If you choose a wrong set of co-workers, you'll practice wrong things in your business. If you choose a wrong set of friends, you'll practice wrong things in your social life. Run with those who do drugs, and you'll wind up doing the same.

But—the flip side—those who walk with the wise learn from them. You need someone who will say, "I'm not sure how healthy that is. I'm glad you asked me. Let's talk about it." And that per-son will help point out the traps you could fall into if you kept tracking in that direction. A couple more statements on this same advantage:

He whose ear listens to the life-giving reproof will dwell among the wise. He who neglects discipline despises himself, but he who listens to reproof acquires understanding. The fear of the Lord is the instruction for wisdom, and before honor comes humility (Prov. 15:31–33).

I like the way Solomon calls this counsel "life-giving reproof." That's exactly what it is!

Now for the second advantage of accountability: *When we are regularly accountable, we are more likely to see the whole picture.* When we have a sounding board, an accountable partner or group who trafficks in truth, we're more likely to see the whole picture. I notice that my life tends to get quite narrow if my world is reduced to my own perspective—just a restricted, tight radius. But with the counsel of a friend, my world expands. I become more aware; I gain depth and I discover innuendo and I find another vista or dimension I would have missed all alone with my two-by-four mind. "Iron sharpens iron, so one man sharpens another" (Prov. 27:17).

Let me expand on that refining process a little. One woman sharpens another; one homemaker sharpens another; one dentist sharpens another (no pun intended); one attorney sharpens another; one physician sharpens another; one businessman sharpens another; one salesman sharpens another; one minister sharpens another. Why? Because the world in which one person lives is too limited and restricted. When rubbing shoulders with another, we gain a panoramic view, which allows us to see the whole picture. "As in water face reflects face, so the heart of man reflects man" (Prov. 27:19).

That's so picturesque! People provide a clear reflection of what is in the heart. A mirror goes only skin deep. The counsel of a friend reflects what is down inside.

Plato, in his *Apology,* wrote, "The life which is unexamined is not worth living." If you are not reflecting on your life, I have news for you: It isn't long before you'll accept mediocrity. Are you doing what you did last year and perhaps the year before that? If so, you're becoming less effective. We need the discipline of self-examination in order to achieve excellence.

The third advantage of accountability: *When we are regularly accountable, we are not likely to get away with sinful and unwise actions.* "Faithful are the wounds of a friend, but deceitful are the kisses of an enemy" (Prov. 27:6).

I've thought a lot about that proverb. Not only because I have been wounded (in the right way) by counselors who had my good at heart, but because I have been curious about how it works in any life. I did an analysis of verse 6 and found that the original Hebrew text reads something like this:

> Trustworthy are the bruises caused by the wounding of one who loves you, but deceitful are the kisses of one who hates you.

Among other things, that limits those who wound us to those who love us. This tells me that not everyone has a right to climb into our life and come down on us with a rebuke. No, that is a privilege and responsibility of someone with whom we have established a love relationship. A love relationship, based on time spent together and a deep knowledge of each other, provides the oil rebukes need in order for them to be accepted. There are times when it is necessary for us to be bruised by a friend's straight talk.

I can't remember where I first read the following words but I will never forget them: "Apart from blunt truth, our lives sink decadently amid the perfume of hints and suggestions."

AN HONEST EVALUATION OF OURSELVES

It is possible to read a chapter like this and never take it personally. Some read it and think, "I have to get my husband to read this!" Or, "It's too bad my pastor hasn't read this chapter. Maybe I can loan him the book—and underline certain statements in chapter 8!" Bad idea. Instead of wishing someone else were reading this, let's play like it's just the two of us. I have the privilege of writing about something that is very, very personal to you—*your* life, *your* private world. To make it palatable, allow me to ask you a few questions. I would like you simply to answer them "Yes" or "No." They are hard questions, I warn you. And you may be embarrassed if someone saw your answers, perhaps, because you wouldn't be able to explain them fully. So just think your answer, okay? Take your time, however. Don't answer too quickly.

Question 1. <u>Can you name one or more people outside your family to whom you have made yourself regularly accountable?</u>

And before you answer, this is what I mean. That person has quick and easy access to your life. He (or she) is free to ask you things like "What's going on?" and "Why?" This person wouldn't hesitate to probe if he were concerned about something you were doing that seemed unwise or hurtful. This friend usually knows your whereabouts and can regularly vouch for your motives. He or she has your private phone number. He isn't afraid to interrupt you. There's a well-developed love connection between you. You've helped cultivate it. Do you have at least one person like that, preferably two or three?

If your answer is "No," rather than just stopping here with a deep sigh, thinking, *I'm out of luck,* take this as a challenge. Say to yourself, "I need to search for someone, a person that I know will take that kind of time with me. And I'm going to invite that person to begin a friendship. We're going to have a meal or two together, and we're going to get to know each other, and I'm going to see if perhaps this is the one to whom I should open my life." I plead with you, don't put it off.

Question 2. <u>Are you aware of the dangers of unaccountability?</u> Again, before you answer, I'm talking about dangers like unattractive blind spots, unhealthy relationships, unchecked habits, unspoken motives that will never be known without such a friend. Are you aware of where these dangers will lead if unaccountability continues? Be honest now. Ponder the consequences of an unaccountable life.

Maybe you have to admit that you've been far too proud, lived much too secretly. When I decided to let down my guard a number of years ago, I wrote out this simple prayer to God. It helped break down my resistance to the counsel of others.

> Lord, I am willing
> To receive what You give
> To lack what You withhold
> To relinquish what You take
> To suffer what You inflict
> To be what You require.
> And, Lord, if others are to be
> Your messengers to me,
> I am willing to hear and heed
> What they have to say. Amen.

Question 3. <u>When was the last time you gave an account for the</u> <u>"private areas" of your life to someone outside your family?</u> Like your finances, sizable purchases, or your pattern for giving? Does anyone know how much (or how little) you give? Does anyone give you counsel on what seems wise and what seems a bit irresponsible in the use of your money? Has someone ever talked to you about sacrificing in the realm of finances? They won't without your invitation.

How about occupational diligence? Does anyone know how much or how little time you really spend at the office? Is anybody aware of the attitude you have there, so that he or she is able to help you see its impact on the lives of others? Maybe someone needs to say you're working *too many* hours. Does someone have a right to that secret world of yours?

How about a schedule of activities? Have you had anyone pull up to you recently and say, "You know you're just too busy. You're away from home too many hours. Why do you say yes so often?" You may be approaching "burnout" without realizing it.

How about addressing your lust? Does anybody know how much you struggle with pornography? Anyone know what you check out at the video stores, or which magazines you linger over? How about a level of entertainment that you've decided you can get away with because nobody knows? Those aren't petty questions; they're hard ones.

I warned you I'd be writing straight talk. I care about your remaining strong and eaglelike. I care about your soaring. I care if you've begun to slump and settle for mediocrity. And I think you care too. I think you really *want* to impact others. Remember my paraphrase of Solzhenitsyn's statement? "One person of truth impacts the whole world."

Recently I read about a woman who, on the advice of her doctor, had gone to see a pastor to talk about joining the church. She had recently had a facelift and when her doctor dismissed her, he gave her this advice:

> "My dear, I have done an extraordinary job on your face, as you can see in the mirror. I have charged you a great deal of money and you were happy to pay it. But I want to give you some free advice. Find a group of people who love God and who will love you enough to help you deal with all the negative emotions inside

of you. If you don't, you'll be back in my office in a very short time with your face in far worse shape than before."[3]

Wise counsel!

Those heroes who soar high above the level of mediocrity possess vision, apply determination, and maintain priorities. But how is it they keep from danger and do not suffer a fall from those heights? By now you know the secret. Accountability—they don't avoid the hard questions.

Enemy-occupied territory—that is what the world is. Christianity is the story of how the rightful King has landed in disguise, and is calling us all to take part in a great campaign of sabotage.

C. S. Lewis
1952

Part Three

Combating Mediocrity Requires Fighting Fiercely

Winning
the Battle
over Greed

9

I n our nation of fast foods and quick fixes, the great hope of Americans is overnight change. Many are too impatient to wait for anything and too lazy to work long and hard to make it happen. We want what we want when we want it, and the sooner the better—which explains our constant pursuit of hurry-up formulas. Everything from diet fads promising rapid weight loss to immediate financial success through clever schemes captures our fancy and gets our vote. The famous showman P. T. Barnum knew what he was talking about, didn't he? Promise instant anything and some sucker will bite. Everybody, it seems, expects instant transformation.

All this reminds me of a funny story I heard recently. A fellow was raised in the back hills of West Virginia—I mean, so far out in the sticks, never in his life had he even seen a big city, to say nothing of modern inventions and neon lights. He married a gal just like himself and they spent all their married years in the backwoods. They had one son, whom they creatively named

Junior. Around the time Junior reached his sixteenth birthday, his dad began to realize it wouldn't be too many years before their son would become a man and would strike out on his own. It troubled him that his boy could reach manhood and wind up getting a job in the city, not prepared to face the real world. He felt responsible and decided to do something about it.

He and his wife started saving for a trip the three of them would take to the city. About three years later the big day arrived. They tossed their belongings in the ol' pickup and started the long journey over winding, rough roads to the city. Their plan was to spend several days at a swanky hotel and take in all the sights. As they approached the outskirts of the metropolis, Papa began to get a little jumpy: "Mama, when we pull up at th' hotel, you stay in th' truck while Junior an' I go in an' look around. We'll come back and git ya, okay?" She agreed.

Flashing neon lights and uniformed doormen greeted them as they pulled up. Mama stayed put as Papa and Junior walked wide-eyed toward the lobby. Neither could believe his eyes! When they stepped on a mat, the doors opened automatically. Inside, they stood like statues, staring at the first chandelier either of them had ever seen. It hung from a ceiling three stories high. Off to the left was an enormous waterfall, rippling over inlaid stones and rocks. "Junior, look!" Papa was pointing toward a long mall where busy shoppers were going in and out of beautiful stores. "Papa, looka there!" Down below was an ice-skating rink—*inside.*

While both stood silent, watching one breathtaking sight after another, they kept hearing a clicking sound behind them. Finally, Papa turned around and saw this amazing little room with doors that slid open from the center. "What in the world?" People would walk up, push a button and wait. Lights would flicker above the doors and then, "click," the doors would slide open from the middle. Some people would walk out of the little room and others would walk inside and turn around as, "click," the doors slid shut. By now, dad and son stood *totally* transfixed.

At that moment a wrinkled old lady shuffled up to the doors all by herself. She pushed the button and waited only a few seconds. "Click," the doors opened with a swish and she hobbled into the little room. No one else stepped in with her, so "click," the doors slid shut. Not more than twenty seconds later the doors opened again—and there stood this fabulously attractive blonde, a young woman in her twenties—high heels, shapely body, beautiful face—a real knockout! As she stepped out, smiled, and turned to walk away, Papa nudged his boy and mumbled, "Hey, Junior . . . *go git Mama!*"

Seems like everybody these days is looking for a room like what Papa thought he had found. Just push the right button, wait momentarily for the door of opportunity to slide open, then "click," magic! In only a matter of seconds we are instantly transformed. Whom are we kidding? That makes a pretty good joke, but when it comes to reality, nothing could be further from the truth. This is especially true when it comes to the cultivation of character. Honestly, I know of nothing that takes longer, is harder work, or requires greater effort than breaking the old habits that hold us in the grip of mediocrity. No eagle instantly or automatically soars!

This constant struggle to cultivate and maintain good character explains why I think of this third section of the book as a combat zone—a series of four chapters that portray the scene of a fierce fight. There are four major enemies that must be identified, attacked, and conquered if we hope to achieve and maintain excellence: *greed, traditionalism, apathetic indifference,* and *joyless selfishness.* And we shall take them in that order. But keep in mind that each one of these opponents of excellence dies a slow and painful death. About the time we think we've got 'em whipped, they're back on their feet and coming at us from another angle.

GREED UNDER THE SCOPE

Let's take a brief yet close look at greed. Practically speaking, greed is an inordinate desire for more, an excessive, unsatisfied hunger to possess. Like an untamed beast, greed grasps, claws, reaches, clutches, and clings—stubbornly refusing to surrender. The word *enough* is not in this beast's vocabulary. Akin to envy and jealousy, greed is nevertheless distinct. Envy wants to have what someone else possesses. Jealousy wants to possess what it already has. But greed is different. Greed is forever discontented and therefore insatiably craving, longing, wanting, striving for more, more, more.

Perhaps there is nothing more tragic to behold than a greedy person—a person who is never fully at rest, always in pursuit of something else, something more, something beyond. The bondage this creates serves as an anchor so huge and heavy, no set of wings, no matter how massive, can lift its victim to soar.

FOUR FACES OF GREED

The first and most common face greed wears is the green mask of money, money, money! Greed is an excessive motivation to have more money. It is a face we see all around us. Most people I meet in the workplace want more money for what they are doing. Before challenging that, stop and think of those you work around. Most are woefully discontented with their salary. And by the way, you don't have to be rich to be greedy. I know more people who haven't enough money who are greedy than I know who have more than they need. Most often, greed appears as a gnawing, ruthless hunger to get more, to earn more, and even to hoard more money.

Second, greed often wears the face of things, material possessions. Greed is an excessive determination to own more things. Again, think before you reject that thought. We never quite have enough furniture. Or the right furniture. Have you noticed? We never have the right carpet or just the drapes we'd like to have. And then there's the woodwork like we've always dreamed of having. Or the car we've always wanted to own. Whether it's little trinkets we happen to collect or some big thing like a home or an RV or a boat—it's always something. It's that driving desire to own more things. To say it straight, greed is raw, unchecked materialism.

Third, greed can wear the face of fame. Greed is also an excessive desire to become more famous, to make a name for oneself. Some are so determined to be stars, to be in lights, they'd stop at nothing to have people quote them or to be seen in celebrity circles. Thankfully, not all who are famous fall into the greedy category. It's wonderful to meet people who are stars and don't know it.

While my family and I were at a Dodgers game last summer, I saw some little fellows waiting for autographs from some of the players in the Los Angeles Dodgers' organization. It was terrific to watch some of those fine athletes—big, strong, and muscular—drop down on one knee and pull a little boy over closer and say, "Sure, I'll sign that," and then write his name on the kid's baseball. Each boy walked away with a new hero added to his list. Approachable professional athletes, politicians, and teachers who take time for young people can make an enormous impression for good!

I remember when I lived in Boston, our older son was just a little bit too young to go to the games. On one occasion I spoke at the Red Sox' pregame chapel. Afterwards I was given a baseball signed by every player who came to the chapel service as a thank-you gesture. They told me to take it home and give it to Curt. They thought he would like that. So did I! Written all over the ball were these famous names. I was careful not to smear the autographs as I took this baseball home to Curt. I rushed into the house and yelled, "Curt, look, this is a new baseball from the Red Sox!" The little guy held it, frowned, and said, "Gee, Daddy, somebody *wrote all over it!*" My little guy was just a couple of years too young to realize what a treasure it was to have a baseball signed by celebrities.

Isn't it great to find famous men and women who are still accessible? They're still real, still vulnerable, still able to put their arms around a little kid, still able to take time for their family, for people. Greed for fame doesn't have to happen.

Fourth, greed can wear the face of control. Such greed is an excessive need to gain more control—to gain mastery over something or someone, to always be in charge, to call all the shots, to become the top dog, the king of the hill. The great goal in many people's lives is to manipulate their way to the top of whichever success ladder they choose to climb.

At the risk of sounding terribly simplistic in my analysis, greed can be traced back in Scripture to that day our original parents, Adam and Eve, fell in the garden. When they turned their attention from the living God back to themselves, greed entered and polluted the human bloodstream. It has contaminated human nature ever since. In order for our greed to be controlled, a fight is inevitable. It is a battle for you, and it is a battle for me—a bloodless yet relentless warfare.

Our Lord realized what a hold material things can have on

humanity. In no less than seventeen of His thirty-seven parables, Jesus dealt with property and the responsibility for using it wisely. One of those stories seems significant enough for us to examine.

GREED EXPOSED AND DENOUNCED

What we find in Luke 12:13–34 is one of the clearest and most forthright discourses on greed that you'll find anywhere in all of literature. It's not difficult at all to understand. But be fore-warned: It will take us the rest of our lifetime to obey!

Let me summarize the Luke 12 account in a simple manner. It seems to fall neatly into four parts. In verses 13–14, there's a dialogue. In verse 15, Jesus gives a brief principle. Then in verses 16–21, there's a story that He tells about a greedy man who made his living as a successful farmer. Then in verses 22–34 we shall find a series of truths.

The Dialogue

> And someone in the crowd said to Him, "Teacher, tell my brother to divide the family inheritance with me." But He said to him, "Man, who appointed Me a judge or arbiter over you?" (vv. 13–14).

Out of the crowd emerges a man who boldly tells Jesus what to do. Interestingly, he neither asks a question nor makes a request. The man doesn't graciously say "Please." There isn't even a "Sir." He has the audacity to instruct Jesus on what to do. Realizing how complicated and counterproductive such family squabbles can be, Jesus refrained. He never got involved in issues that weren't related to the big-picture purpose of His goal on earth. I have always respected that about Christ.

By the way, there's a great lesson to be learned here in bowing out of other people's business. People who want to rope us into the petty details of their lives will toss issues in our direction that we have no right to get involved in. When little would be gained from running that rabbit trail, we must have the foresight and discipline to say, "I'm not qualified to address that. I'm really not the one you ought to talk to." It is comforting to remember that Jesus didn't attempt to meet *every* person's need or become entangled in *every* person's affairs. He was selective. Those needs He did meet were directly related to His big-picture mission. No wonder He, like none other who ever lived on this vast globe, maintained a high-level commitment to excellence. He never lost sight of His priorities.

But apparently Jesus heard in the tone of the man's voice, or realized from the issue that was raised (a family inheritance), that this was a perfect place to address the bigger issue of greed. After all, that is what prompted the man's opening statement to Jesus, when he asked Jesus to take sides. Instead, He stated a principle for all to follow.

The Principle

> And He said to them, "Beware, and be on your guard against every form of greed; for not even when one has an abundance does his life consist of his possessions" (Luke 12:15).

Don't miss the pronouns. In verse 14, "He said to *him*." But in verse 15, "He said to *them*." Jesus answers the man in verse 14, but then He turns to the crowd and speaks to *them* about a broader subject. In doing so, He declares a warning: "Watch out—be on guard!" About what? "Be on your guard against every form of greed." Jesus employs the word *form*. Earlier I used the word *face*. Greed has many faces, but Jesus' word is better. "Every FORM of greed, whether money or things or fame or control, in whatever form it may appear, watch out."

The Greeks had a curious word they used when referring to *greed*. The word used in verse 15 means "a thirst for having more." To illustrate, it's probably fanciful yet fairly descriptive to think of a fellow who is thirsty taking a drink of *salt* water, which only makes him thirstier. His thirst causes him to drink even more, which ultimately results in making him terribly sick. And if he continues to drink he could die. That's the whole point of greed. You'll want more and more of something that really isn't good for you. And in the getting of it, you'll suffer the painful consequences. That is why Jesus warns, "Beware. Be on your guard. This thing is like a cancer—an insatiable leech that will suck the life right out of you." Enough will never be enough, which explains the reason our Lord adds: ". . . for not even when one has an abundance does his life consist of his possessions." Life does not—*cannot*—revolve around things if one hopes to achieve true excellence. The battle with greed must be won if we hope to soar.

The Parable

> And He told them a parable, saying, "The land of a certain rich man was very productive. And he began reasoning to himself, saying, 'What shall I do, since I have no place to store my crops?' And he said, 'This is what I will do: I will tear down my barns and build larger ones, and there I will store all my grain and my goods. And I will say to my soul, "Soul, you have many goods laid up for many years to come; take your ease, eat, drink and be merry."' But God said to him, 'You fool! This very night your soul is required of you; and now who will own what you have prepared?' So is the man who lays up treasure for himself, and is not rich toward God" (Luke 12:16–21).

Before we call down wholesale condemnation upon this farmer, let's be sure we understand that the man is not wrong because he is successful and prosperous. There isn't a word here or anywhere else in Scripture against well-earned or well-deserved success or financial prosperity. This man is clearly a success; he has worked long and hard. Furthermore, he's not wrong because he is lazy. Neither do we find one word here about the man's being dishonest. He hasn't earned a dishonest living. On the contrary, he's apparently been very diligent and careful as a farmer. He's planted and he has harvested. In previous days he prepared the soil and faithfully rotated the crops. It seems that he's done everything correctly. And so what he sees as he looks outside the windows of his farmhouse is a bumper crop. It must have been beautiful to behold. There's nothing wrong with a bumper crop—or with any of the things that brought him to prosperity. Then, what is wrong?

I find three glaring, tragic failures about this man.

First: <u>He didn't really know himself</u>. It never entered his mind that he might not live for many years to come; he talked to his soul as if he were immortal. He also never stopped to consider that his abundance would never, ever satisfy his soul down deep inside. He was so preoccupied with the temporal that he didn't bother to give eternal thoughts the time of day. Such horizontal thinking is the epitome of a mediocre lifestyle.

Are you ready for a shocking thought? Some of you reading these words right now may very well be dead in a year. Some of you won't be alive in five years. We simply don't have many years. And it seems that so many people are dying younger these days. We haven't yet eradicated heart disease, cancer, or the AIDS virus.

The farmer in Jesus' story didn't really understand himself because he didn't stop to think that his abundance in crops would not bring ultimate satisfaction. Remember what he said? "Take your ease, eat, drink, and be merry." Those are words of false satisfaction. Elsewhere, Scripture calls it presumption. He's thinking that by getting more, there'll be a sense of satisfaction in his soul.

I was speaking to a businessman at breakfast just this past week who has finally come to terms with his business. With a burst of emotion he said to me, "Chuck, that business was my god! I was anxious, preoccupied, seldom at home, and nursing an ulcer. I thought my work would bring me the satisfaction I needed. But I have finally come to see that it won't. At last I am operating my life with an eternal dimension in mind. I have put the Lord in a perspective I've never had Him in before, and I've never been happier." There was contentment written all over that man's face. He had come to know himself—realistically, spiritually, deeply. That's what the farmer in Jesus' parable missed. He didn't realize that he wouldn't live forever and never even stopped to think about it.

Second: He didn't really care about other people. His remarks are thoroughly, completely, unashamedly full of himself. He is occupying the throne of his own life. In the English version of my Bible, I count six "I's" and five "my's." Never once do we find "they," "them," "their"—no, not even once. Why? Because he doesn't care about "they," "them," and "their." He cares only about "I," "me," and "my." Greed personified.

William Barclay writes:

> It was said of a self-centered young lady, "Edith lived in a little world, bounded on the north, south, east, and west by Edith."[1]

Have you ever spent much time around people like that? Sure you have. It's all around us! As I said earlier, it's in our bloodstream. From our earliest years we bear the marks of greed.

To date, Cynthia and I have three darling (and amazingly intelligent!) grandchildren. We love it! And we're looking forward to having *more* of them. I joked with our two married kids, "Keep having 'em. They are just great. Bring 'em over when they're clean and cute and smell great. Take 'em home when they don't." It's wonderful! But there is something funny about these adorable little people. They're all born with their granddaddy's problem—*selfishness.* They all grab and grasp. They all want, take, keep. "Mine! Mine! Mine!" Funny, no one had to teach them that word. It's built into their nature. A stubborn desire for more is like a massive muscle flexing inside each one of them. Already their parents (and grandparents) are having to do battle with their vigorous greed. Winning the battle over greed is a lifetime assignment.

Third: <u>The man didn't really make room for God.</u> He lived his entire life in the tight radius of himself, just as if there were no God. Imagine the shock when the death angel said to him, "You fool! Tonight is curtains! It's over, man—it's all over. Then to whom are you going to leave all these things? Who will have the right to these things that you've prepared?"

There once lived a French artist who read this story Jesus told. Afterwards, he produced a masterful representation of it on canvas. Maybe you've seen it or read about it. It's one of the few paintings painted *on both sides* of the canvas. On one side there is this rather portly farmer sitting at his desk. In front of him are several bags bulging with money. Through the window behind him you can see crops glistening in the evening sun; they're starting to lean over, heavy with grain, with corn. Nothing but dark green fields as far as the eye can see. And sitting on a long shelf above the farmer's head are more bags of money. He has the marks of abundance all around him, sort of like a Silas Marner sitting alone at the desk. He's got that faraway look in his eye like, "What will I do with it now?"

The painter read the story again with a sigh. He frowned at what he had painted. Dissatisfied, he flipped the canvas over and began the same picture on the other side. Same man, same desk, same window and bumper crops, same little bags of money, same shelf above the man's head. But this time he painted everything covered with a thin layer of dust. And something else has been added, too. The death angel is standing near with his hand on the man's shoulder and his lips are pursed as if to be saying, "Fool."

A Series of Truths

On the basis of that story, Jesus presents what appears to be a mini Sermon on the Mount. And in some ways it is. Notice what comes next: "He said to His disciples. . . ." (See the difference? In verse 14 He spoke to the man, and in verse 15 He addressed the crowd. But finally He gets alone with His twelve and talks with His closest friends—the disciples.)

> And He said to His disciples, "For this reason I say to you, do not be anxious for your life, as to what you shall eat; nor for your body, as to what you shall put on. For life is more than food, and the body than clothing. Consider the ravens, for they neither sow nor reap; and they have no storeroom nor barn; and yet God feeds them; how much more valuable you are than the birds! And which of you by being anxious can add a single cubit to his life's span? If then you cannot do even a very little thing, why are you anxious about other matters? Consider the lilies, how they grow; they neither toil nor spin; but I tell you, even Solomon in all his glory did not clothe himself like one of these. But if God so arrays the grass in the field, which is alive today and tomorrow is thrown into the furnace, how much more will He clothe you, O men of little faith! And do not seek what you shall eat, and what you shall drink, and do not keep worrying. For all these things the nations of the world eagerly seek; but your Father knows that you need these things. But seek for His kingdom, and these things shall be added to you. Do not be afraid, little flock, for your Father has chosen gladly to give you the kingdom. Sell your possessions and give to charity; make yourselves purses which do not wear out, an unfailing treasure in heaven, where no thief comes near, nor moth destroys. For where your treasure is, there will your heart be also" (Luke 12:22–34).

As I study Jesus' magnificent talk, four major truths emerge. The first comes from several negative commands like: "Don't be anxious" and "Don't seek what to eat or wear." He's saying, "Don't be preoccupied. Don't let your life revolve around your wardrobe or your coiffure." Don't have your life revolve around things that are going to burn up and be gone in a matter of time. And again, "Don't be afraid."

Here's what I learn from all these negative commands. *Those who lose the battle with greed are characterized by anxiety and a pursuit of the temporal.* I'll not elaborate on that, but it deserves some meditation. Read it again to make sure you've let it sink in.

I also notice several positive commands in Jesus' speech: "Consider the ravens" and "Consider the lilies." Also, "Seek His kingdom." (Of course, you remember that one since we've mentioned it numerous times in earlier chapters.) These positives lead me to a second major truth: *Those who win the battle over greed realize their value in God's sight and simply trust Him.*

When we arrive at Jesus' powerful conclusion (vv. 33–34), a third truth emerges: *Overcoming greed requires deliberate and assertive action.* "Sell! Give! Make!" Those are demanding imperatives. Take your time, and study what Jesus said about each one of them. It isn't simply a stimulating idea from one of today's theologians. It isn't some slogan from the headquarters of some denomination. This is *Jesus'* teaching. And He was teaching His first converts, His early disciples. "Make deliberate and assertive decisions, men, regarding greed. Don't allow it in your life. And as soon as you see it coming, kick it out." That's the underlying idea.

There's nothing in the world wrong with making a nice living. Nor is there anything wrong with being eminently wealthy if you earn and handle it correctly. But there's something drastically wrong when you keep it all to yourself! God gave it to you so you could, in turn, give it back to Him, to others—yes, in *abundance.* The only reason I can imagine for God's allowing anyone to make more than one needs is to be able to *give* more. We certainly can't take it with us, that's for sure.

I have a close friend in the ministry who traveled across the country for a week of meetings. The only problem was, his baggage didn't make it. As I recall, the bags went on to Berlin! He really needed a couple of suits. So he went down to the local thrift shop and was pleased to find a row of suits. When he told the guy, "I'd like to get a couple of suits," the salesman smiled and said, "Good, we've got several. But you need to know they came from the local mortuary. They've all been cleaned and pressed, but

why I said earlier that I think of this third section of the
combat zone, where fierce fighting takes place. Because
the time to address all the opponents of excellence, I am
limit the four chapters in Part Three to four of the
enemies we can encounter.

ter 9 we squared off with *greed*. We weren't two pages
ubject before we realized what a choking grip greed can
I wrote some suggestions on how to win the battle over
hopes of helping you not to "let the world around you
ou into its own mold." In this chapter we face a second
ss aggressive than greed in principle but far more subtle
ance—*traditionalism*.

IDENTIFYING THE DRAGON

e careful to identify the right opponent. It isn't tradition
s traditionalism. I'm not trying to be petty, only accu-
right kind of traditions give us deep roots—a solid net-
eliable truth in a day when everything seems up for
nong such traditions are those strong statements and
s that tie us to the mast of truth when storms of uncer-
eate frightening waves of change driven by winds of
my book *Growing Deep in the Christian Life,* I address
hose essentials: believing in the authority of holy Scrip-
wing and loving God, bowing to the Lordship of Jesus
ommitting ourselves to others, and becoming people
e encouragement. Such traditions (there are others, of
e valuable absolutes that keep us from feeling awash in
f relativism and uncertainty.

you haven't noticed, we are specifically commanded
o the traditions of faith: "stand firm and hold to the
which you were taught" (2 Thess. 2:15). Even though
ie majority, in fact—will elect to walk a contrary path,
rding to the tradition" which Scripture clearly asserts,
tructed to stay on target (2 Thess. 3:6).
tand now, I'm thinking of the big picture, where truth
, not tiny scenes of lesser importance, where mere taste
m are a matter of preference. Some insist, for example,
rotestants must conduct themselves according to the

they were used on stiffs. Not a thing wrong with 'em; I just didn't want that to bother you." My friend said, "No, that's fine. That's okay." So he hurriedly tried some on and bought a couple for about twenty-five bucks apiece. Great deal!

When he got back to his room, he began to get dressed for the evening's meeting. As he put one on, to his surprise there were no pockets. Both sides were all sewed up! Though surprised, he thought, *Why of course! Stiffs don't carry stuff with 'em when they depart!* The suits looked as if they had pockets, but they were just flaps on the coat. My friend told me later, "I spent all week trying to stick my hands in my pockets. Wound up having to hang my keys on my belt!" The minister was reminded all week long that life is temporal. And he probably preached all the better for that thought!

Finally, a fourth truth comes from Jesus' words ". . . where your treasure is, there your heart will be." *Personal valuables— real valuables—are sealed in our hearts.*

Combating mediocrity requires fighting fiercely. Don't ever forget it! The greed of our lives won't be conquered without a fight. Greed and brokenness cannot coexist. When Jesus, our Lord, finally surrendered to the Cross, totally broken before the Father, He turned it all over to Him. He said, "If it is at all possible not to allow this to happen, let the cup pass from Me— take it from Me; nevertheless, Your will be done, not Mine." That is the maximum statement of brokenness. Put yourself in His place. Dare to say the same prayer He uttered. "If it's Your will, Lord, that I have any of this, then fine. But if it's Your will that it all be taken away, take it all—even my life—because I'd rather be broken on earth and rich in heaven than have my way down here and be poor up there."

These thoughts remind me of one of the most helpful poems I ever committed to memory:

TREASURES

One by one God took them from me,
All the things I valued most,
Till I was empty-handed;
Every glittering toy was lost.

And I walked earth's highway, grieving,
In my rags and poverty,
Till I heard His voice inviting,
"Lift your empty hands to Me!"

So I turned my hands toward heaven,
And He filled them with a store
Of His own transcendent riches
Till they could contain no more.

And at last I comprehended
With my stupid mind and dull,
That God could not pour His riches
Into hands already full![2]

—Martha Snell Nicholson

That'
book as
I haven'
forced
toughes

In ch
into the
get on u
greed ir
squeeze
foe, no
in appea

Let's
per se; i
rate. Th
work of
grabs.
principl
tainty
doubt.
many o
ture, kn
Christ,
of genu
course)
a world

In ca
to cling
tradition
many—
"not ac
we are i

Unde
is at sta
and cus
that all

For years I have appreciated J.
from Paul's letter to the Rom
originally appeared in the apostl
century-one pen, it is as relevant
today: "Don't let the world aroun
mold" (Rom. 12:2, *Phillips*).

Great advice! Whoever decid
heights, well above the level of
through the flatland fog which ha
sameness. It isn't uncommon fo
American poet and artist e. e. c
truth about humans, wrote:

. . . to be nobody but yourself in
night and day, to make you ever
hardest battle which any human
fighting.[1]

tradition of the Reformers, "just because the Reformers did it that way." While I appreciate those great men, I disagree. John Calvin wore a hat in church. That's enough for some to say, "Everybody should do the same." But before every man and woman planning to worship next Sunday runs out and buys a hat, something needs to be said as to *why* Calvin wore a hat. Actually there are two reasons: "because the church had (a) drafts and (b) pigeons."[2]

There is a great deal of difference between tradition and traditional*ism*. Jaroslav Pelikan puts his finger on the crux of the issue: "Tradition is the living faith of those now dead; traditionalism is the dead faith of those still living."[3]

By traditionalism, I have in mind mainly an attitude that resists change, adaptation, or alteration. It is holding fast to a custom or behavior that is being blindly and forcefully maintained. It is being suspicious of the new, the up-to-date, the different. It is finding one's security, even identity, in the familiar and therefore opposing whatever threatens that. And if you'll allow me one more, it is substituting a legalistic system for the freedom and freshness of the Spirit—being more concerned about keeping rigid, manmade rules than being flexible, open to creativity and innovation.

By now you've guessed where I stand. Clearly, my position is on the side of openness, allowing room for the untried, the unpredictable, the unexpected—all the while holding fast to the truth. When this philosophy is embraced, eagle eggs are laid, eagles are hatched, and eagles are given room to fly. When traditionalism rules the roost, you can expect nothing but parrots—low-flying creatures that stay on a perch and mimic only what they are told to say. Believe me, there are plenty of people around who feel it is their calling to tell others what to do and what to say. They are self-appointed wing-clippers who frown on new ways and put down high flight. To use J. B. Phillips' words again, they work hard to "squeeze you into their mold."

A New Venture

When my wife and I decided to link arms and venture into a radio program, we had zero experience. Neither of us had a background in reaching the public via the media, nor did we know much of anything about the complicated intricacies of a non-profit corporation. To quote an attorney of ours, we didn't start at scratch, we started "*below* scratch"! Thankfully, there were a few close and competent friends who helped us slide out of the boat into the ocean without hurting ourselves, but since that time we have taught ourselves to swim through the swift currents of this particular extension of our lives. The result? An innovative, one-of-a-kind radio outreach named "Insight for Living" that doesn't pattern itself after any other program on the air. Why should it? Duplications are a drag. I'm not suggesting that ours is the only effective radio ministry. Of course not! But it *is* unique, from start to finish.

The systems we use, we designed. The techniques we employ, we devised. My style is my own—in no way do I attempt to be like or sound like or compete with any other person or broadcast. Why should I? I'm *me*—and I'm an eagle. To be like someone else is to become a parrot. No, thanks. The fund-raising letters are strictly mine—I write every word of them. The philosophy behind them is ours, not some professional organization that provides a script for us to follow. Our mailings are dreamed up, designed, and produced within our own organization by people we have employed—people who possess incredibly innovative, creative skills. How we appreciate them and love them!

We're not the biggest (never worry over size) but we are determined to remain a pacesetting organization. We're certainly not the richest (never worry over finances) but we do employ vast vision while maintaining a close watch over our expenditures, always refusing to cut quality for the sake of quantity. Yes, always. Our policies are of the highest standard of integrity—that, we *do* worry over. And every thing we promote, produce, proclaim, and provide has one identifying mark: EXCELLENCE. Whether it's a cruise we sponsor or a brochure we design, a conference we participate in or a study guide we make available to our listeners, excellence is our middle name.

And why not? We represent the King of kings. If I may put this in today's terms, He is a class act—absolute tops. Lord, in fact! We're the ones who ought to cause the world to turn its head, not the other way around. Eagles don't have any business scratching around like a cage of parrots or a pen full of turkeys. Let me put it straight: Long enough have evangelicals been the ugly ducklings of Christendom!

Do we get criticism? Of course! Can't let that worry us, though. There will always be those who think we should do this or should not do that. Because we have always refused to consult the party line and get in step with what the so-called "experts" suggest, we are often told, "This won't work, you'll see," or "You should do that, instead," or "You can't. . . . You're being unrealistic." But it's amazing! Most (I'm resisting saying *all*) of the things we were told could not be done *are* now being done. We're doing them, by the grace of God. The things we were told would never fly, not only flew—they soared!

Cynthia and I are neither brilliant nor worldly wise, but we do learn fast and we stay flexible, always open to innovative ideas. Mainly, there is too much eagle in either one of us to be satisfied with the dull, standard operating procedures established by the lowest common denominator of human opinion. If a fresh idea, never tried before, makes sense, we'll give it a whirl! If it fails, we learned. If it works, we get all the more excited.

I will be quick to add that we openly acknowledge God's gracious faithfulness and forgiveness as we have grown and groaned together—and we are equally grateful for a carefully selected board of directors. They know how to direct and respond to these two eagles without clipping our wings. We are accountable to them but not intimidated by them. Not one, by the way, is bound by traditionalism. They would not be on our board if they were. Why? Because traditionalism is a vicious dragon that must be slain if we hope to move into the twenty-first century with excellence, enthusiasm, momentum, and relevance. Traditionalism breeds parrots; it must not be tolerated. If you're fighting it, good for you! Don't stop. That old dragon is bad about squeezing the very life out of its victims, so never stop fighting. It's a matter of survival.

FIRST-CENTURY TRADITIONALISM

In Jesus' day the dragon of traditionalism reared its ugly head in a different way from what it does today. In the first century traditionalism was synonymous with Pharisaism. The Pharisees embraced it, promoted it, and modeled it. Whenever Christ encountered them, He encountered *it!* When others were cheering Him, the Pharisees were frowning Him down. A classic case in point? That time He was confronted by the sourpuss group while He was having dinner with a roomful of sinners. Maybe you don't know the background. Allow me:

A fellow named Matthew (called Levi by Dr. Luke) was invited to leave his profession as a tax-gatherer and become a disciple—a close follower of Jesus. He did. In fact, he threw a party at his place in honor of the Master. I suppose we could call it a farewell celebration as Levi left his career.

Naturally, the place was packed with guys Levi had run around with for years—fellow tax men and other cronies, none of them religious but all of them his friends and colleagues. Here's the way Dr. Luke describes the scene:

> And after that He went out, and noticed a tax-gatherer named Levi, sitting in the tax office, and He said to him, "Follow Me." And he left everything behind, and rose up and began to follow Him. And Levi gave a big reception for Him in his house; and there was a great crowd of tax-gatherers and other people who were reclining at table with them (Luke 5:27–29).

I'm smiling as I think about those guys at that meal. Can't you just imagine? Lots of clinking of dishes, loud talking, periodic uproars of laughter, different ones standing up and offering a toast, an all-around fun time. And nobody enjoyed it more than Jesus! (Too bad we don't have a few pictures painted of Jesus at this table.) These were *real* men. No phony-baloney stuffed shirts, no let's-try-to-impress-the-guy-in-the-white-robe clowns. Just upfront sinner types who knew Levi and came to have a good time.

There was plenty of food and lots of wine. Maybe even a first-century "roast" where Levi took it on the chin. There was a lot of telling and sharing and listening to stories. They were having a whale of a good time together, just plain fun—except, of course, for the Pharisees. I can just imagine their standing outside, looking in the window, staring and not smiling. The tax-gatherers and other friends, along with Jesus and His disciples, were reclining at the table together. But when the religious hotshots heard the noise, they began taking verbal shots at Jesus and His men.

> And the Pharisees and their scribes began grumbling at His disciples, saying, "Why do you eat and drink with the tax-gatherers and sinners?" (Luke 5:30).

You see, the main problem was that the disciples of Jesus were mixing with and enjoying themselves among the sinner types. The Pharisees believed (and taught!) that they should remain separate from these types. They should not associate with sinners, and they should *absolutely* not be having fun together. I mean, the very idea! By the way, did you notice that Luke first refers to "tax-gatherers and other people" (v. 29)? But note the difference when he quotes the Pharisees. The phrase changes to "tax-gatherers and *sinners*" (v. 30).

"How could You, Jesus—You, of all people—how *could* You sit down at a meal and enjoy eating and drinking with these tax-gatherers and sinners? Ugh! I mean, what will people say? What about Your testimony?"

The disciples are speechless, probably because they are scared spitless. They don't know what to say. Most Jews back then were paralyzed in their thoughts when Pharisees confronted them; but never Jesus. Completely unintimidated by the presence of Pharisees, He gave them a straight answer. I love that about Him. Jesus looks right into their eyes and says: ". . . It is not those who are well who need a physician, but those who are sick" (v. 31). It was another say of saying, "Knock it off!" (Swindoll paraphrase). But it sounds better to say, "What these people need is healing. Since I'm a healer, since that's what I'm about, then I don't want to run around with people who think they don't need healing. These people are sick. They make no bones about it; they don't hide it. They need help. That's why I'm here."

If that isn't enough to slam them to the mat, read on: "I have not come to call righteous men but sinners to repentance" (v. 32). Stab . . . twist. I think if I had been at the table I would have said (in Aramaic, of course), "All right, Jesus, go for it!" I probably would have whistled and applauded, too! Jesus was right on target when He answered, "I've not come to call people who think they are righteous, but people who *know* they are sick. That's My ministry, plain and simple. They need Me and are open. You don't think you need Me, so you're closed!"

Well, if you think the Pharisees left Him alone after that, you don't understand the nature of the dragon, traditionalism. All that meant to them was that the coin had been flipped and it was time to kick off. The violent game was on, and the Pharisees answer Jesus with:

. . . "The disciples of John often fast and offer prayers; the disciples of the Pharisees also do the same; but Yours eat and drink" (v. 33).

That is supposed to be a sarcastic put-down. "You may have time for this jesting, but not us! This is serious business. We're into fasting. You and Your people are in there eating and drinking with those nasty sinners and having fun. Don't You know that life is much too serious for all this?"

Look at the answer.

And Jesus said to them, "You cannot make the attendants of the bridegroom fast while the bridegroom is with them, can you?" (v. 34).

What a superb rebuttal! Back then, as long as the bridegroom was around, it was nonstop eating and drinking, laughing and having fun—constant rejoicing. But when the bridegroom left, it got sad because everyone had to go back to work. A lot of serious stuff also began to happen. And Jesus (referring to Himself) said, in effect, "The bridegroom is among His friends. This is not the time to fast and look somber and sad and act as if we're mad at the world. There will be a time for that later."

"But the days will come; and when the bridegroom is taken away from them, then they will fast in those days" (v. 35).

"At that time, the time I go to the cross and die, you won't hear any laughing. You won't hear the clinking of goblets. There will be no feasting then because everything will be serious. I'll be gone."

The Pharisees were strangely silent. They stared, struggling to grasp His meaning. Apparently, they were unable to piece it together so Jesus tells them a brief story. If I live to be one hundred years old, I will never cease to be amazed at what a marvelous communicator He really was. Nobody ever slept when Jesus was speaking. His talks were always brief and to the point—a rare skill among preachers! Furthermore, He referred to things that anybody could understand. He was never interested in impressing His audience with some profound, ultra-deep statement— even though He could have easily wowed them and caused them to leave His presence, saying, "What was that all about?" "I don't know, but it was deep, man. Nobody understood it." That may be our style but it certainly wasn't Jesus' style. His words penetrated with deadly accuracy. When He got through talking, listeners were yanking big darts out of their bodies. He was forever stabbing them awake with the truth. Notice His approach in verse 36. He does it in a simple, disarming way. He does it with comments having to do with old and new garments, with old and new wine.

. . . "No one tears a piece from a new garment and puts it on an old garment; otherwise he will both tear the new, and the piece from the new will not match the old" (v. 36).

Anyone who has had new clothing shrink would understand. Even today, if you take an old garment and cover a tear with a new patch, you know it is going to shrink. Ultimately, it may tear away. That's what verse 36 is all about. Well, not altogether. He is using clothing as His subject, but He has something deeper in mind (would you believe, traditionalism?). You see, these Pharisees were committed to the old. They majored in *ancient* history, and they swore by the Law. They were set in concrete into the precepts and statutes of the Law. They could quote those words exactly as they appeared on the ancient scroll of the Torah. To make matters worse, they added over six hundred additional rules (really!) so everybody would understand how *they* interpreted the way everyone should live. And they were rigid about it! You see, they are the "old garment." Jesus' point: You can't match something new with something old. It will tear away.

He drives His point home by speaking of wine:

"And no one puts new wine into old wineskins; otherwise the new wine will burst the skins, and it will be spilled out, and the skins will be ruined" (v. 37).

In fact, when Matthew tells the story, he adds, "Neither will be preserved. You'll lose both skin and wine." I don't know much about wine, but I do know if you take fresh wine and pour it into an old, worn-and-brittle wineskin bag that is no longer supple, you're in for a leaky surprise. It won't be long, thanks to fermentation, before the wine's change will cause the bag to bulge and stretch. Finally, it will rip just like an old used balloon. It won't hold it.

Just as Jesus wasn't talking about literal old and new fabrics, neither is He now talking about literal wine and wineskins. This is a parable, remember—a story that uses the literal and familiar to teach the spiritual and unfamiliar. Jesus' audience understood that these words were missiles carrying a massive payload.

Sometimes, even today, we'll use words that everyone understands should not be taken literally. I carry my family around in my wallet. If you ask, I'll show you my family. "No," you say, "you don't actually carry your family around in your wallet." You're right, I really don't. I carry a *picture* of them. But I pull it out and say, "Here's my family." But, there again, the words I use can't be taken literally. You understand that it is just a picture of my family. Jesus' story is simply a picture of something far more significant. He presses His point home:

"But new wine must be put into fresh wineskins" (v. 38). Hmmmm. All of a sudden, the picture is coming into clear focus, which makes the Pharisees terribly nervous.

You know why? Because Jesus says, in effect, "You like the old."

"And no one, after drinking old wine wishes for new; for he says, 'The old is good enough' " (v. 39).

The old Judaic-traditionalism skin could not contain the new wine of the revolutionary gospel Christ was offering. It split the skin. There they stood, representing all those manmade regulations, observing this revolutionary, risky message about liberty, grace, freedom, forgiveness, deliverance from the Law, compassion, and hope. (How new can you get?) But their wineskin couldn't contain it. They were so entrenched and inflexible, the new wine dripped through. Finally, it burst the bag completely. Exposed, they were forced to see that their attempt to squeeze Jesus into their mold had backfired. The old simply could not contain the new.

Oh, but how they loved their own traditions! They preferred them to the Truth of God, believe it or not. Matthew's account includes a rebuke from Jesus to the Pharisees about how they were holding their traditions so tightly that they were resisting God's revelation. His rebuke? "You invalidated the word of God for the sake of your traditions" (Matt. 15:6). Isn't that an indictment? In effect, He is saying, "You are so defensive of your hardened, old wineskin bag, you totally reject the new wine I'm offering you." No eagle ever soared higher or was hated more. Let's face it—truth that sets people free is the greatest threat to traditionalism.

TWENTIETH-CENTURY NEW-WINE TRUTHS

So much for first-century wines and wineskins. Our interest, as I have said before, is not simply to discover and develop truth from ancient times. It is to see how relevant that truth is for *our* times.

A couple of very significant things seem to jump out at me when I think about Jesus' parable. Here's the first one: *God is a God of freshness and change.* That's the wine. In January of every new year, God puts together twelve months of wine. Twelve fresh vats are placed in storage (the contents unknown to us). Each vat will run out in a month. This new wine is vital. It is sparkling, fresh, and ready to fill new skins. God is a God of freshness and change. But wait, before I leave that thought, let me make something very clear: "God Himself isn't changing, nor is His Son. He "is the same yesterday and today, yes and forever" (Heb. 13:8). Isn't that a great thought? God is no different this year than He was last year or a decade ago. Nor will He change one hundred years from now. But even though He is the same, His working is different. It stays fresh. His ways and methods are forever fresh, unpredictably new.

I find that thought woven throughout the Scriptures. The Old Testament speaks of a new song, a new heart, a new spirit, a new covenant, and new things that God is doing. In the New Testament we're called "new creatures." Through Him "all things become new." We're told that we have been given a "new birth." We are instructed to live by a "new commandment." We are people with "a new self," living in "a new man." We are even looking forward to a "new heaven and new earth." The last reference to *new* in the entire Bible is very near the end, in Revelation 21:5 where our Lord says He's "making all things new."

I need to warn you, if you like things to stay the same, you're going to be terribly uncomfortable in heaven. Everything is going to be new. God is a God of freshness and change. He flexes His methods. He alters His way so much, it's as if you've never seen it before. You can't imagine what it may be like next time. How does this personally apply? My answer is found in the first verse of Ephesians, chapter 5:

> Therefore be imitators of God, as beloved children; and walk in love, just as Christ also loved you, and gave Himself up for us, an offering and a sacrifice to God as a fragrant aroma.

God says we are to be "imitators" of Him which really means we are to "mimic." Since God is a God of freshness and change, so we should be. If we are to fulfill this command "to be mimics of God, as His beloved children," then I suggest that we stay fresh— that we remain open, innovative, willing to change.

It's been my observation that every generation tends to be more strict and rigid than the last. We tend to tighten the lid tighter on traditionalism. Even though our God of freshness and change has given us all those vats of new wine to use, we'll not let it go; we'll find ways to conserve it, to protect it, to maintain it—to save it for a "rainy day."

Remember the manna God gave His people to eat in the wilderness? One of the first things they had to forget about doing was saving it. They wanted to hold onto more of it. Why? Because they were afraid they were going to run out of food. They were afraid fresh manna wouldn't be delivered tomorrow morning. The only time they had to worry about that was on Friday because when Saturday came, there wouldn't be a delivery. But God even took care of that! On Friday they were to gather a two-day supply that would stay fresh and not spoil. So they had nothing to worry about, everything to enjoy. But still there was that tendency to hoard.

Do you remember the bronze serpent Moses held up in the wilderness when the people were being bitten by snakes and dying? God provided that bronze serpent for their healing. But did you know they dragged that serpent around in the wilderness, as well as in Canaan, for generations? Perhaps you didn't realize that. Well, here's the passage that tells it all.

> He removed the high places and broke down the sacred pillars and cut down the Asherah. He also broke in pieces the bronze serpent that Moses had made, for until those days the sons of Israel burned incense to it; and it was called Nehushtan (2 Kings 18:4).

There they were, still hanging onto that old bronze snake they'd been dragging around all those years. What was it now? It was just Nehushtan—meaning, "a piece of brass." What were they supposed to have done? Get rid of it! Instead, they were *worshiping* it. If we are going to "mimic God," we must stay fresh and open. Dump the Nehushtans! Otherwise, we won't stay flexible, creative. Those who resist mediocrity are models of innovation.

Now for the second significant fact I see from Luke, chapter 5: *New wineskins are essential, not optional.* Every age knows the temptation to try to restrict God's dealings. The majority of people in this world are maintainers. Once we get things set, we don't like them changed.

Let me give you a couple of illustrations. Sometime after beginning my pastorate in California, I looked closely at the order of service and decided we had done the "Doxology" at the beginning of the service long enough! So I put it at the *end* of the service. A number of people asked, "How can we sing it at the end? I mean, I'm not sure it will *work* at the end." (That made me smile, I confess.) It worked. In fact, only on rare occasions now do we even sing it. But when we do, it is more meaningful than ever!

But the one that really threw the congregation a curve was when we had the audacity to put the announcements at the *beginning* of the worship service. Can you believe I actually took them out of the sacred central part of the worship service (though I have never heard a worshipful announcement in my entire life)? Announcements can become a sacred cow. No, they're just wineskin. We continually look at the worship service and think of fresh skin in which to pour fresh wine. We try new things all the time. It's wonderful! Some still get a little nervous at times. I love that look on their faces. It says, "Does Chuck know this is going on?" when actually I was in on the planning, all along. I mean, you name it—it's new skin—it's just a bag. But what it holds is significant. It's the innovation of it all that keeps it fresh, vital, creative, new. Let me go further.

There was a time when aviation in missions was unheard of. Then along came a man like Jim Truxton (who is a part of our congregation, by the way). And he and a few committed people said, "There's no reason there couldn't be an arm of missions that becomes a flight service for people living out in the bush. We'll fly people and supplies in and out." Enter the birth of Missionary Aviation Fellowship. Unheard of, but it worked! And now they are using helicopters. Of course!

One of my mentors at Dallas Theological Seminary tells me about the time when the first chalk talk was used in his church many years ago. Many frowned and muttered, "They use that in the secular world, don't they? We don't believe in chalk talks in the church. Next thing you know, somebody will use a flannel-graph board." How liberal can you get? Hey, that stuff is wine-skin; that's *all* it is. Now it's films and television and computers and other yet-to-be discovered inventions. It is new styles of music. It is new methods that assault the mindset of the old lifestyle. It still makes many uncomfortable because it's threatening. But it has nothing to do with the wine. If it does, there is something wrong with it. It is only the skin. The wine stays fresh because it is from God. But the skins? That's where we need to flex.

We must guard against wrapping the Christianity of the 1980s and 1990s in the garb of the 1960s! If we're not careful, we'll become so committed to "the way we were" we'll dull the cutting edge of relevance and leave this generation in the dust. I repeat: NEW WINESKINS ARE ESSENTIAL. Organizations don't change; people change. Churches don't flex; people flex. There is no flex in walls or wood. No flex in the stone or structure. It is in us. We're the skin. If we hope to soar into the 1990s, we *must* come to terms with rigidity. The dragon of traditionalism *must* be slain!

TWO PENETRATING QUESTIONS

Here are a couple of probing questions: First, *is the wine still fresh*? Or are you living on wine from yesteryear? Are you tapping into that fresh wine that is still bubbling, still sparkling, still exciting? Or do you have to go back to early 1970—or September of 1977? "Great time back then, great progress! God did great things." But what about today? People need to know how Jesus Christ addresses today's issues in today's world. He wants to know how fresh the wine is. You may be thinking, "That sounds pretty radical, Chuck. I don't know. I've gone along with you for nine chapters, but, man, this one is getting pretty loose." For you, especially, I bring this reminder: "And the threshing floors will be full of grain, and the vats will overflow with the new wine and oil" (Joel 2:24).

Joel, the prophet, is looking far into the future. Imagine this: He's got his sights trained as far away as the 1980s and 1990s. "There will be an overflow of new wine," he says. But that isn't all.

> "Then I will make up to you for the years that the swarming locust has eaten, the creeping locust, the stripping locust, and the gnawing locust, my great army which I sent among you" (Joel 2:25).

What does God call the locust? "My great army which I sent among you." It's as if He is saying, by way of application, "I will discover that mentality, that traditionalism, that old enemy of freshness, and I'll say to the locust, 'Sic 'em.' They'll come in and eat away. They'll gnaw away. They are My army."

But did you notice what the Lord promises? He promises to make up to you for the years the locust has eaten, once the pests have been removed:

> "And you shall have plenty to eat and be satisfied, and praise the name of the Lord your God, Who has dealt wondrously with you; then My people will never be put to shame. Thus you will know that I am in the midst of Israel, and that I am the Lord your God and there is no other; and My people will never be put to shame.
> "And it will come about after this that I will pour out My Spirit on all mankind; and your sons and daughters will prophesy, your old men will dream dreams, your young men will see visions" (Joel 2:26–28).

What a promise for the future—and for *today!* Through his scriptural binoculars, the prophet is seeing the future. How are the dreams coming along? How about the visions? Any fresh, creative ideas? We must have new thoughts and dreams for these new times.

In 1984 *Esquire* magazine released a special issue entitled "Golden Anniversary Collector's Issue," which included an anthology of fifty different men and women who are called "American originals." And when you read through the smaller print, you see that the magazine's subtitle, "Man at His Best," is correct. I spent the better part of a week several years ago leafing through it, reading various authors' works and studying more about these great personalities, most of whom are instantly recognizable.

Except for a very brief reference to a theologian, only one well-known Christian appeared in the anthology. Of the fifty who made a difference in the last fifty years, only a couple of Christians appear. I realize *Esquire* is not a Christian publication. I also know they are not looking into our ranks that closely. And, of course, some who were named could have been Christians. But honestly, *where* are all the Christians? Which high-flying eagles will make any difference during the next fifty years? Do you want a challenge? Plan now to make a difference. Do you know what I noticed about each person named in that special issue of *Esquire?* Each one is an eagle—there's not a parrot in the whole group. Eagles make things happen; they are the ones, as I said in an earlier chapter, who challenge our world to "break a vase!" In this chapter I come with another plea: Make a difference!

There's a second question on my mind: *Is the wineskin still flexible?* Now what do I mean by flexible? All right, let's start with the word *mobile.* Are you ready to move? I know, I know, you just got your stuff together. You finally got that last payment out of the way. You finally got settled down. Don't bet on it. This year a whole bunch of people will be on the move. And you may be one of them.

Here's another word: *change.* Are you open to change in your whole career? Are you willing to risk? Are you flexible enough to innovate? Are you willing to tolerate the sheer possibility of making a massive change in your direction for life? People who make a difference have supple wineskins. They can be stretched, pulled, pushed, and changed, "Lord, is it South America? Great! Or Indonesia? I'll do it. I'll move or change my profession. *Fine!*

Are You leading me into a new venture? I'll do it. Count me in!"
That's the spirit! It may mean moving across the street. It may
mean moving across the States. It may mean moving across the
seas. How flexible are you? It may not involve a move at all, only
a willingness.

Read these words very carefully. They are dragon-slaying
words!

> . . . Today's followers of Christ must learn the full signifi-
> cance of the pattern of the children of Israel in the desert, who
> went or stopped when the cloud moved or stayed. They must
> learn to wait upon the Lord, to be sensitive to his leadings and to
> depend less and less on the arm of flesh. . . .
>
> In many ways, we Christians today are reliving the New Testa-
> ment age. These are days of rapid church growth, and yet also of
> uncertainty, apostasy, threatening persecution and, above all,
> the expectation of the return of Christ. This was the situation of
> the early church. First-generation Christians thought Christ
> would come back. He didn't. . . .
>
> The church seems impotent before the ecological crisis, for
> example, or in the face of mindless technology or the worldwide
> web of political power and intrigue. But the weapons of our war-
> fare are spiritual, not carnal. Using the world's weapons, the
> church does not stand a chance. But when the church uses God's
> weapons (Eph. 6:14–17), it is the world which becomes weak.
>
> These are not days for the church to turn inward, curl up in a
> corner and passively await the end. The world has yet to see what
> the Spirit can do.[4]

Stop letting the world around you squeeze you into its own
mold. Out with the dragon of traditionalism! This is a new year, a
new generation, a new era.

Removing
the Blahs
from Today

11

Monotony and mediocrity mesh like teeth in gears. One spawns the other, leaving us yawning, bored, and adrift. In referring to monotony, I do not have in mind a lack of activity as much as a lack of purpose. We can be busy yet bored, involved yet indifferent. Life becomes tediously repetitious, dull, humdrum, pedestrian. In a word, *blah*.

Who would ever expect such a thing to be an enemy? Seems too mild, too passive to even mention. Not so! It is one of the deadliest darts in the Devil's quiver. Once it strikes, the poison spreads rapidly, leaving us listless, careless, and disillusioned. Our vision gets blurred and our shoulders start to stoop. We become putty in the enemy's hand. That explains why C. S. Lewis wrote:

> The safest road to Hell is the gradual one—the gentle slope, soft underfoot, without sudden turnings, without milestones, without signposts (*The Screwtape Letters,* letter 12).

> The long, dull, monotonous years of middle-aged prosperity or middle-aged adversity are excellent campaigning weather [for the Devil] (*The Screwtape Letters,* letter 28).[1]

Why, certainly! In our world of four-day work weeks, lengthy vacations, and extended periods of leisure, more and more wonder what to do with their time. That's one kind of *blah*. Far more subtle, however, is the tedious sameness that accompanies routine of any kind. Even a routine that results in good pay and great popularity.

Look into the faces of entertainers *off* the stage. Talk to physicians *out* of the office and hospital corridors. Those in the political arena are equally susceptible. Both John Dean (in his book *Blind Ambition*) and Chuck Colson (in *Born Again*) confessed that boredom accompanied their lives in the busyness of all their high-profile activities. Strangely, on the heels of Richard Nixon's landslide victory, Colson admitted that he should have been exhilarated, but he felt empty. Athletes often feel the same. Ministers aren't immune, either. Cartoonist Ralph Barton, although successful and in demand, took his own life, leaving a note nearby that included these words, "I am fed up with inventing devices to fill up twenty-four hours of the day."

None of these people were standing around collecting dust. They were skilled, competent, responsible individuals, but monotony siphoned the joy and motivation from their tank. Assignments lacked meaning. Work lacked purpose. Boredom held them back, like an iron anchor that had slipped out of the boat and snagged and dragged on the bottom. Show me an individual who once soared, whose life was characterized by enthusiasm and excellence, but who no longer reaches those heights, and I'll show you a person who has probably become a victim of the *blahs*.

A *blah* attack may sound harmless, but it can leave us in an emotional heap, seriously questioning if life is worth it. Yes, those "long, dull, monotonous years of middle-aged prosperity or . . . adversity" are enough to bring even the strongest eagle down with a thud.

A section on fighting fiercely would certainly be incomplete if we failed to address the *blahs* of monotony and indifference. It is essential that we be engaged in a winning battle against this enemy if we hope to achieve excellence. The two cannot coexist. Surely, if this sneaky opponent of excellence is that powerful, there ought to be some insights and techniques that help us fight it out in the trenches. Indeed there are! In fact, I have often used the same ones I want to mention in this chapter and have found them effective. Believe it or not, they find their source in a prayer written by Moses many centuries ago.

A PRAYER WITH A PUNCH

Psalm 90 is the only psalm specifically attributed to Moses. He may have written others, but we know for sure he wrote this one. Remember Moses? Most think of him as a man of action, an aggressive leader, point man in the exodus, outspoken giver of the Law. But it is easy to overlook the repetitious, monotonous routine he endured. Between ages forty and eighty, Moses led his father-in-law's flock of sheep in the desert. Following the exodus, he led the Hebrews another forty years as they wandered across and around the wilderness. I'd say he knew about the *blahs*. Same terrain, same scenes, same route, same ornery people, same negative outlook, same complaints, same miserable weather, same *everything!* The prayer he wrote could have been his means of maintaining sanity! Moses addresses his Lord specifically (vv. 1, 2, 13, 17) and spells out His personal involvement in everyday affairs.

Breaking the Spell

Frequently, our problem with boredom begins when we fall under monotony's "spell." In this quasi-hypnotic state, we get sucked into a bland, "who cares?" mentality. Mediocrity and passive cynicism await those who let themselves get trapped. How to cope? We must direct our attention (as Moses does) to (a) the right object that we might gain and (b) the right perspective.

Lord, Thou hast been our dwelling place in all generations. Before the mountains were born, or Thou didst give birth to the earth and the world, even from everlasting to everlasting, Thou art God (Ps. 90:1–2).

As this ancient shepherd-leader did, we too must begin by crying out to our God: "Lord!" What a relief to be able to call on Him! In doing so, it helps to rehearse before Him our real place of residence. It isn't here on this measly piece of real estate called Earth. It is with Him. Did you get that? "Lord—*You* are my home . . . my habitation . . . my hiding place."

Moses goes even further, in the opposite order of creation. Originally, God made this world, the mountains, dry land, and finally mankind. Moses turns it around:

World ◄——— Mountains ◄——— Dry Land ◄——— Man

If we take our minds as far back as possible, we arrive at the vanishing point of the past—infinity. Moses is saying: "God, even at the vanishing point of the past and the future—the most distant place we can imagine—You are there!"

We can't fathom such a journey. We can only imagine it. But when we go as far back as possible in our minds (the vanishing point of the past) and step off, there is God. And when we project ourselves to the vanishing point of the future, the misty infinity of tomorrow, again there is our God.

What he is saying is this: As I go from the vanishing point of yesterday to the vanishing point of tomorrow and find that God is present, then there is not a place in the entire scope of my everyday existence where God is not there. And to make it even more personal, as Francis Schaeffer put it, "He is there and He is not silent." There is purpose, there is meaning in the presence of God. Even in the things that we may consider to be pointless, insignificant, trivial.

I find it amusing to read certain critics who say that Moses groveled in a sort of ignorant theology. Frankly, I find from this psalm that he possessed a rather sophisticated theology. The man who wrote the creation story had a pretty good grasp of what it was all about. And this psalm reveals that, to him, God was in it all, even when he led those stubborn woolies across the backside of the desert. Even when he led those wayward people through the wilderness. To make it much more personal—even during *your* drab and seemingly meaningless assignments of life, He is there! He cares! He knows! Thoughts like that help us soar, don't they?

And don't miss the right perspective: "From everlasting to everlasting, Thou art *God.*" From my yesterday to my tomorrow—God. From the little involvements to the big ones—God. From the beginning of school to the end of school—God. From the assignments that will never really make the headlines (which seems to me mere busy work) all the way to those things that gain international attention—God. From my children's earliest years to our last year together—God! You are in it, Lord. You're there! Yes, even when everything goes wrong.

> Verdi's opera "La Traviata" was a failure when it was first performed. Even though the singers chosen for the leading roles were the best of the day, everything went wrong. The tenor had a cold and sang in a hoarse, almost inaudible voice. The soprano who played the part of the delicate, sickly heroine was one of the stoutest ladies on or off stage, and very healthy and loud.
>
> At the beginning of the Third Act when the doctor declares that consumption has wasted away the "frail, young lady" and she cannot live more than a few hours, the audience was thrown into a spasm of laughter, a state very different from that necessary to appreciate the tragic moment!
>
> Who doesn't have days like that when everything goes wrong, when we become overwhelmingly conscious of our frailty and imperfection? At those times it is good to remember this is not our world. The earth is the Lord's. "You cannot stir a flower without troubling a star." And so the sooner we learn to walk closely with God, who is in charge and who does not change, the happier we will be.[2]

We entertain the feeling on those "bad" days that we deserve better, almost as though we own our lives. When, in fact, it is in the menial assignments of life that God reminds us, "No, I own your life. You are Mine. I have purpose in this that seems to you so purposeless." Try this. The very next time you feel those clammy, cold fingers of the *blahs* reaching around you, remember, "From yesterday until tomorrow, You, O Lord, are there, You care!" It will help you mount up with wings as an eagle. I know. I have put it to the test numerous times.

Probing the Soul

So much for breaking the spell. Probing the soul takes up where that leaves off. As I probe my soul during times of such wrestlings, almost without exception, I find three thoughts washing around in my head. First, I think: Life is so short. We really don't have many years. And to spend them doing dumb stuff seems like such a waste. If that isn't depressing enough, you come across the words of some clown who writes that most of those who fill the pages of *Who's Who* were or are under thirty years of age! You had every intention of being there too, but you are now fifty-six and, would you believe, fast approaching sixty! You feel more like you belong in *Why Me?* You're still doing the assignments that will never make the headlines. Is life really short? Yes.

> Thou dost turn man back into dust, and dost say, "Return, O children of men." For a thousand years in Thy sight are like yesterday when it passes by, or as a watch in the night. Thou hast swept them away like a flood, they fall asleep . . . (Ps. 90:3–5).

Talk about vivid word pictures! Life moves so rapidly it is as if we have been swept through time like a *flood.* Quickly passing as a three-hour *watch* in the night, like *yesterday!* And then we fall asleep and die.

> . . . In the morning they are like grass which sprouts anew. In the morning it flourishes, and sprouts anew; towards evening it fades, and withers away (Ps. 90:5–6).

Another reminder of the brevity of life. "Toward evening it fades, and withers away" like *grass.*

Those thoughts have a way of haunting a person who really wants his life to amount to more than just a tiny period printed on the page of time, don't they? We want to offer at least a sentence. But what I see growing out of these lines in Moses' prayer is that it is God who controls our marks in this world. He sets the limit. In fact, He's the One who says, "Return, O children of men." And without hesitation, they return. What seems all-important can change almost overnight. When the Controller says, "Return," it's amazing how quickly that return can occur.

I was intrigued several years ago when reading about some ghost towns littered across the plains of Nevada. The writer pointed out that there was every indication between the middle and the end of the 1800s that these towns would flourish forever. There were people by the thousands. There was gold in abundance. There were new buildings, vast plans, a spirit of excitement. There was wild and wooly entertainment at every corner —houses and hotels, brothels and taverns, mines and money. The Gold Rush looked as if it would last forever. But suddenly, everything screeched to a halt. Almost overnight those bustling, loud population centers became vacant dust collectors. The sound of the cash register ceased. Today, except for a handful of eccentric desert dwellers, the stores and streets are empty. Those windswept ghost towns are now silent, hollow shells along forgotten sandy roads. Whatever happened to the boomtowns of Nevada? May I suggest a very simple answer? The Lord said, "Return, O cities of Nevada."

The Kennedy family also comes to mind when I think of this kind of dramatic change. I vividly remember the upward swing and enormous popularity of the whole Kennedy clan as they came on the scene in the 1960s. It was meteoric. It looked as though we would have Kennedys in leadership for two or three decades! And what happened? In the briefest period of time, a few rapid-fire events changed everything: John was murdered— assassinated; Robert was assassinated; and Ted was stigmatized—a scandal and a fractured marriage dogging his heels. What really happened? No one can fully explain, but it seems as if God said to a family that looked like it would continue in leadership forever, "Return, O Kennedy family." Sovereignly, He puts up one and sets down another.

Why do I mention those two examples? Because they perfectly describe life. What often looks as if it is here to stay and make a perpetual impact can be frighteningly temporary. When God says, "That's it; that's curtains," it's only a matter of time. It is the perspective in all of this that holds us together. Our God is in complete control. He lets nothing out of His grip. He starts one and stops another. He pushes one ahead and holds another back.

Look again at Moses' prayer. He brings up a second thought that plagues me when the *blahs* come: My sins are so obvious. Do you ever feel like that in the midst of this routine called life and time? Sure you do. Moses did, too.

> For we have been consumed by Thine anger, and by Thy wrath we have been dismayed. Thou hast placed our iniquities before Thee, our secret sins in the light of Thy presence. For all our days have declined in Thy fury; we have finished our years like a sigh (Ps. 90:7–9).

Remember the secret sin that haunted Moses—the murder of that Egyptian? I wonder how many rocks he walked around in the desert only to hear that same skeleton rattle. I cannot imagine how many days he must have finished with "a sigh." Couldn't hide it, couldn't dodge it, couldn't deny it. "My sins are so obvious, Lord. How can I put it all together? I am weary of feeling the stinging reminder of Your wrath!" Immediately on the heels of those feelings, Moses writes:

> As for the days of our life, they contain seventy years, or if due to strength, eighty years, yet their pride is but labor and sorrow; for soon it is gone and we fly away (v. 10).

These are the words of a man who feels cornered by an attack of the *blahs.* Few in the Christian family bother to address the ever-present feeling that says down deep inside, "My sins are so obvious." At the end of a week, that thought hangs in our head. And even at the beginning of the next week, we face another seven days, only to be reminded how obvious our sin is.

That is bad enough, but when Moses tosses in God's "wrath," it is sufficient to make the strongest saint throw in the towel. One notable Bible teacher explains all this in these words:

> Surely this phrase "the wrath of God" is greatly misunderstood. Many think, invariably, of some sort of peeved deity, a kind of cosmic, terrible-tempered Mr. Bang, who indulges in violent uncontrolled displays of temper when human beings do not do what they ought to do. But such a concept only reveals the limitations of our understanding. The Bible never deals with the wrath of God that way. According to the Scriptures, the wrath of God is God's moral integrity. When man refuses to yield himself to God, he creates certain conditions, not only for himself but

for others as well, which God has ordained for harm. It is God who makes evil result in sorrow, heartache, injustice, and despair. It is God's way of saying to man, "Now look, you must face the truth. You were made for Me. If you decide that you don't want Me, then you will have to bear the consequences." The absence of God is destructive to human life. That absence is God's wrath. And God cannot withhold it. In His moral integrity, He insists that these things should occur as a result of our disobedience. He sets man's sin and His wrath in the same frame.[3]

I think what he's saying is that our Lord is not some tyrannical God who stomps across heaven like the giant in *Jack in the Beanstalk,* swinging a club and waiting to give us a smashing blow to the head. No. Rather, it is as if He says to us, "You're Mine and I want you to walk in step with Me. I've arranged a plan so that walking with Me will result in a righteous lifestyle. If you make a decision *not* to walk with Me, I've also arranged consequences that will happen and you must live with them."

Yes, life is short. Yes, our sins are obvious; no one can deny that. And if those thoughts aren't hard enough to handle, there's a third feeling: My days are so empty. Listen to Moses' grand desire:

> So teach us to number our days, that we may present to Thee a heart of wisdom (Ps. 90:12).

Now Moses isn't suggesting that we keep a calendar, obviously. Nor does He mean we need to remember when our birthday is or simply how old we are. It is much deeper than that.

Look at the word *teach*—"teach us." The word means "cause to know." And the word *number* means "to reckon" or "assign" or "appoint" something. One lexicon suggests the phrase "that we may present to Thee" could be rendered "that we may gain." All these observations lead me to this paraphrase of verse 12:

> "So cause us to know how to assign significance to our days so that we may gain the ability to see life as You see it."

To say that in the form of a prayer: "Lord, in the daily, monotonous assignments of life, cause me to learn how to view each day as You look at it."

Think of the person who is in sales. He faces the competitive battle of a monthly quota. He fights that tough assignment (talk about boring!) to keep himself clothed and his family fed. How does verse 12 apply? "Lord, show me, in the struggle to meet my quota, how to see all this as You see it." How about the teacher? "Show me, as a teacher who faces the same routine in classes week after week, year after year, the ultimate investment I am making in these lives." Or what about those in vocational Christian service? "Lord, cause me to see that when I carry out my call to ministry, there are dimensions of meaning far beyond what I am able to understand or see." And the homemaker? "Help me, Lord, to see the value of my role as a mother with three, four, five kiddos." Or, "Show me as one who has no children, your plan for me." Or perhaps, "In our home without the children any longer—now only a couple drawn back together—teach us the wisdom of taking life a day at a time. Cause us to learn how to make these days *significant* days. Help us to keep on soaring!"

Bringing the Song

After breaking the spell and probing the soul, the psalmist introduces us to a very special song, "Do return, O Lord; how long will it be? And be sorry for Thy servants" (Ps. 90:13). The idea is for God to have pity upon them. The song continues: "O satisfy us in the morning with Thy lovingkindness, that we may sing for joy and be glad all our days (v. 14). It sounds to me as if Moses has broken through the *blahs*. I don't know about you, but with me it often happens in the morning. The night before may have seemed dark and dreary. Those night hours are often the backwash of boredom. By morning, however—usually early, when there's sort of a fresh breath of air, the smog is gone, and the day is cool—it is amazing how God brings something fresh. Psalm 30:5 also describes this feeling of renewal.

> For His anger is but for a moment, His favor is for a lifetime; weeping may last for the night, but a shout of joy comes in the morning.

The Living Bible puts it like this: "Weeping may go on all night, but in the morning there is joy."

Ruth Calkin describes God's faithfulness in the very middle of our "aching exhaustion":

IN THE MORNING

Today, Lord,
I have an unshakable conviction
A positive, resolute assurance
That what You have spoken
Is inalterably true.

But today, Lord,
My sick body feels stronger
And the stomping pain quietly subsides
Tomorrow . . .

And then tomorrow
If I must struggle again
With aching exhaustion
With twisting pain
Until I am breathless
Until I am utterly spent
Until fear eclipses the last vestige of hope
Then Lord—
Then grant me the enabling grace
To believe without feeling
To know without seeing
To clasp Your invisible hand
And wait with invincible trust
For the morning.[4]

Want a little extra advice without extra charge? (I have learned this lesson the hard way.) If you are facing a tough assignment and it's possible to wait until the morning to deal with it, then wait. This is especially true if the decision that you must make will affect other lives and could hurt them if you handle things wrongly. Just hold off and sleep on it. If you must spend a restless night turning and tossing with your decision, so be it. That struggle may last "all night long." Somehow a freshness of thought, even new joy, bursts into bloom the next morning. I cannot explain it, but a new gladness comes.

After the satisfaction that comes from fresh joy in the morning, there is restoration: "Make us glad according to the days Thou hast afflicted us, and the years we have seen evil" (Ps. 90:15).

The phrase "according to the days Thou hast afflicted us" seemed troubling to me when I first read it. Then I noticed that the marginal reference in my New American Standard Bible suggests "Make us glad *as many days* as Thou hast afflicted us." Now I understand. "Lord, when You bring satisfaction to what seemed to me to be a monotonous life, that satisfaction is in proportion to the days that once seemed meaningless." *The Living Bible* says, "Give us gladness in proportion to our former misery." God has a way of balancing out the good with the bad.

Finally, after all that, there is motivation:

Let Thy work appear to Thy servants, and Thy majesty to their children (v. 16),

and confirmation:

And let the favor of the Lord our God be upon us; and do confirm for us the work of our hands; yes, confirm the work of our hands (v. 17).

Confirm means "to give meaning, to make permanent." It is this idea: "Cause me to see it as significant." Instead of my thinking of these days as just about as futile as emptying wastebaskets, help me to see the significance of them in light of Your plan. When God confirms the work of our hands, He helps us see the value of the routine, the importance of what we once considered mundane, humdrum—the same ol' thing.

HANG IN THERE! IT IS WORTH IT

After having lunch with a couple of friends at the Orange County Medical Center several years ago, I was surprised to see a deep impression in the grass right next to the sidewalk. Strangely, it was the outline of a human body. I stopped, frowned, and studied the impression. The grass was still pressed down flat. I could detect where the head had been. It had gone through the sod so deeply that the dirt could be seen. I was stunned, my stomach turned. My companions stood silently beside me as I stared down. Finally, I asked, "What is that?"

"See that window way up there on the fifth floor?" One friend pointed up as the other spoke. "A woman jumped from that window early this morning. This is where she landed."

I confess that immediately I imagined an aged person who could see no end to the tunnel of pain—someone who probably thought, *It's no use . . . my life is finished.* Staring down again, I asked, "Was it an older person?"

"Oh, no," he responded. "Matter of fact . . . a mother of five. She was still in her thirties—a rather attractive young woman."

"Five kids? In her thirties? What in the world drove her to this? How could it be?" I'll never forget my friend's answer.

"Those who were around her a lot got to know her. On a number of occasions, they had heard her say, 'Life just doesn't have any more meaning. I'm empty. All I face is a lifetime of more demands, endless chores, no relief!'"

What did she lack? She lacked the "confirmation of the work of her hands," as Moses put it. She lacked any sense of permanence or significance in the monotonous assignments of life.

For sure, one of the toughest assignments in all of life is staying by the stuff at home, handling the endless, thankless tasks of parenting—and seeing meaning and purpose in it day after demanding day. Dealing with the constant demands of children and teenagers is extremely difficult, but oh, *so* important! If that is your lot, hang in there, my eagle friend! Those eaglets may be overly demanding today, but someday you will look back with a smile and say, "It really *was* worth it all!"

Some time back we had a young medical intern in our church who set all kinds of academic records. I distinctly remember talking with him one Sunday morning. I started the conversation, "Well, my young doctor friend, how are you doing?"

He lit up: "Really great!"

"That's good," I smiled. "I'm glad to hear it."

He went on, "This is the first weekend I've had off in I forget how many weeks." He continued, "You know, Chuck, something bothers me. I'm surrounded by a large number of Jews in my training. I wonder at times what meaning there is in all of this—if I should really move in and openly declare where I stand. Actually, they *know* where I stand. But it's almost as though we live in that quiet world of two bubbles. They know where I stand, and I know where they are. We do things together and watch each other, but we're not building many bridges. I feel as if I should be moving in."

I pressed him, "You're sure they know that you're committed to Jesus Christ and Him only?"

"Yes, there is no question about it."

"Then they know where you are. God is working, even though you may not be able to see it. Believe me, they are watching!"

I then told him about a doctor friend of mine whose practice is with a medical group on the East Coast. This friend is virtually surrounded by non-Christians—not only his patients, but those other physicians in the group. He often struggled with the day-by-day *blahs,* wondering, *Is any of this making an impact?* But one day he discovered otherwise. Here's the story he told me:

"One of the guys in the group owns his own airplane and flies regularly. He also has a lot of other things going on outside of his own marriage. Other women, other affairs. I've never condemned him, but he knows where I stand. I thought he wasn't even hearing what I was saying, just enduring the monotonous routine of practicing medicine (even that gets monotonous, seeing one patient after another, after another, after another). I thought the guys in the group had just written me off. But the other day as I was packing my things, planning to move, the playboy physician said to me right out of the blue, 'Before you move, I want to talk to you. My life is *100 percent empty.* You told me once that any time I wanted to, I could come and talk to you. I've been watching your life, day after day. I've watched almost every move you make. That's why I'm here. You've got something I don't have. What is it?'" You can guess the outcome. One doctor led the other to an understanding of Christ. And the playboy physician decided to put his faith and trust in the Great Physician.

In the monotonous assignments of daily living, God can take something that seems routine and dull and use it as a platform on which to do His significant work. Remember this: Those who achieve excellence are faithful in the tedious, monotonous details of life. It is there amidst the *blahs* of boredom that we rise above the level of mediocrity and soar. One final warning before I wrap up this chapter: Watch out for those long, dull middle-aged years of prosperity and adversity. They kill more eagles than all the other years combined.

Becoming a Model of Joyful Generosity

12

I promised myself when I started this book that I would not let it degenerate into a grim-faced, morbid monster. That's a tough promise to keep, especially in a section dealing with enemies like greed, traditionalism, and indifference. Maybe it is time to look up and stretch, to remind ourselves that fighting may be a part of life—but it isn't *all* of life. Some don't want us to believe that. A you-better-get-with-it doomsday face is fast becoming the identifying mark of the Christian. And that's too bad—tragic, in fact.

I am genuinely concerned that joy is being replaced with a host of pathetic substitutes, none of them nearly as important. Don't think the world overlooks this fact, either. A man was standing behind a woman at the check-out counter of a local grocery store. He was well-dressed and his facial expression was quite stern. The woman glanced back at him a time or two as she finished unloading her basket. Finally, unable to restrain herself any longer, she asked the serious-looking gentleman, "Excuse me, but do you happen to be a minister?"

"No, I'm not," he replied. "I've just been sick for a couple of weeks."

There seems to be more of everything these days than joy. There's certainly more Bible study than joy. There is more prayer than joy—more church attendance, more evangelism, more activity, even more discernment than joy. And those of us who are leaders in religious service are often a major cause.

Some Christians look like they've been baptized in lemon juice. Many have such long faces they could eat corn out of a Coke bottle! There are some exceptions, but therein lies the problem. Why are the joyful ones the exceptions?

If I read the Book correctly, joy is the runner-up virtue. If the "fruit of the spirit" is listed in the order of importance, love gets the blue ribbon, joy the red, right? If God awarded us medals, as they do in the Olympics, love would win the gold, joy the silver, and peace the bronze. I call that second-place finisher significant! Where are all the silver-medal eagles? We need more!

Check out the average ministerial staff or, for that matter, the faces at a pastor's conference. Believe me, I have. Listen for frequent laughter. Look for joyful spirits. You'd think the morticians had landed! You'll probably find a fair amount of love, lots of compassion, a good deal of purity, patience, hope, and gentleness. And all that is marvelous. But where's the joy? Why have we relegated joy to the nonessentials, for that matter, to the suspicious? What's wrong with a well-developed sense of humor? It really concerns me that congregations seldom enjoy real laughter, those delightful lighthearted times when the nervous system gets flushed out, cleansed by joy. I find it amazing that the only ones on this planet who have every right to smile at the future and enjoy life seldom do. Why, you'd think we have been hired to carry the weight of the world on our shoulders!

I know, I know—"life is serious business." If I hear that one more time, I think I'll gag. I fully realize that too much humor can become offensive. I recognize that it can be taken to such an extreme that it is inappropriate. But doesn't it seem we have a long way to go before we are guilty of *that* problem? The final result of a joyless existence is sad—a superhigh-level intensity, borderline neurotic anxiety, an absence of just plain fun in one's work, a lack of relaxation, and the tendency to take ourselves much too seriously. We need to lighten up! Yes, spirituality and fun do go well together.

Scripture speaks directly to this issue, you know—especially the Proverbs.

> A joyful heart makes a cheerful face, but when the heart is sad, the spirit is broken (Prov. 15:13).

Amazing how that proverb goes right to the heart of the problem (no pun intended). We're not talking about a person's face here as much as we are about the heart. Internal joy goes public. We can't hide it. The face takes its cue from an inside signal. "All the days of the afflicted are bad, but a cheerful heart has a continual feast" (v. 15).

Isn't that a delightful way to put it? A cheerful heart serves the rest of the body (and others) a "continual feast." And what a sumptuous banquet! A well-developed sense of humor reveals a well-balanced personality. Maladjusted people show a far greater tendency to miss the point in a funny remark. They take jokes personally. They take things that are meant to be enjoyable much too seriously. The ability to get a laugh out of everyday situations is a safety valve. It rids us of tensions and worries which could otherwise damage our health. You think I'm exaggerating the benefits? If so, maybe you've forgotten another proverb: "A joyful heart is good medicine, but a broken spirit dries up the bones" (Prov. 17:22).

Isn't that eloquent? Look even more closely. Literally, it says, "A joyful heart causes healing." What is it that brings healing to the emotions, healing to the soul? A joyful heart. And when the heart is right, a joyful countenance accompanies it.

I mentioned our radio program, "Insight for Living," earlier in this section of my book. When I decided to go on radio, I specifically chose not to alter my style of communication. It is my nature and approach to enjoy a good laugh on occasion—to tell a joke—to find a little humor rather regularly. That is my style in life, so I figured, why not continue it in my teaching? It would be inauthentic for us to edit out all the fun and joy. So we decided to leave it in. I cannot tell you how many times I have heard from listeners who write in and say, "Chuck, don't stop laughing!" Some have gone even further: "You can stop teaching, but don't stop laughing. You're the only laughter we hear over the radio." Several have even admitted, "Yours is the only laughter I hear in our home."

I think it was Erma Bombeck who said, "We sing 'Make a joyful noise unto the Lord' while our faces reflect the sadness of one who has just buried a rich aunt who left everything to her pregnant hamster." I've laughed with Erma for years. She's the one who says that God understands even her shallow prayers that implore, "Lord, if You can't make me thin, then make my friends look *fat!*"

If I may press the point, eagles who soar, who pursue excellence, who are determined to live high above the level of mediocrity must remember the value of joy. Yes, there are times of great grief and sadness. No, life isn't a big bowl of cherries. But in complete candor, I cannot grasp how anyone can justify a continual long face. Surely, God never intended such! And it isn't just a matter of personality. Or simply a matter of temperament. It's mostly a matter of the heart and often a matter of habit. We need to be ever alert to joylessness—an enemy that will break and enter, robbing us of one of life's most prized possessions.

Joylessness is never a more evident enemy than when the subject of giving surfaces. But if I read God's Book correctly, He takes no delight in a grim giver, but rather in a cheerful one. He loves it when hilarity and generosity meet at the offering plate! When they do, I have this sneaking suspicion that He smiles broadly. To the surprise of many, the Bible frequently connects a laughing heart with a giving hand. So I think it might be best to approach this subject of joy from the viewpoint of being generous as well. First, I want us to see the statement in the New Testament that gives us the overriding principle in a few words, and then I'd like us to observe several examples or models of joyful generosity.

A STATEMENT WORTH PONDERING

Two letters in the New Testament were written to the church at Corinth. Both were from the same man, Paul, who spent a little over a year and a half getting that particular church established. The Corinthian church was loaded with potential. It had numerous spiritual gifts and fine teachers. It had money and influence. It was a place you and I would have wanted to attend had we lived in first-century Corinth. It was winsome and exciting. Probably the best description is *contagious*. But it also had some people who reverted to carnality. These people had made great promises to God regarding their commitment, but only a few months later they'd grown cold and backed off. They needed to be reminded of what they had promised God. That is part of the reason Paul wrote them—actually, the major reason he wrote them the second letter.

You see, many miles removed from Corinth was another church, much older, and struggling financially. I'm referring to the mother church in Jerusalem. That church, though older, was now economically strapped. Their need for assistance was acute. So Paul was involved in raising funds for the Jerusalem church, a project which brought him to the region of Macedonia, just north of Corinth.

Even though the Macedonian Christians were also in an economically depressed area, Paul appealed to them, urging them to respond to the needs in Jerusalem. They gave generously—abundantly, in fact. A year earlier the Corinthians also had promised to give to this need. When word reached Paul that the Corinthians had long since set aside this project and had failed in their efforts to raise the funds that they promised to give, he decided to write them to remind them of their previous commitment.

> For it is superfluous for me to write to you about this ministry to the saints; for I know your readiness, of which I boast about you to the Macedonians, namely, that Achaia has been prepared since last year, and your zeal has stirred up most of them. But I have sent the brethren, that our boasting about you may not be made empty in this case, that, as I was saying, you may be prepared (2 Cor. 9:1–3).

In other words, Paul is saying that if he were to bring some Macedonian Christians with him to Corinth and have them pick up the measly Corinthian offering to take back to Jerusalem, he would be red-faced. Why? Because it was the Corinthian example (Paul had mentioned them to those in Macedonia) that prompted the Macedonians to give over and above their ability. So he writes to spur them on. Drawing on an age-old agricultural analogy, he begins:

> Now this I say, he who sows sparingly shall also reap sparingly;
> and he who sows bountifully shall also reap bountifully (2 Cor. 9:6).

In effect, Paul is saying, "There is a basic principle I taught you while I was with you in Corinth. If you plant only a little bit of seed, you'll get a meager harvest. But if you plant a lot of seed, you'll harvest an abundance. Which makes better sense?" He goes further: "Let each one do just as he has purposed in his heart; not grudgingly or under compulsion; . . ." (2 Cor. 9:7). The word *grudgingly* means "reluctantly," the idea of holding onto something because you don't want to part with it.

If you have little children or if you have been around little ones, then you've seen the same scene dozens of times. The child gets a toy. He's the older of the two. Let's say he's got this special little truck he loves to play with. He plays with it so much he virtually wears all the paint off the little thing. One day he leaves it sitting on the toy box. Nobody is touching it. Along comes little sister who toddles up to the table and reaches her tiny hand over to pick up the truck, only to have it snatched away by young King Kong, as he yells, "That's *my* truck!" He doesn't want to part with something he considers that important. When his mother makes him let her play with it, he "grudgingly" does so. It means reluctantly giving up something because it represents so much.

In the 2 Corinthians passage, we are also instructed not to give under compulsion. That means "feeling forced because of what someone may say or think." You see, compulsion results in even greater reluctance. When we are compelled to do something, we are all the more reluctant to give it up.

To return to my truck story, when Mom looks down and says, "Let her play with it," it's doubtful that he would ever say, "Why, of course! Here, Sis, I'm sorry I was selfish." You're smiling. Older kids *never* say that! Instead, you hear, "That's mine! That's mine!" And you have to pull his grip loose to wrench that little truck out of his hand. He doesn't want to give it up. Strangely, our compulsion makes him grip it even tighter.

Those are the word pictures implied here regarding giving. I find it almost amusing that the standard approach in fund-raising today is causing people to feel forced, compelling them to give. If God means what He says (doesn't He always?), then there's got to

be another way. To the shock of most people, the other way is
JOY! Generosity prompted by joy.

I've built to the climax that appears at the end of verse 7:
". . . for God loves a cheerful giver."

In the ancient days when the Greek text was written, interesting
things occurred in the formation of words in a phrase or sentence.
When words were placed out of order at the beginning of a sentence, it was usually for the purpose of emphasis. Guess what
appears first in this last sentence: *cheerful,* not *giver.* Not even
God. No, the word *cheerful* is the first major word to appear in the
text. "For the cheerful one, who is a giver, God prizes." If I may
return to my earlier example, "It's the *cheerful* giver who gets the
silver medal; it's the *cheerful* giver who gets the red ribbon."

Hover for a moment over the key word, *cheerful.* In Greek it is
the term *hilaros,* from which we get our word *hilarious.* It is such
an unusual word it appears nowhere else in all the New Testament. Several times it surfaces in the Old Testament Greek version of the Bible (the Septuagint), but never any other place in all
the New Testament. Literally, the sentence reads, "For the hilarious giver God prizes." Do you know why He prizes the hilarious
giver? Because the hilarious giver gives so generously. He has no
special possession or gift or skill or amount of money that he
grips tightly. No, when the heart is full of cheer, it is amazing how
it causes the pockets to turn inside out. Unlike the mediocre
majority, those who soar are full of joy that expresses itself in
greathearted generosity.

At our church in Fullerton, California, the First Evangelical
Free Church, we needed about eight thousand dollars for a group
of high schoolers to go to Paraguay one summer. The teens had
raised most of their support, but they came up eight thousand
dollars short. We presented the need, and in less than twenty-four
hours *more* than eight thousand dollars was given. Because we're
rich? No. Because I begged? No. You know better than that! Compulsion backfires, remember. Simply because cheerful hearts
created a spirit of such generosity, the momentum accomplished
the goal.

But wait, let me quickly state that I'm not limiting these
thoughts to money. I'm talking about being joyfully generous
with our time and talents, too. I also have in mind compassion,
possessions, and skills. Such joyful generosity is beautifully illustrated in other places of Scripture.

Examples Worth Remembering

In the Old Testament

Way back in the Book of Exodus, we find a classic example of joyful generosity. The people of God are now out of Egypt and on their trek across the wilderness en route to Canaan. Smack dab in the middle of no-man's land, God gives them an architectural plan for a portable worship center. Look:

> Then the Lord spoke to Moses, saying, "Tell the sons of Israel to raise a contribution for Me; from every man whose heart moves him you shall raise My contribution. And this is the contribution which you are to raise from them: gold, silver and bronze, blue, purple and scarlet material, fine linen, goat hair, rams' skins dyed red, porpoise skins, acacia wood, oil for lighting, spices for the anointing oil and for the fragrant incense, onyx stones and setting stones, for the ephod and for the breastpiece (Exod. 25:1–7).

Wait. Hold on, here. I ask you, couldn't Bill Cosby do a number on these verses? "I want you to raise a contribution. I want you to get porpoise skins and acacia wood and oil for lighting and rams' skins dyed red. And I want something to go on a breastplate. And I want onyx stones and setting stones." Give me a break! What is that all about? What are they going to do? I would love to see Cosby do a take-off on those words!

Why do all this? Read on:

"And let them construct a sanctuary for Me . . ." (v. 8). Are you ready? It was a fund-raising drive for a building, right from the Bible! Some of you, I'm sure, are ready to slam the book shut. You've heard enough! But hang with me. The plot thickens and the response becomes so joyful that the scene gets downright contagious. These people were told to construct a first-class portable building, a tabernacle, which they were to carry across the wilderness. It would be a structure for worship in which God Himself would dwell. His *Shechinah* (a bright, blinding light) would dwell in its most sacred center, the "holy of holies." Actually, He had never resided in a place on earth before. So we can be sure this structure would be built exactly as He specified.

> "According to all that I am going to show you, as the pattern of the tabernacle and the pattern of all its furniture, just so you shall construct it" (v. 9).

And beginning at verse 10 of Exodus, chapter 25, all the way through to chapter 35, God presents the specifications, the inspired drawings to Moses. In these plans God tells the Israelites everything they are to make and how they are to make it. It was an ingenious plan, brilliantly thought through and beautifully designed.

You can probably guess what followed. Earlier Moses was there by himself. But now he brings the people in, because that is where the funds will come from. In chapters 35 and 36, Moses assembles all the congregation and breaks the news to them.

> And Moses spoke to all the congregation of the sons of Israel, saying, "This is the thing which the Lord has commanded, saying, 'Take from among you a contribution to the Lord; whoever is of a willing heart, let him bring it as the Lord's contribution: gold, silver, and bronze, and blue, purple and scarlet material, fine linen, goats' hair, and rams' skins dyed red, and porpoise skins, and acacia wood, and oil for lighting, and spices for the anointing oil, and for the fragrant incense, and onyx stones and setting stones, for the ephod and for the breastpiece (Exod. 35:4–9).

Go back and underscore a phrase you may have passed over: "whoever is of a willing heart." In essence, Moses is saying, "We want no one to give grudgingly or under compulsion to participate, only *willing hearts.*" (Sound vaguely familiar?) And then what? ". . . let him bring it as the Lord's contribution."

Moses goes even further.

> "'And let every skillful man among you come, and make all that the Lord has commanded: the tabernacle, its tent and its covering, its hooks and its boards, its bars, its pillars, and its sockets; the ark and its poles, the mercy seat, and the curtain of the screen; the table and its poles, and all its utensils, and the bread of the Presence; the lampstand also for the light and its utensils and its lamps and the oil for the light; and the altar of incense and its poles, and the anointing oil and the fragrant incense, and the screen for the doorway at the entrance of the tabernacle; the altar of burnt offering with its bronze grating, its poles, and all its utensils, the basin and its stand; the hangings of the court, its pillars and its sockets, and the screen for the gate of the court; the pegs of the tabernacle and the pegs of the court and their cords; the woven garments, for ministering in the holy place, the holy garments for

Aaron the priest, and the garments of his sons, to minister as priests'" (vv. 10–19).

By now, I really believe the people's mouths must have dropped open and their hearts began to beat faster. "Ah, are we going to have a great place of worship! God is going to dwell among us. This is my chance to use my skill, my talents, my treasure, my craft, to assist in providing a place where God's people will meet for worship. What a privilege . . . what an opportunity!"

Now read very carefully, paying close attention to the comments related to their "hearts" and their "spirits."

Then all the congregation of the sons of Israel departed from Moses' presence. And everyone whose heart stirred him and everyone whose spirit moved him came and brought the Lord's contribution for the work of the tent of meeting and for all its service and for the holy garments (vv. 20–21).

What could these nomads possibly give? They're in the wilderness. They're living in tents. Well, they had some valuables they had taken with them when they left Egypt. And not one of them held tightly to those possessions.

Then all whose hearts moved them, both men and women, came and brought brooches and earrings and signet rings and bracelets, all articles of gold; so did every man who presented an offering of gold to the Lord. And every man, who had in his possession blue and purple and scarlet material and fine linen and goats' hair and rams' skins dyed red and porpoise skins, brought them. Everyone who could make a contribution of silver and bronze brought the Lord's contribution; and every man, who had in his possession acacia wood for any work of the service, brought it. And all the skilled women spun with their hands, and brought what they had spun, in blue and purple and scarlet material and in fine linen. And all the women whose heart stirred with a skill spun the goats' hair. And the rulers brought the onyx stones and the stones for setting for the ephod and for the breastpiece; and the spice and the oil for the light and for the anointing oil and for the fragrant incense. The Israelites, all the men and women, whose heart moved them to bring material for all the work, which the Lord had commanded through Moses to be done, brought a freewill offering to the Lord (vv. 22–29).

I love that scene! By the hundreds, by the thousands, by the tens of thousands they came with their offerings, bringing them before their Lord in the wilderness. Skilled men stood ready with saw and hammer and chisel. Skilled ladies stood by with their needle, thread, and fabric to do the fine embroidery and needle-point that would be a part of the veil (the curtain that would divide the holy place from the holiest of all) and the other beauti-ful tapestries and curtains. The tabernacle was a beautiful, skill-ful work of art, masterfully engineered. There would be those who worked in gold, silver, and fine gems who would finish the precious metals and the jewels just as God directed through the skill He had given them. God really "broke a vase" when He designed this baby! It must have been something to behold.

Now this is where the story gets really exciting. You are going to meet a couple of men you've probably never heard of before. That is the way it often is with skilled craftsmen, in this case, the construction superintendents.

> Then Moses called Bezalel and Oholiab and every skillful per-son in whom the Lord had put skill, everyone whose heart stirred him, to come to the work to perform it (Exod. 36:2).

There is no guilt. There is no external compulsion, no manipula-tion whatsoever. Rather, with joyful hearts moved and stirred, they came eagerly to work on this project.

> And they received from Moses all the contributions which the sons of Israel had brought to perform the work in the construc-tion of the sanctuary. And they still continued bringing to him freewill offerings every morning (v. 3).

Morning after morning God continued to stir the hearts of peo-ple. As a result they brought bracelets and brooches, jewels and earrings, along with pieces of gold and bronze and silver. True joy had invaded the camp. There were miles of smiles. God Himself must have smiled back at such joyful generosity.

> And all the skillful men who were performing all the work of the sanctuary came, each from the work which he was performing, and they said to Moses, "The people are bringing much more than enough for the construction work which the Lord commanded us

to perform." So Moses issued a command, and a proclamation was circulated throughout the camp, saying, "Let neither man nor woman any longer perform work for the contributions of the sanctuary." Thus the people were restrained from bringing any more. For the material they had was sufficient and more than enough for all the work, to perform it (vv. 4–7).

That's right. I'm not kidding, Moses had to issue a command: "No more offerings. Please don't give any more!" How would that come across on a Sunday morning at your church? "Folks, we're not going to take an offering today because you people have unloaded the truck on us for the last two Sundays, so we're going to pass it up today! Do not give any more!" Don't get your hopes up! But the truth is this: When there is such a spirit of hilarity, when genuine joy overflows, people do have to be *stopped* from giving! Because our ability so outstrips the need, we can't keep handling all the funds that would pour into the treasury. What a wonderful change of scenery: "The people were restrained from bringing any more."

Can you imagine the joy? The camp of Israel was never happier. You could have heard singing among the carpenters working with wood, singing among the jewelers, singing among the ladies who worked with their fabrics and their design and other pieces of art. What a place to be! What an absolutely irresistible magnet in the wilderness! But "Operation Tabernacle" is just one scene. The tent of worship was built and God met with the people. They praised His name and found cleansing and forgiveness in that tabernacle for years, really for centuries.

Now here is another scene. Tragically, the Hebrews later forgot God and were swept away into captivity in Babylon. They finally left Babylon, faltering in their steps, stumbling back to Jerusalem to rebuild the city which had been destroyed by the heathen. They returned to their beloved Zion. Nehemiah led one of the groups back, and he wasn't there long before he realized the wall around the city had to be rebuilt or the people would be plundered by enemies. Finally, after surveying the need, he came before the people and presented a challenge in hopes of raising their support and getting them involved:

Then I said to them, "You see the bad situation we are in, that Jerusalem is desolate and its gates burned by fire. Come, let us

rebuild the wall of Jerusalem that we may no longer be a re-
proach" (Neh. 2:17).

By the way, we must not hurry over the intrinsic motivation
Nehemiah used in that speech. He appealed to their heart when
he said, "Can you imagine what people all over the region are
saying about our God? They're saying, 'You're telling me that
your God is great? Look at the awful place you live in. This place
is the pits!'" As the people began to imagine such thoughts, they
were motivated from within to respond. When they considered
the need, their patriotic pride pushed them into action. Winston
Churchill, a master of intrinsic motivation, constantly rallied the
people of the British Isles by reminding them of the importance
of upholding their British heritage. He linked them with the
pride of their fortune.

Well, that was Nehemiah's approach: "How good it would be to
have a wall that stands tall and strong around this city, men and
women, one that represents the strong name of our God, so that
when the enemy looks over at us and sees us dwelling in peace in
Zion, they will say, 'My, their God is the One to revere!'"

Who knows? Sir Winston Churchill may have learned how to
do it from Nehemiah. Remember the Prime Minister's words?

> I have not become the King's First Minister in order to preside
> over the liquidation of the British Empire (Speech at the Lord
> Mayor's Day Luncheon, London [Nov. 10, 1942]).

> I have nothing to offer but blood, toil, tears, and sweat (First
> statement as Prime Minister, House of Commons [May 13,
> 1940]).

> Never give in, never give in, never, never, never, never—in noth-
> ing, great or small, large or petty—never give in except to convic-
> tions of honor and good sense (Address at Harrow School [Oct. 29,
> 1941]).[1]

Hitler laughed at Great Britain. But Churchill and the Britons
had the last laugh. May I repeat? He appealed to the intrinsic
motivation of the people of Great Britain. That is what Nehemiah
does here.

> And I told them how the hand of my God had been favorable to me, and also about the king's words which he had spoken to me. Then they said, "Let us arise and build." So they put their hands to the good work (Neh. 2:18).

What do you see in that statement? I see cheer. I see motivation. I don't hear any grumbling. And I don't find anybody feeling under pressure. Everyone says, "Let's do it. It's only right. Let's go for it! Lead us, Nehemiah, and we will do it." And that is exactly what happens. They put their hands to the work.

> So we built the wall and the whole wall was joined together to half its height, for the people had a mind to work (Neh. 4:6).

The word translated "mind" in this verse is literally, "heart." It is like the line out of the popular song of yesteryear, "You gotta have heart." When eagles soar, they "gotta have heart." When we keep pursuing a standard of excellence, surrounded by mediocrity, we "gotta have heart."

And those Hebrews definitely had heart! They stayed at it against incredible odds until they finished the task.

> So the wall was completed on the twenty-fifth of the month Elul, in fifty-two days. And it came about when all our enemies heard of it, and all the nations surrounding us saw it, they lost their confidence; for they recognized that this work had been accomplished with the help of our God (Neh. 6:15–16).

Isn't that great? Those on the outside couldn't deny the incredible feat these Hebrews had accomplished. As they walked by the completed wall, they looked at it with a whole different perspective, wondering, *What kind of God do they serve?*

You have to realize that for the longest time these enemies had been badgering the people of Israel—taunting, tempting, and insulting them, trying their best to shut down "Project Rebuild." Really, their scheme was to rob them of their joy—the fuel of morale. But that wall kept going up against all odds until finally the enemy stuffed his hands in his pockets and said, "I can't believe it. They got that thing built." The Hebrew's success in rebuilding the wall reminds me of the verse, "He who sows bountifully shall also reap bountifully" (2 Cor. 9:6).

In the New Testament

When we arrive at the New Testament, one of the first things we encounter is a set of gifts brought by some wise men to the King. We are less than two full chapters into the New Testament before we come across a few men, called magi, who have come to visit the baby Jesus.

> And when they saw the star, they rejoiced exceedingly with great joy. And they came into the house and saw the Child with Mary His mother; and they fell down and worshiped Him; and opening their treasures they presented to Him gifts of gold and frankincense and myrrh (Matt. 2:10–11).

What characterized the attitude of these visitors? Joy. Exceedingly great joy. And what was the result? Great generosity. They gave gold, frankincense, and myrrh to this little Child. Oh, I know all sorts of symbolic things have been said, but if you'll allow me the simplicity of literalism, they brought what they had. And they lavished upon Him sheer extravagance—they worshiped as they gave expensive gifts. Why? Because they had cheerful hearts.

I could go on. Rather obscure men like Epaphroditus and Onesiphorus gave themselves to Paul, as did Dr. Luke. The church at Philippi, out of great joy, gave more than once to Paul, over and above his needs, so that he could say from their example, "I have learned to abound." What joy Paul modeled! In fact, have you thought lately about our ultimate home in heaven? Take a quick glimpse now:

> And I saw the holy city, new Jerusalem, coming down out of heaven from God, made ready as a bride adorned for her husband. And I heard a loud voice from the throne, saying, "Behold, the tabernacle of God is among men, and He shall dwell among them, and they shall be His people, and God Himself shall be among them, and He shall wipe away every tear from their eyes; and there shall no longer be any death; there shall no longer be any mourning, or crying, or pain; the first things have passed away" (Rev. 21:2–4).

What will be the eternal sound of heaven? No tears, pain, or sorrow. Sounds like laughter and joy to me! Count on it—heaven will be the first place where joy will be in the majority.

Joyful Generosity Can Be Ours Today

We've spent sufficient time on biblical examples. Let's think about how we can bring some much-needed joy back into our lives today. I have four suggestions in mind.

1. <u>Reflect on God's gifts to you.</u> In case you need a little help, read through Psalm 103:

> Bless the Lord, O my soul; and all that is within me, bless His holy name. Bless the Lord, O my soul, and forget none of His benefits; who pardons all your iniquities; who heals all your diseases; who redeems your life from the pit; who crowns you with lovingkindness and compassion; who satisfies your years with good things, so that your youth is renewed like the eagle. The Lord performs righteous deeds, and judgments for all who are oppressed (Ps. 103:1–6).

The psalmist lists several benefits to prod our thinking. As we reflect on God's gifts to us, it's helpful to be specific.

Do you have eyesight? It's a gift. Do you have a good mind? It's a gift. How about dexterity in your fingers? Or special skills that allow you to work in your occupation? Do you have leadership abilities that cause others to follow? A good education? Do you have the ability to sell? These are all gifts. Has He given you a family? Has He given you sufficient clothes? How about a nice, warm, soft bed at night or a comfortable place to live in the hot summer? Why, some even have more than one home! These are all gifts from God's hand. Reflect on His numerous gifts to you. It will increase your joy. And a smile will soon replace that frown.

2. <u>Remind yourself of God's promises regarding generosity.</u> God promises if you sow bountifully, you will reap bountifully. If you give in abundance, a tabernacle can be erected. If you work hard with one another, a wall can be built. So give! Give abundantly! Even extravagant giving is honored by God. I've never known anyone who went bad because he or she was *too* generous. Remind yourself of His promises regarding generosity and start releasing! My good friend, Ron Blue, has helped Cynthia and me more than any other person when it comes to generosity. By his example and professional financial assistance, he has challenged us and shown us ways to increase our charitable contributions to incredible proportions. I strongly recommend your reading

Master Your Money by Ron Blue.[2] Don't be afraid of outgiving God. It is absolutely impossible to do that. He will keep every one of His promises related to generosity. Try Him!

3.   <u>Examine your heart</u> (this is going to be the tough one). I don't want you to examine your tax records from last year. That will merely speak to your mind. I want you to talk to your heart. I don't want you to examine your neighbor or some other person, because you will be better than your neighbor or whichever individual you choose. Don't even compare yourself with the way you used to give, because you probably are doing better than you used to do. I challenge you to *examine your heart.*

Here are some questions for you to ask yourself:

- Do I really believe there is a need?
- Am I responding out of pressure or because I really care?
- Is my gift an appropriate expression of my income or is it more of a last-minute, unplanned get-it-over-with act?
- Have I prayed, or is this impulsive giving?
- Is joy prompting me? Am I genuinely thrilled about what God is doing in my life as well as through my giving?
- Does generosity characterize my life?

4.   <u>Glorify God by being extremely generous.</u> I think a unique way to look at it is to scare yourself a little. Remember when you didn't have much and you gave more than you should have given, at least for logic's sake? You scared yourself a little, didn't you? Wasn't that fun? Wasn't that absolutely delightful? And the good news is you made it. You didn't starve. Chances are good you are still rather well fed. And sufficiently clothed. But are you joyful? Honestly now, has the enemy, Joyless Living, taken charge of you? If so, I can guarantee that you have become less generous. How about cultivating extreme generosity? Talk about being a rare species of eagle!

I find it interesting that most people picture their heavenly Father as frowning and wringing His hands or sort of pulling His beard when His Son left heaven. I don't think so. I wonder if there wasn't a smile in heaven. Even when our Lord faced the cross and thought of dying in agony, what spurred Him on was "the joy that was set before Him." And can you imagine the shout of joy from heaven when the resurrection occurred? "Raised from the dead! That's My Son!" How about when the Father welcomed Him back to the throne! I would imagine the greatest joy possible surrounded that reunion. And speaking of the greatest—

God	the greatest Giver
so loved	the greatest motive
the world	the greatest need
that He gave	the greatest act
His only Son	the greatest gift
that whosoever	the greatest invitation
believes in Him	the greatest opportunity
should not perish	the greatest deliverance
but have eternal life	the greatest joy

Do you want to know the endless source of joy? Jesus Christ. Through Him alone we receive salvation—an act of love, fulfilled with joy, resulting in peace. Thanks be to God for His indescribable Gift. All that He is and all that He provides is enough to make me laugh out loud!

We've spent enough time in the combat zone. While here, we have taken on four of the more prominent enemies of soaring: greed, traditionalism, indifference, and joylessness. These opponents of excellence, as we have learned, will not surrender easily. On the contrary, they are so entrenched, they require strong and consistent bombardment. But the good news is this: *They can be overcome!* May God give us strength to face each one without fear.

Must one point out that from ancient times a decline in courage has been considered the first symptom of the end?

Aleksandr I. Solzhenitsyn
1978

Part Four

Resisting Mediocrity Includes Standing Courageously

Standing Alone When Outnumbered

13

One of the great American myths is that we are all a bunch of rugged individualists. We would like to think that, but it simply is not true. There are some exceptions, of course, but for the majority it is not that way at all.

Deep within, we imagine ourselves as a mixture of Patrick Henry, Davy Crockett, John Wayne, and the prophet Daniel! But the truth of the matter is that most of us would do anything to keep from being different. We'd much rather blend into the woodwork. One of our greatest fears is being ostracized, rejected by "the group." Ridicule is a pain too great for most to bear.

There are other fears—fear of being made to look foolish, fear of standing out in a crowd, fear of being talked about and misunderstood. Rather than rugged individualists, we are more like Gulliver of old, tied down and immobilized by tiny strands of fear, real or imagined. The result is both predictable and tragic: loss of courage.

> We can see these symptoms . . . throughout society, but the most visible one is loss of courage. People stand by and watch a fellow citizen being beaten or stabbed and they do not interfere. They are afraid. Our political leaders watch Communism gobble up other nations and they do nothing. They are afraid. People complain in private about the state of affairs but will not speak out in public. They are afraid. . . .[1]

Because this is true, I have decided to combine the final four chapters of my book under one major heading: Courage. Living above the level of mediocrity includes standing courageously. In the final analysis, whoever decides to soar will be forced to face and come to terms with the great temptation to conform. This is obvious since those who don't want to soar will ridicule those who do. Eagles will always be outnumbered. Standing alone when outnumbered and opposed can be an uncomfortable, threatening experience.

Over thirty years ago I worked as a machinist in a shop where the vast majority were members of the local union. It didn't take me long to realize that the maintenance of a mediocre standard was one of the unwritten laws of that shop. Pressure was applied to anyone who worked unusually hard or produced more than the lower-than-average quota. Why? It made all the others look bad, and there was no way they would tolerate such a thing! Mild suggestions, if unheeded, would be followed by gentle nudges. Then, if still unheeded, the nudges would be followed by direct confrontation. If *that* was ignored, there were stronger measures taken to maintain the level of mediocrity. They would have no part of excellence. Conform or else! We had our moments, to say the least.

Such pressure is not uncommon in numerous slices of life. The hard-charging high achiever at school is usually viewed with suspicion, not respect. Instead of others in the class picking up the pace and trying their best to do better, they would rather put down the student out front and make him or her look foolish. The same can be true on a sales team or for that matter in a residential neighborhood. People don't want anyone to soar, especially if they prefer to slump! Chances are good that you feel the same pressure I'm illustrating. If not, color yourself fortunate. Few are the places today where eagle types pursuing excellence are admired and encouraged to reach greater heights. Because this is so common, I feel we need to seriously consider what is involved in standing courageously.

A Brief Analysis of Conformity

Earlier I mentioned the significance of certain lines from chapter 12 of the Letter to the Romans. I'd like us to return to that thought and spend a few more minutes on the overall setting in which that line occurs.

> I urge you therefore, brethren, by the mercies of God, to present your bodies a living and holy sacrifice, acceptable to God, which is your spiritual service of worship. And do not be conformed to this world, but be transformed by the renewing of your mind, that you may prove what the will of God is, that which is good and acceptable and perfect (Rom. 12:1–2).

Allow me to mention six observations from those two verses:

1. This truth is mainly for the Christian. "I urge you, *brethren*. . . ." If I haven't made this clear before, I need to say it straight now. Apart from a personal and vital faith in Jesus Christ, it is impossible to wage a winning effort against the system called "the world." Trying to soar on one's own, overcoming the powerful magnet of the majority without help from above, would be a frustrating and counterproductive effort. Only God can give us such transforming power through our faith in His Son.

2. There is an urgency in this message—intense urgency, in fact. Paul doesn't say, "Oh, by the way, it might be nice if . . ." No, he says, "I *urge* you." The writer is pressing his pen hard; he feels passionate about this. And so must we. No one ever eased effortlessly out of conformity.

3. This urgency is related to a sacrifice. The point being, the process of commitment is a "holy sacrifice." We never sacrifice something easily. The whole idea of sacrifice is yielding something that is important to us—releasing, giving over, letting go, surrendering. The urgency will call for sacrifice. Notice that the sacrifice is not only "holy," it is a "living" sacrifice. One of the

major problems of a living sacrifice is that it keeps crawling off the altar!

4.   This sacrifice touches two realms: the inner person and the outer person. The *inner person* is addressed in the word *present*—"I urge you . . . to present your bodies." This is a decision we make deep down inside ourselves. Next is the *outer person,* "your bodies"—that part of you that touches the system around you. "I urge you by the mercies of God," says Paul, "that you Christians make a deep-down, gut-level decision to present your bodies."

Listen to the words of the late Donald Barnhouse:

> There are two things involved here—our innermost self that does the presenting and our bodies that are presented. It should almost go without saying that it is useless to give our bodies if we have not, first of all, given ourselves.[2]

This matter of presenting our bodies is a very practical thing. I had to consciously come to terms with it when I went overseas in the Marine Corps for many long months. I knew before I ever set foot in the barracks that more than likely, most of the forty-seven other guys would be just alike, especially in the moral realm. Marines have never been known for their moral virtue (you're smiling). I knew my buddies were going to be unfaithful. I knew they were going to traffic in sensual things. I knew in my heart they would buy into the world's system. While on that massive troop ship steaming across the Pacific, I can recall as clearly as if it were yesterday thinking hard about the issue of conformity. I had enough sense to say, "Lord, God, I give myself to You during these months in front of me. I don't want to come off as a self-righteous monk who stands aloof, but I do desire to walk a path that honors Your name. Therefore, Lord, I need Your strength to stand alone. I present my body to You . . . for Your glory."

I'm not talking out of theory. I know firsthand that this kind of commitment works. During those months when I was sur-rounded by fellow Marines with totally different moral standards from those I held, I did not yield to peer pressure. I did not con-form. I remained faithful to my wife. By God's grace and power, I maintained a walk with Jesus Christ. I do not intend to sound like a goody two-shoes. I want to verify that *it works.* Therefore, I can say to you teenagers who wake up on Monday morning and know that when you go to school you're going to be surrounded by the system, *you can handle it!* You *cannot* counteract it alone, however. You're too weak and it's too appealing, too attractive. But by presenting yourself to the Lord on a day-by-day basis, almost until it is a habit, you can handle it. To do so, there must be a harmony—an agreement—in your inner and outer person.

5.   The sacrifice is essentially a spiritual one. As far as God is concerned, a consistent godly life is well pleasing, acceptable to Him. As far as you are concerned, it is an act of worship. It is a "spiritual service of worship."

I need to be very candid here. If you are a "Sunday Christian," you will not stand alone when outnumbered. Anybody can soar—anyone can walk in victory while sitting in church. But the kind of "service of worship" Romans 12:1–2 is talking about affects your Monday, your Thursday, your Saturday lifestyle— your entire week, in fact, all fifty-two of them every year. So at the deepest level there is the presenting of oneself to God—at lunch time, if you please; before a date; during a date; before a trip; in the middle of a vacation. During any scene in which you find yourself, you give yourself to God. "Lord, in this body there are certain drives and many desires. In my eyes, there are interests that are not from You. In these ears of mine and in these hands and in various parts of my body there are things that are attracted, like a magnet, to the world system. Therefore, I deliberately and willingly give You my eyes, my ears, my senses, my thought processes as an act of worship. I am Yours, Lord. Please take control of each one of these areas."

All this brings me to a final observation:

6.   This sacrifice leads to a practical and radical decision. Look again at the second verse: "Do not be conformed to this world (that is the practical decision), but be transformed by the renewing of your mind (that is the radical decision)." I mentioned J. B. Phillips' paraphrase of this verse in chapter 10, but it's worth repeating: "Don't let the world around you squeeze you into its own mold" (Rom. 12:2). *The Living Bible* says, "Don't copy the behavior and customs of this world." Many read that and think only of hairstyle or clothing, which could be merely a superficial application. But it seems to me, what Paul had in mind is that the whole world system is at odds with God.

We are like tiny islands of truth surrounded by a sea of paganism, but we launch our ship every day. We can't live or do business in this world without rubbing shoulders with those driven by the world's desires. God calls very few to be monks in a monastery. So we must make a *practical* decision not to be conformed while we are in the system, and at the same time, we must make a *radical* decision to give God the green light to transform our minds.

Let me clarify those thoughts. First, what does it mean to be *conformed?* The word means "to assume an outward expression that does not come from within." When I conform to something, I masquerade; I wrap myself in a mask that isn't true to what I am on the inside. Deep inside of me is the Person of Jesus Christ. When the outside of me is involved in actions that are un-Christlike, I am conforming. But when the living Christ within me is expressed on the outside, I am not conforming. I am being authentic. When He lives out His life through me, there is genuine expression, not a masquerade.

Second, what does it mean to be *transformed?* That word is different from *conformed.* The biblical term means "an outward expression that comes from within." Not only is it different, but it is the antithesis of *conform.* The Greek word underlying the term *transformed* here is the verb *metamorphoō,* from which come the English words *metamorphose* and *metamorphosis.* To be "transformed" is to be "metamorphosed."

When a grub becomes a butterfly, there has been a metamorphosis, a radical transformation. When a tadpole becomes a frog, there has been a transformation. When the real Christ expresses Himself through our lives, there is evidence of dramatic change. What occurs is nothing short of a striking, radical transformation. And how does it occur? Paul says, "Do this by the renewing of your mind." In my opinion, that is where the techniques begin. For there to be victorious transformation rather than defeating conformity, there must be renewing thoughts.

In order for you and me to keep ourselves from conforming, we must have a renewed mind. The primary battleground, as I wrote at the beginning of this book, is the mind—that inner part of our being where we decide who we are and where we stand. As someone once wrote, "We are not what we are. We are not even what others think we are. We are what we think others think we are."

At the deepest level, even though the majority may not want to admit it, most people are conformists. That is why it is correctly termed a radical decision. Only a radically different mindset can equip folks like us to stand alone when we're outnumbered. Conformity will always be there inviting us in, appealing to our insecurities, painting a comfortable, rosy picture that says, "Aw, come on and join us. Why be so different?"

FOUR OBJECTIVES OF THE WORLD SYSTEM

The world system is committed to at least four major objectives, which I can summarize in four words: fortune, fame, power, pleasure. *First and foremost: Fortune, money.* The world system is driven by money; it feeds on materialism. I've already said a lot about this, but eagles don't soar until they realize the reality of this constant pull. *Second: Fame.* That is another word for popularity. You wrestle with it, your kids are wrestling with it, your grandkids will wrestle with it. Fame is the longing to be known, to be somebody in someone else's eyes. I'm not referring to being someone's hero, but someone's god. I'm talking about a celebrity mindset. *Third: Power.* This is having influence, maintaining control over individuals or groups or companies or whatever. It is the desire to manipulate and maneuver others to do something for one's own benefit. *Fourth: Pleasure.* At its basic level, pleasure has to do with fulfilling one's sensual desires. It's the same mindset that's behind the slogan: "If it feels good, do it." The world is ruthless and relentless as it works overtime to communicate this fortune-fame-power-pleasure syndrome.

Deposit your child into a system like that with no information, little help or technique on how to handle it, and I can almost guarantee you that in only a matter of months that youngster will think like, look like, sound like, and worst of all, *act* like the system. If your child's close friends are into profanity or immorality, chances are good your son or daughter will conform. If they are into alcohol or drugs, you can expect the same at home.

Several years ago I stumbled upon a verse of Scripture that seemed to leap off the page. Right in the middle of 1 Corinthians 15, which is a chapter on the doctrine of resurrection, is this very practical thought: "Do not be deceived: 'Bad company corrupts good morals'" (v. 33). *The Living Bible* puts it this way: "Don't be fooled by those who say such things. If you listen to them you will start acting like them."

Monkey see, monkey do. When we spend enough time around those in a particular scene, our actions usually become similar. It is just the way we're made. And it is especially true if the one in the minority is insecure and unsure. If you doubt that, you are merely deceiving yourself. Wake up, eagle! Realize the overwhelming power of peer pressure on you as well as your kids. Some call it the "herd instinct." All things being equal, if you run with bad company, you will be corrupted. The good won't rub off on them. Their bad will rub off on you. It's like putting on a pair of white gloves on a muddy day and picking up that mud and mixing it around in your hands. Interestingly, the mud never gets "glovey," but the gloves get muddy. Never saw "glovey" mud in my entire life!

AN OLD SCENE WITH A MODERN MESSAGE

In light of what 1 Corinthians 15:33 says about the dangers of peer pressure, let's look at Deuteronomy 6:10–15. The people being addressed in this scripture are the new-generation Hebrews we discussed earlier—those who lived to see the Promised Land after wandering in the wilderness for forty years until they buried all those who had doubted Moses' leadership. Except for Caleb and Joshua, only the young Israelites survived. Now they are on the verge of invading Canaan. Just before entering it, Moses pulls them aside and gives them a few warnings. In no uncertain terms, he tells them about the perils lurking in the shadows once they take up residence in that new territory. Though Moses himself would not be going in with them, he loved them too much to simply step aside and hope for the best. He wanted them to be aware of what they would soon encounter. I suppose we could call his words "good fatherly advice." In any case, Moses' counsel would later come back to haunt the Hebrews. Read carefully his words of advice.

"Then it shall come about when the Lord your God brings you into the land which He swore to your fathers, Abraham, Isaac and

Jacob, to give you, great and splendid cities which you did not build, and houses full of all good things which you did not fill, and hewn cisterns which you did not dig, vineyards and olive trees which you did not plant, and you shall eat and be satisfied, then watch yourself, lest you forget the Lord who brought you from the land of Egypt, out of the house of slavery. You shall fear only the Lord your God; and you shall worship Him, and swear by His name. You shall not follow other gods, any of the gods of the peoples who surround you" (Deut. 6:10–14).

Today, we'd say, "You are going to be tempted to go along with the crowd, so watch it! You must continue to swear by one name— the name of the living God—even though you will be surrounded by people who don't!"

For the Lord your God in the midst of you is a jealous God; otherwise the anger of the Lord your God will be kindled against you, and He will wipe you off the face of the earth (Deut. 6:15).

Don't think for a moment that God doesn't care about the conduct of His chosen ones. He is jealous for our love and allegiance. Look back over Moses' words. Notice his repeated reminders of what God had done for them: cities they had not built, houses full of things they had not filled, wells they had not dug, trees they had not planted. How easy it would be for them to feel indulged! And how dangerous! In light of all those things they would soon get for nothing, he warned them against the ultimate trap: forgetting the Lord their God. Between the lines, I think he was urging them to keep on standing alone: "Don't yield to peer pressure! Maintain your distinctiveness! Be very courageous! Remember, you are unique!" Sounds a lot like the advice parents give their older teenager just before he (or she) leaves for college, doesn't it?

Four Practical Principles for Today

As I think about Moses' warnings, four principles emerge— each one leading to the next.

1. Getting something for nothing can breed irresponsibility. When a lot of things are suddenly laid in our laps, it is easy to pick up an attitude of "Who needs God?" Sort of a spoiled-child syndrome. Too many toys, too much luxury, all too easily acquired—

a breeding ground for irresponsibility. You and I have seen it happen.

2. Irresponsibility creates a careless attitude. When there is an abundance of things freely unloaded, a carelessness emerges—an inability to discern the right scale of values. "What does it matter?" or "Who really cares what I do with it?" That's the reason for the warning: "Watch yourself, lest you forget the Lord."

3. Carelessness leads to a loss of standards. Those Hebrews would soon be surrounded by a majority of people who worship other gods. If the Hebrews became careless about their spiritual standards the most natural response would be for them to embrace the same gods of the people around them. In fact, that is exactly what they did! Carelessness creates a loss of spiritual, moral, and ethical standards. That is why Moses said, "Fear only the Lord your God; and . . . worship Him."

4. A loss of standards prompts personal insecurity. Think about this one, especially. That is precisely the problem of second- and third-generation Christians. Parents, you and I forged out our theology. Many of us got saved off the street. Originally, we didn't know the Lord from a lizard. Out of the blue we were brought face to face with the claims of Christ, and we surrendered to Him. Then things changed, especially for our kids. We gave birth to a generation who have fought for nothing. They've been given virtually everything on a silver platter. Our kids don't know what it is to be on the street, spiritually. They have heard the name of Jesus all their lives. In most cases, they have never had to struggle to forge a theology of their own, so they don't really care. Watch out—it won't be long before they get picky and spoiled and even careless with spiritual things. That's when real trouble starts.

Here is your son, raised by a family who cares, in a good church, surrounded by good people who love the Lord Jesus. He's got all the breaks! Then why in the world is he on drugs? What is it that turned him off, spiritually? Why isn't he an eagle like his mom and dad? Take another look at those four principles just mentioned. The syndrome sucked him in! He's part of that irresponsibility which breeds carelessness, which in turn leads to a loss of standard and ultimately results in insecurity.

How can we stop this downward spiral syndrome? Let me suggest four mind-renewing thoughts that have certainly helped me.

They are brief yet powerful statements we can say to ourselves and ultimately pass on to our offspring.

First: "*I am responsible.*" I said that to myself so many times in the Marine Corps that I got sick of hearing myself say it! "Swindoll, *you* are responsible." Nobody was around, no parents, no wife, nobody who knew me. I had no reputation to uphold, no fear of being "found out." And so I began to renew my thought life with, "I am responsible." To this day, I still repeat those three words in my mind. With a family it works out this way: "Son, daughter, you are responsible."

Second: "*I must not forget.*" Remember Moses' counsel? Though centuries old, it is still relevant.

". . . watch yourself, lest you forget the Lord who brought you from the land of Egypt, out of the house of slavery" (Deut. 6:12).

You see, when you haven't been brought out of Egypt, when you haven't had to fight to survive, it is easy to forget God. Your kids and mine don't know a thing about Egypt. We do, but they don't. We must not forget the Lord our God. And neither can we afford to let them forget.

Third: "*I am accountable.*" I am accountable to God whether I'm in Fullerton or Asia, at the tip of South America or at the North Pole. I am accountable to my Lord.

Fourth: "*I get my standard and security from Him.*" Not from my friend, not from my business, not from my neighbors—not even from within myself. Christ is my surety. Don't be fooled by the crowd. I remember an old saying, "There's safety in numbers." Well, not always. Sometimes there's danger in numbers. Just because "everybody's doing it" doesn't mean it's either safe or right.

All this reminds me of a story I read years ago about a bright young fly who unfortunately sought safety in a crowd.

Once a spider built a beautiful web in an old house. He kept it clean and shiny so that flies would patronize it. The minute he got a "customer" he would clean up on him so the other flies would not get suspicious.

Then one day this fairly intelligent fly came buzzing by the clean spiderweb. Old man spider called out, "Come in and sit." But the fairly intelligent fly said, "No, sir. I don't see other flies in your house, and I am not going in alone!"

But presently he saw on the floor below a large crowd of flies dancing around on a piece of brown paper. He was delighted! He was not afraid if lots of flies were doing it. So he came in for a landing.

Just before he landed, a bee zoomed by, saying, "Don't land there, stupid! That's flypaper!" But the fairly intelligent fly shouted back, "Don't be silly. Those flies are dancing. There's a big crowd there. Everybody's doing it. That many flies can't be wrong!" Well, you know what happened. He died on the spot.

Some of us want to be with the crowd so badly that we end up in a mess. What does it profit a fly (or a person) if he escapes the web only to end up in the glue?[3]

It takes courage to think alone, to resist alone, to stand alone—especially when the crowd seems so safe, so right. But remember God. Keep flying high, eagle—far above the glue that snares the crowd. Up there it doesn't just seem safe and right, it *is* safe and right.

Standing Tall When Tested

14

A few years ago psychologist Ruth W. Berenda and her associates carried out an interesting experiment with teenagers designed to show how a person handled group pressure. The plan was simple. They brought groups of ten adolescents into a room for a test. Subsequently, each group of ten was instructed to raise their hands when the teacher pointed to the longest line on three separate charts. What one person in the group did not know was that nine of the others in the room had been instructed ahead of time to vote for the *second*-longest line.

Regardless of the instructions they heard, once they were all together in the group, the nine were not to vote for the longest line, but rather vote for the *next*-to-the-longest line. Here are the charts as they appeared before each group when the votes were taken.

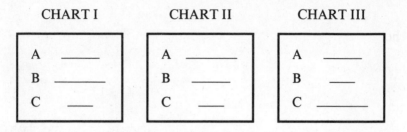

CHART I   CHART II   CHART III

The desire of the psychologists was to determine how one person reacted when completely surrounded by a large number of people who obviously stood against what was true.

> The experiment began with nine teen-agers voting for the wrong line. The stooge would typically glance around, frown in confusion, and slip his hand up with the group. The instructions were repeated and the next card was raised. Time after time, the self-conscious stooge would sit there saying a short line is longer than a long line, simply because he lacked the courage to challenge the group. This remarkable conformity occurred in about seventy-five percent of the cases, and was true of small children and high-school students as well. Berenda concluded that, "Some people had rather be president than right," which is certainly an accurate assessment.[1]

That basic test was removed from any feeling of emotion. It was simply a logical examination to see how a person handled group pressure. My point? It is one thing for peer pressure to be determined in a classroom. Things are safe under the watchful eye of a professional psychologist. It is another thing entirely when it happens to be your child or mine (or you or me!) who is surrounded by a majority that says, "The-next-to-longest line is really the longest line." The moral and ethical implications that accompany such an experiment are frightening.

I want to make a forceful statement here, but one I believe with all my heart. *If your child is not taught how to stand alone when surrounded by those who put him to the test, he won't be able to stand tall.* He or she will go through self-doubts, then uncertainty, and finally slump into complete conformity. If our kids are not given a good deal of practical help on how to handle peer pressure, chances are good they will fail when the tests come. Let me illustrate. Let's say your son has been raised in a Christian home, has gone to school in Christian schools, has run with Christian friends, and has spent all his formative years in that rather sheltered environment. To make matters more complicated, you have said little about the "real world" and done nothing to equip him for what he is sure to face. When he goes off to college he is thrust into a school that is not Christian. He is surrounded by young adults who, for the most part, are not Christians. Almost overnight, he is introduced to an environment he hardly knew existed. That is where the rubber meets the road. That is when all theory either works or goes down the tube—when he will either stand tall and model secure courage even though outnumbered or begin to waver. The test is on! That's one of the toughest assignments for moms and dads—to get our offspring ready for life's examinations without damaging their self-esteem in the process. Somehow the eaglet must learn to fly on its own, but no responsible eagle just abandons the nest, thinking, "Sure hope the little guy makes it!"

A LITTLE MORE HISTORY, PLEASE

In chapter 13 we spent time studying the theoretical warnings in Deuteronomy. Now let's go to reality. We find it in the Book of Judges. I want to show you what happened to those Hebrews who heard the great words Moses delivered as they were about to enter the Promised Land. Waiting just around the corner were the Canaanites. Why?

> And they were for testing Israel, to find out if they would obey the commandments of the Lord, which He had commanded their fathers through Moses (Judg. 3:4).

God had warned the Hebrews that the Canaanites would be all around them: "They will be there, you'll see. I'm leaving them there for one reason: a test! And when you arrive, you'll have to drive them out. If you don't, they're going to take over. Those tough-minded people are in the conquering business. They have many gods, and none of them will lead you to the true God of heaven. On the contrary, they will try to draw you into their lifestyle. Your God, Jehovah, will take you through this time of testing, but you must stand tall as I've commanded you. *Do* it." So they did—at least at the beginning. But by and by, they began to compromise.

The former president of The Navigators, Lorne Sanny, made an interesting comment to me several years ago. He said, "If I could wrap up all of my father's counsel into one sentence, it would be four words, 'Get with it, son.'" That's not bad counsel, is it? That's what God said to Israel. "All right, get with it, sons. When you go into the land, take it. Stand alone. If you don't, you'll lose."

Let's go back to the first chapter of Judges and take a look at the situation when the Hebrews encountered the Canaanites. Three things characterized their lives when they moved from theory into reality.

1.   They were alone and uncertain. The Israelites felt just like you feel when you face your first day on a new job, or when you come to the first day on the campus and you're a greenhorn freshman, or your first day in boot camp. Another example might be the way you feel when you first move out on your own and you discover you are the only one in your apartment complex who has strong moral convictions.

I once heard of a large apartment house in a metropolitan area where the residents were expected to participate in their favorite game. It came at the close of their weekly party when all the gals tossed their apartment keys out into a big pile near the swimming pool. All the guys then rushed to the pile and grabbed a key. Obviously, each guy would then spend the night with the girl whose key he had retrieved. In a case like that, either you stand alone or you don't. By the way, that kind of thing is not uncommon—and it doesn't occur just in California!

The Hebrews were alone and they were uncertain.

> Then Judah said to Simeon his brother, "Come up with me into the territory allotted me, that we may fight against the Canaanites; and I in turn will go with you into the territory allotted you" (Judg. 1:3).

Although God was with them, their leaders were dead and they really felt alone. They didn't know which direction to go. There was no manual to follow, so they decided to slug it out in teams.

The Lord had simply told them, "When you get into the land, drive them out." They got into the land, but then they began to wonder, *Joshua's dead. Moses is dead. Wonder where we go from here?*

By the way, that is often the way your kiddos feel. They can't admit it in so many words, but that's how they feel. You are not there (and they don't want you there!). Yet in their hearts, they wonder, *To whom do I turn now?* They feel insecure and uncertain. And to make matters more complicated, the world *feeds* on uncertainty and aloneness. The majority preys on the unsuspecting. When in doubt, conformity is always ready to be called into action! The insecure will do anything to be a part of the group, to break that feeling of loneliness or isolation.

2. Those Hebrews were inexperienced and vulnerable. They had not seen firsthand God's mighty works in Egypt and the wilderness. The generation Moses and Joshua had addressed had died off.

> And all that generation also were gathered to their fathers; and there arose another generation after them who did not know the Lord, nor yet the work which He had done for Israel (Judg. 2:10).

How about that? The generation of combat troops who sat at Moses' feet and fought alongside Joshua, those veterans who had been involved in the victories that brought them into the land of Canaan were now gone from the scene. In their place there emerged the next generation. Two things were true of those new folks: they didn't know the Lord, and they didn't know what He had done in the previous years. They lacked the knowledge of what brought them there; they had no awareness of what their liberty had really cost!

Something massive is lost when a nation loses its historical and spiritual heritage. If for no other purpose, that alone is reason enough for us to be good students of history. It builds deep roots into our character to know the price others paid for what we enjoy, to be aware of the things God did on behalf of our parents and our grandparents.

We must never forget the importance of a historical and spiritual heritage in the training of our children. How does one go about such training? It's simple. Let them know what God has done in your life. And rehearse before them the significant battles of the past! Don't hesitate telling them what God did. If you fail to do that, how will they ever know?

I didn't know much about my own father's spiritual condition for the longest time. I'm honest—I'd lived with my dad for years. In fact, after my mother died, he moved in with us out here in California and stayed with us for several years. Yet, I still didn't know where he stood spiritually. Late one evening, years ago, I could wait no longer to find out.

I slipped into his room and said, "Dad, I want to talk to you about something that is very important. I want to talk to you about your relationship with the Lord. I have never heard you tell how you came to know Christ." Then I came right out and asked him, "Do you know the Lord?" That's when he first described to me what God had done in his life. Beginning with his boyhood, I journeyed with him through his spiritual pilgrimage as he reviewed his experiences at various stages of his life. Now there I was, a man more then forty years old, listening to my dad, and I was choking back tears of delight as he related his story to me. What a great time we had together that evening. I received full assurance of his salvation. What a relief! And on top of that, I gained fresh courage to soar even higher.

That's what can happen in the lives of your kids when they become acquainted with the victories you've experienced. They want to hear how you came to know the Lord. And they need to hear what God has done in your life. It brings them special delight and it gives them extra courage. And by the way, *don't leave out the failures.* Don't paint some flawless picture as though you qualify to sit for a modern-day portrait of Saint Francis of Assissi. (They know better than that!) Say to them, "when I got to that place in my life, I blew it! But let me tell you what God did in spite of that." Our kids can also learn from our failures.

What I have been illustrating here are the kinds of things that make up one's spiritual heritage. And that is precisely what those ancient Hebrews failed to relate to the next generation. They didn't do their homework. Deuteronomy 6 says, in effect, "Tell your kids." But the parents died and the kids didn't even know the Lord. Maybe they were too busy fighting battles. That can happen, can't it? No wonder the new generation was so vulnerable! They had never gone to battle. They didn't know how to handle life in the trenches. They were not hardened, made tough by enduring the rigors of war. They had never experienced opposition firsthand. So there they stood, not knowing the Lord, not knowing their history, and absolutely inexperienced in warfare.

It's a foolish, apathetic mistake to pamper and indulge our younger generation. Instead, we need to provide them with techniques for doing battle. Let's take a quick peek at Proverbs 29.

> The rod and reproof give wisdom, but a child who gets his own way brings shame to his mother (v. 15).

The marginal reference in my New American Standard Bible gives "But a child *left to himself*" as a more literal translation for "who gets his own way." Interestingly, the Hebrew text uses just the word for *left* and leaves it at that. "But a child *left* brings shame to his mother." Meaning what? Left in his room? No. It suggests "left in the same condition in which he was born." A child left without training will bring shame to his mother.

You might be engaged in spiritual activities day after day, even teaching Bible classes on a regular basis. You can be a faithful preacher, an evangelist, a Christian worker, a solid Christian businessman, and still omit the training of those little ones. And guess what? Chances are good they will grow up lacking the things that made you great. They *must* have your help.

Because those ancient Hebrews didn't have help from their parents, they didn't know how to handle hand-to-hand combat— not just physically, but especially spiritually and emotionally. In today's terms, they were spiritual wimps, ready to be picked off like sitting ducks.

Thus far we have considered two things that characterized the lives of the Hebrews as they encountered the Canaanites. They were alone and uncertain. And they were inexperienced and vulnerable. But there's a third characteristic we must not overlook.

3.   They were surrounded and outnumbered.

> These nations are: the five lords of the Philistines and all the Canaanites and the Sidonians and the Hivites who lived in Mount Lebanon, from Mount Baal-hermon as far as Lebo-hamath. And they were for testing Israel, to find out if they would obey the commandments of the Lord, which He had commanded their

fathers through Moses. And the sons of Israel lived among the Canaanites, the Hittites, the Amorites, the Perizzites, the Hivites, and the Jebusites (Judg. 3:3–5).

You're probably thinking, *Who in the world were all those "ites"? Why mention them?* They were the Canaanites, the various tribes poised for battle—tough-minded heathen who weren't about to give up their territory without a fight.

If you ever want an eye-opening experience, do a little study on the Canaanites. You will find, to your amazement, that pornography originated with them. You will also find that idolatry reached its most debasing level among the Canaanites. And you will find that it wasn't uncommon for the social diseases to devastate those ancient communities. One archaeologist writes this:

> New vistas of knowledge of Canaanite cults and their degrading character and debilitating effect have been opened up by the discovery of the Ras Shamra religious epic literature. . . . These cults were utterly immoral, effete, and corrupt, dangerously contaminating. . . .[2]

Those words describe the neighborhood the Hebrews moved into! Today, it would be like moving from a solid, sheltered home in Montana or Nebraska to live in downtown Los Angeles, San Francisco, New York, or Miami, surrounded by the dangerous, sleazy scenes that are so common among those sidewalk jungles. Day in, day out, day in, day out, that's where the Hebrew kids played. That's where they lived and moved and chose their circle of friends. No wonder God said, "Be distinct! Stand tall when tested by the Canaanites! If you don't, they'll ruin you."

And so, how do the Israelites react? Again, there are three reactions.

First of all, there was lack of total obedience. In Deuteronomy 7:1–2, we read where the Lord had in essence said, "Don't let any of them live. Annihilate them." Well, they did that for a while, and they did a pretty good job of fighting. They were battling under Judah and under various tribes. But finally, when the going got tough and the battles got long, they backed off and let the enemy live.

Now the Lord was with Judah, and they took possession of the hill country; but they could not drive out the inhabitants of the valley because they had iron chariots (Judg. 1:19).

Very interesting. I cannot help but wonder: *They could not or they would not?* You see, they came up against a tough group of Canaanites. And so their thinking probably went something like: *Hey, they're way down in the valley. What does it really matter? They won't bother anybody down there.* What a subtle inroad of limited courage! Someone once wrote, "Sow a thought, reap an act. Sow an act, reap a habit. Sow a habit, reap your character. Sow your character, reap your destiny." In the valley of the Canaanite country those Israelites sowed a thought: *Aw, let's not get so fanatical about this. A few Canaanites won't hurt. God's on our side.* So they left the door open. Notice how others followed suit. It's an incredible example of erosion. One compromise led to another, until what had begun as a tiny hole in the dike had become a deadly rupture.

But the sons of Benjamin did not drive out the Jebusites who lived in Jerusalem; so the Jebusites have lived with the sons of Benjamin in Jerusalem to this day (Judg. 1:21).

And further . . .

But Manasseh did not take possession of Beth-shean and its villages, or Taanach and its villages, or the inhabitants of Dor and its villages, or the inhabitants of Ibleam and its villages, or the inhabitants of Megiddo and its villages; so the Canaanites persisted in living in that land (v. 27).

Again and again (vv. 28–32), right down the line we find that God's people failed to destroy the inhabitants of the land.
Finally:

Naphtali did not drive out the inhabitants of Beth-shemesh, or the inhabitants of Beth-anath, but lived among the Canaanites, the inhabitants of the land; and the inhabitants of Beth-shemesh and Beth-anath became forced labor for them (v. 33).

Did you catch that? The enemy is no longer down in the valley. Hebrews and Canaanites are now *living* together. The Hebrews started thinking, *Why sweat it? We'll just make these people serve us. We'll use them as forced labor. What harm can that do? No sense wasting all that manpower.* But the wicked and immoral ways of the conquered Canaanites eventually conquered their captors.

Got the picture? Are you seeing the analogy, my eagle friend? Standing tall when tested takes courage—constant, relentless, never-give-up courage! You can be sure that the old flesh will fight for its arousal and satisfaction. All it takes is a little rationalization—just a little. Just look the other way. Just shrug it off. Don't sweat it. And before long you have a rattlesnake in your sleeping bag.

After a few fast-moving years, that little tolerance of rebellion in your home leads to a child you can no longer handle. And by the time he reaches his teen years, he rules the place. If you compromise, you will ultimately have to pay the fiddler. The way of the transgressor is indeed hard!

What exactly happened? Three things, actually.

First, remember, *they lacked total obedience.* They rationalized around it; they mentally imagined obedience, but they acted out compromise.

Second, they suffered a loss of spiritual distinctiveness. Because they lacked total obedience, they decided to leave the Canaanites in the valley. Instead of destroying them, the Hebrews used the Canaanites as forced labor, but eventually the Israelites themselves bowed down to the Canaanite gods.

> Then the sons of Israel did evil in the sight of the Lord, and served the Baals, and they forsook the Lord, the God of their fathers, who had brought them out of the land of Egypt, and followed other gods from among the gods of the peoples who were around them, and bowed themselves down to them; thus they provoked the Lord to anger (Judg. 2:10–12).

Can you believe it? They forsook the Lord and served Baal and the Ashtaroth. Frankly, in my study of Ashtaroth, I discovered there isn't much I would be free to discuss in this book about the subject. It includes some of the most debasing, obscene things you can imagine. In fact, one writer, although apparently an unbeliever, wrote, "The author now begs freedom from more de-

tail." You seldom come across an author who says that. He chose
not to add any more descriptive explanations concerning the worship of Ashtaroth. And yet those Hebrews bowed down and
served that idol. How could they? Why did they? The answer can
be given in one word: *Compromise.* Through compromise their
spiritual distinctiveness was eroded.

The third Israelite reaction was a looseness of marital ties.

> And they took their daughters for themselves as wives, and gave
> their own daughters to their sons, and served their gods (Judg. 3:6).

Never fails, does it? Let a nation drift morally and before long the
same values or lack of values will move right into the home.
The Israelites chose immoral friends, and before long their marital ties were loosened.

> And the sons of Israel did what was evil in the sight of the Lord,
> and forgot the Lord their God, and served the Baals and the
> Asheroth (v. 7).

Sow the wind and, for sure, you'll reap the whirlwind. Eagles may
be strong birds, but when the wind velocity gets fierce enough, it
takes an enormous amount of strength to survive. Only the ultra-
powerful can make it through the whirlwind.

Evangelist Billy Graham, while speaking to a packed house
at the Urbana '84 Student Missions Convention in Illinois, addressed the importance of Christians being people of great inner
strength.

> Not long ago *Newsweek* magazine reported on what it called
> the new wave of mountain men. It's estimated that there are some
> sixty thousand serious mountain climbers in the United States.
> But in the upper echelon of serious climbers is a small elite group
> known as "hard men." For them climbing mountains and scaling
> sheer rock faces is a way of life. In many cases, climbing is a part
> of their whole commitment to life. And their ultimate experience
> is called free soloing: climbing with no equipment and no safety
> ropes.
>
> John Baker is considered by many to be the best of the hard
> men. He has free-soloed some of the most difficult rock faces in
> the United States with no safety rope and no climbing equipment

of any kind. His skill has not come easily. It has been acquired through commitment, dedication and training. His wife says she can't believe his dedication. When John isn't climbing, he's often to be found in his California home hanging by his fingertips to strengthen his arms and hands.

Where are the hard men and women for Jesus? Where are those who will bring all their energies to bear for the sake of Christ? That's the kind of people it's going to take to spread the gospel around the world in these closing years of the twentieth century.[3]

THREE ENCOURAGEMENTS FOR STANDING TALL

Before closing this chapter allow me to offer three suggestions for standing tall.

First: *Standing tall starts with the way we think.* It has to do with the *mind.* As I've said so often, being a person of inner strength is really a mental factor: excellence starts in the mind. It has to do with the way we think about God, ourselves, and others. Then it grows into the way we think about business, the way we think about dating, the way we think about marriage and the family, the way we think about the system that is designed to destroy faith and bring us down to a lower standard.

Second: *Standing tall calls for strong discipline.* This has to do with the *will.* Disciplining the eyes, the ears, the hands, the feet. Keeping moral tabs on ourselves, refusing to let down the standards. People of strength know how to turn right thinking into action—even when insistent feelings don't agree.

Third: *Standing tall limits your choice of personal friends.* This has to do with *relationships.* What appears harmless can prove to be dangerous. Perhaps this is as important as the other two factors combined. Cultivate wrong friendships and you're a goner. This is why we are warned not to be deceived regarding the danger of wrong associations. Without realizing it, we could be playing with fire. That is exactly how the ancient Hebrews met their Waterloo.

Several weeks ago, a personal friend of mine told me a true story that illustrates so vividly the reality of what I've been saying all the way through this chapter.

Two young women from Southern California spent the day doing some last-minute Christmas shopping in Tijuana, a

Mexican border town several miles below San Diego. After a successful day of bargain hunting, they returned to their car. One of the ladies glanced down in the gutter and noticed something moving, sort of squirming, as if in pain. As they bent down and looked closer, the two women saw what appeared to be a dog—a tiny Chihuahua—struggling for its life. It was breathing heavily, shivering, and barely able to move. Their hearts went out to the pathetic little animal. Their compassion wouldn't let them drive off and leave it there to die.

They decided to take it home with them and do their best to nurse it back to health. Afraid of being stopped and having the little creature detected by border patrol officers, they carefully placed it on some papers among their packages in the trunk of their car. No problem. Within minutes they were back in California and only a couple of hours from home. One of the women held the sick little Chihuahua the rest of the way home.

As they pulled up in front of one gal's home, they decided she would be the one to keep the little orphan through the night and do everything she could to help it regain strength. She tried feeding it some of her food, but it wouldn't eat. She patted it, talked to it, cuddled it, and finally wrapped it in a small blanket and placed it beneath the covers on her bed to sleep beside her all through the night. She kept feeling it to make sure it was okay.

By early the next morning she could see it was not doing at all well. Before dawn she decided to take it to an emergency animal clinic nearby. Handing the weakened animal to the doctor on duty, she began to describe all the things she had done to help the tiny creature.

He quickly interrupted her and asked, "Where did you *get* this animal?"

For fear of being reprimanded for bringing an animal across the border, she told him that she was keeping it for a friend who had found it.

"I'm not letting you leave," he insisted sternly, "until you tell me where you got this thing."

She said, "We were shopping in Tijuana and found this little Chihuahua in the gutter near our car. Our hearts went out to it when . . ."

"This is no Chihuahua, young lady. What you brought home with you is a rabid Mexican river rat!"

What appeared to be harmless to these two young women proved to be extremely dangerous. The same is true of relationships—peer pressure can be downright deadly. Standing tall when testing comes (and teaching our young to do the same) reflects the way we think about God, ourselves, and others. It isn't easy. It takes strong discipline to maintain high, personal standards and to avoid undesirable friendships. But most of all it takes courage. Without courage we can forget about soaring above mediocrity.

Standing Firm When Discouraged

15

Even eagle types have down days—blue days; dark and dismal days; the kind of days my keen-thinking friend, the late Joe Bayly, once portrayed so vividly in his "Psalm in a Hotel Room."

> I'm alone Lord
> alone
> a thousand miles from home.
> There's no one here who knows my name
> except the clerk
> and he spelled it wrong
> no one to eat dinner with
> laugh at my jokes
> listen to my gripes
> be happy with me about what happened today
> and say that's great.
> No one cares.
> There's just this lousy bed

expect to cash in on the benefits of His instruction. So you see, application is the essential link between instruction and change.

Imagine, if you will, that you work for a company whose president found it necessary to travel out of the country and spend an extended period of time abroad. So he says to you and the other trusted employees, "Look, I'm going to leave. And while I'm gone, I want you to pay close attention to the business. You manage things while I'm away. I will write you regularly. When I do, I will instruct you in what you should do from now until I return from this trip." Everyone agrees. He leaves and stays gone for a couple of years. During that time he writes often, communicating his desires and concerns. Finally he returns. He walks up to the front door of the company and immediately discovers everything is in a mess—weeds flourishing in the flower beds, windows broken across the front of the building, the gal at the front desk dozing, loud music roaring from several offices, two or three people engaged in horseplay in the back room. Instead of making a profit, the business has suffered a great loss. Without hesitation he calls everyone together and with a frown asks, "What happened? Didn't you get my letters?" You say, "Oh, yeah, sure. We got all your letters. We've even bound them in a book. And some of us have memorized them. In fact, we have 'letter study' every Sunday. You know, those were really great letters." I think the president would then ask, "But what did you *do* about my instructions? And, no doubt, the employees would respond, "Do? Well, nothing. But we read every one!"

In the very same way, God has sent us His instruction. He has preserved every word of it in a Book, the Bible. It's all there, just as He communicated it to us. When He returns for His own, He is not going to ask us how much we memorized or how often we met for study. No, He will want to know, "What did you *do* about my instructions?" He promises us hope—relief from discouragement. Yes, it's available. And we can actually stand firm through discouraging times but only if we apply His instructions.

Hard as it may be for you to believe, you will be able to walk right through those "gray slush" days with confidence. The One who gives perseverance and encouragement will escort you through the down days, never leaving you in the lurch. Discouragement may be awful, but it is not terminal. You will soar again.

GUIDELINES FOR HANDLING DISCOURAGEMENT

From this nugget of truth in Romans 15, let's return to the Old Testament Book of Judges for a brief look at the life of a man you may have never even heard of. He was an ancient eagle type named Gideon. Before meeting him, however, it will help if we first read the key verse of the Book of Judges. It is the very last statement in the book and succinctly reveals why Judges is a record of defeat and failure.

> In those days there was no king in Israel; everyone did what was right in his own eyes (Judg. 21:25).

The first half of the verse explains the latter. There was no monarch in charge, no one to give direction or set the pace, no one to model truth or instruct the people in righteousness. The result was predictable: "Everyone did what was right in his own eyes." "Do your own thing" is not some modern motto. It began in the days of the judges. They were adrift in a sea of shifting feelings and carnal impulses. Each person did what felt good. And so, in light of that, we should not be surprised to read these words earlier in the book: "The sons of Israel did what was evil in the sight of the Lord" (Judg. 6:1). When folks are free to choose the path of least resistance, wrongdoing becomes common-place—it's the direction most choose to go.

Historical Situation

Let's spend a few moments reconstructing the historical scene. We learned in my previous chapter that when the Israelites came into the land of Canaan, they had a chance to drive out all the enemies, as God had commanded; but they compromised. In the final analysis they failed to do that. They left some Canaan-ites in the valley, and that number began to grow. When word of this compromise passed to another tribe of Israel, they followed suit and also left another pocket of idolators in another part of the Promised Land. And it wasn't long before some of the hea-then tribes actually outnumbered the Hebrews. Finally, the tail wagged the dog. The Israelites began to serve the Canaanites' gods. Through intermingling of lifestyle and intermarriage, it soon reached a point where it was hard to tell an Israelite from a Canaanite. By failing to stand courageously, God's chosen people lost their distinctiveness as well as their identity.

But the tragic part of the story is that the consequences of disobedience do not decrease; they intensify. Look for yourself:

> And the power of Midian prevailed against Israel. Because of Midian the sons of Israel made for themselves the dens which were in the mountains and the caves and the strongholds (Judg. 6:2).

In other words, they were forced to live like animals. They had *no homes.* Their "gray slush" days were now coming in spades. Think of the discouragement!

> For it was when Israel had sown, that the Midianites would come up with the Amalekites and the sons of the east and go against them. So they would camp against them and destroy the produce of the earth as far as Gaza, and leave no sustenance in Israel as well as no sheep, ox, or donkey (Judg. 6:3–4).

How demoralizing! Not only were the Israelites stripped of their homes, but they had *no peace* either. When they planted crops to grow food for their families, the Midianites, along with the Amalekites, invaded. They mercilessly destroyed the crops after taking just enough produce for themselves. So the Israelites began to starve. On top of all their other troubles, now they had *no sustenance.*

> For they would come up with their livestock and their tents, they would come in like locusts for number, both they and their camels were innumerable; and they came into the land to devastate it (v. 5).

Try to imagine such a scene. If you've never planted and then lost what you planted, you don't know how discouraging that could be. I, personally, have the gift of killing whatever is green! Whatever I try to plant dies—and I mean fast! Believe it or not, I tried no less than nine different times to plant grass in our front yard. Nine times! I would lie awake at night wondering what demons were out there in the soil stealing those tiny blades of grass from us. I began to feel like an Israelite being invaded by the

Midianites and the Amalekites. But we persevered to the end. Which, being translated, means that I hired a gardener. When I got *my* hands out of the soil, presto! Instant green. He tactfully asked me to look but not touch.

Now in the case of the Hebrews, the reason their crops didn't grow was clear: the enemy devastated their land! Wholesale discouragement swept over everyone: "Israel was brought very low." In fact, one translation says, "Israel was impoverished (MLB)." How true! They had no homes. They had no food. They had no belongings they could claim as their own. They were waist deep in "gray slush" discouragement. People may have talked of those days when courageous eagles once flew, but now none could be seen in the sky. So much for the historical scene.

Spiritual Analogy

Picture for a moment the barrenness and bleakness that happens in a life when compromise occurs. It doesn't come immediately. At first it's fun to run with the wrong crowd. There's some zip, a little excitement; there's a measure of thrill and pizzazz in being a part of the in-group. But inevitably the fleshly investment starts to yield its carnal dividends. And when that happens you suffer as you've never suffered before. At first, it may have seemed a little stimulating for the Hebrews to worship the demonic gods of Amalek and Midian. Finally, however, those idols vomited out tragic consequences upon Israel. So much so that Israel was forced to live in dens like wild animals, discouraged and impoverished. These sad words describe their misery: "Israel was brought very low because of Midian . . ." (Judg. 6:6).

Perhaps the words *"very low"* paint a picture of bleakness that describes you at this very moment. You have ignored God's warnings and pushed your strong convictions aside as you associated with the wrong crowd. But now you are at the end of your rope. You're discouraged. You have failed miserably. And, of all things, you're seeing your life pass in review as you read about the bleak barrenness of this ancient nation. You're thinking, *What a terrible way to live!*

All of us have spent time in that miserable camp called Reaping What Was Sown. En route, there's enough pleasure to make it seem like fun, but when it's all said and done, it's downright awful. There is no discouragement like the discouragement that comes from self-generated wrongdoing. Enduring the consequences of one's own irresponsibility creates feelings of grief and discouragement that defy description. No one ever said it better than F. B. Meyer:

> This is the bitterest of all—to know that suffering need not have been; that it has resulted from indiscretion and inconsistency; that it is the harvest of one's own sowing; that the vulture which feeds on the vitals is a nestling of one's own rearing. Ah me! This is pain! There is an inevitable Nemesis in life. The laws of the heart and home, of the soul and human life, cannot be violated with impunity. Sin may be forgiven; the fire of penalty may be changed into the fire of trial: the love of God may seem nearer and dearer than ever and yet there is the awful pressure of pain; the trembling heart; the failing of eyes and pining of soul; the harp on the willows; the refusal of the lip to sing the Lord's song.[2]

Practical Correction

That's enough about the problem. What we really need are specific suggestions that get us back on track. I find no less than five such guidelines woven through the biblical narrative concerning the Israelites and the Midianites.

1.   <u>Openly acknowledge what caused your condition.</u>

> So Israel was brought very low because of Midian, and the sons of Israel cried to the Lord.
> Now it came about when the sons of Israel cried to the Lord on account of Midian, that the Lord sent a prophet to the sons of Israel, and he said to them, "Thus says the Lord, the God of Israel, 'It was I who brought you up from Egypt, and brought you out from the house of slavery. And I delivered you from the hands of the Egyptians and from the hands of all your oppressors, and dispossessed them before you and gave you their land, and I said to you, "I am the Lord your God; you shall not fear the gods of the Amorites in whose land you live. But you have not obeyed Me""" (Judg. 6:6–10).

That's what I call *direct counsel*. But, you'll notice, it comes on the heels of the Israelites' cry for help. God never holds back when we openly acknowledge the whole truth of our condition. And doing that, by the way, is a mark of excellence. Hold nothing back! Even though it may be painful, total honesty is important. If you are discouraged because of compromise, a truthful acknowledgment of your condition is the place to begin.

Openly admit that you have failed to stand alone as a true child of God and therefore you have begun to live like a heathen Midianite. The problem is you weren't built to live that way. As we have seen throughout the pages of this book, you were meant to soar, not to slump and stumble through life. You have allowed someone else to call your cadence. You're marching out of step with your Instructor. And the Lord speaks directly: "You have not obeyed Me."

What stands out in my mind, though, is the swift and open fashion with which our God deals with wrong. Our problem is that we usually wait much too long to acknowledge our need and call for help.

I love the story that describes Peter when he stepped out of the boat onto the water. As he was walking toward the Lord on the stormy sea (what an incredible experience), he suddenly looked around and was seized with fear. Scripture says, "Beginning to sink, he cried. . . ." Did you get that? *"Beginning* to sink, he cried out." That provides a perfect reminder for what we must do when we find ourselves sinking. Don't wait to cry out. Yell "HELP!" fast.

Are you ready for some superencouraging news? When we openly acknowledge our condition before our God, He won't reject us. Nor will He put us on probation and watch us squirm. On the contrary, we'll find the Lord to be explicitly interested and compassionate, quick to forgive. I find that wonderfully inviting.

And now, back to the story. We're about to meet Gideon:

> And the angel of the Lord appeared to him and said to him, "The Lord is with you, O valiant warrior." Then Gideon said to him, "Oh my lord, if the Lord is with us, why then has all this happened to us? And where are all His miracles which our fathers told us about, saying, 'Did not the Lord bring us up from Egypt?' But now the Lord has abandoned us and given us into the hand of Midian" (vv. 12–13).

While Gideon is evaluating the situation, he is confused. So he says, "Where's the Lord in all of this?" Unlike those around him, his own personal walk with the Lord has been consistent. But he has suffered because the great majority of those around him have not lived pleasing lives before the Lord. Now he's wrestling with doubts. *How much is the Lord really with us?* he wonders. *Has He abandoned us?*

Look at the Lord's answer:

> And the Lord looked at him and said, "Go in this your strength and deliver Israel from the hand of Midian. Have I not sent you?" And he said to Him, "O Lord, how shall I deliver Israel? Behold, my family is the least in Manasseh, and I am the youngest in my father's house." But the Lord said to him, "Surely I will be with you, and you shall defeat Midian as one man" (vv. 14–16).

What confidence-building words! In effect He was saying, "You'll stand firm, Gideon, 'as one man.'" (Never doubt the impact of one strong individual.) And when Gideon was convinced that what he heard came from the Lord, he built an altar.

> Then Gideon built an altar there to the Lord and named it The Lord is Peace. To this day it is still in Ophrah of the Abiezrites (v. 24).

This provides us with the second guideline.

2. Focus directly on the Lord, not on the odds against you. As I sit here today writing these words about standing firm when discouraged, I realize some will think, *Oh, you don't have any idea of the odds that are against me, Chuck. Where I work . . . where I go to school . . . in my particular profession it's filled with skeptics and cynics—I mean, you can't believe the odds against me!* I hear you, but quite frankly, my answer stands. Everything depends on where your focus is. You must discipline yourself to focus directly on the Lord, not on those odds!

At first all Gideon could see were odds. Finally, he heard the Lord's word, "Have I not sent you?" Then Gideon says, "I'm the youngest." He felt incapable. He felt as if he were not the man to do the job. And the Lord said, "Look, I'll be with you. Even though you're one man, you'll do it." And He promised him, "Peace to you, do not fear; you shall not die." How comforting!

Get this straight and never forget it: You will not stand alone when outnumbered or stand tall when tested or stand firm when discouraged if your focus remains on the odds. Your eyes must be trained on the Lord.

It's helpful for me to remember that our eyes are focused on one of four places at all times: on our *circumstance,* on *others,* on *ourself,* or on *the Lord.* If they focus on any one of the first three and not on the Lord, we will drift and ultimately fail. It's only a matter of time. It took awhile, but Gideon finally got his eyes focused on the Lord.

While speaking last week with one of the foremost authorities on eagles, I learned a fact nothing short of fascinating. An eagle's eyes are amazingly keen. It has an unbelievable ability to focus on specific objects that are vast distances away. Remember, as I mentioned in chapter 5, it's not uncommon for these phenomenal birds to spot small fish in a lake miles away.

My point is obvious: If we are hoping to develop eaglelike qualities in our commitment to excellence, we must cultivate a keen focus on the Lord, not on the odds.

The next time we find our friend Gideon, he is all alone, outnumbered, opposed—but definitely *not* discouraged.

> Then all the Midianites and the Amalekites and the sons of the east assembled themselves; and they crossed over and camped in the valley of Jezreel. So the Spirit of the Lord came upon Gideon; and he blew a trumpet, and the Abiezerites were called together to follow him. And he sent messengers throughout Manasseh, and they also were called together to follow him; and he sent messengers to Asher, Zebulun, and Naphtali, and they came up to meet them (vv. 33–35).

What's happening? Gideon is gathering a following. He stood alone. And the Lord had said, in effect, "You stand alone, I'll take care of the odds." Gideon did just that. By the use of a trumpet, he made it known on which side he stood.

3. Declare your allegiance publicly. Somehow that trumpet blast announced something significant to the people in those days. I don't fully understand how they could interpret what it meant. But they interpreted it to mean, "That man is the one to follow." God used the blowing of that trumpet to call a group to follow Him. When Gideon declared his allegiance

publicly, God honored his courage. And others fell in rank behind him.

Have you made it known to others where you stand spiritually? I'm not suggesting a trumpet, but I am suggesting a clarion communication of your allegiance to Christ as Lord.

You may still be single and interested in discovering God's partner for your life. Have you compromised morally, or have you made it clear where you stand? If you have compromised, that explains why you're struggling with such feelings of discouragement. Perhaps not one person you are dating knows where you stand spiritually. If that is true, no wonder you're having such a battle in your intimate life! You have not declared your allegiance. Until you do, you will not stand strong and stable and secure. Don't be afraid to blow the trumpet of your testimony. It is amazing what occurs when you do.

A student on a college campus or a soldier in the military who declares his faith in Jesus Christ is used of God to be a leader for others to rally around. It has also been my observation that those who fail to take a stand are intimidated until they do. But as soon as a stand is taken, it is just beautiful how it disarms the enemy.

The remarkable story of Jim Vaus is such an account. On one occasion years ago, I heard Jim tell about the time he was secretly entangled with the Mickey Cohen gang. What made that rather interesting is that at the same time Jim was also employed by the Los Angeles Police Department. Fun, huh? During that time the Lord brought Jim Vaus to Himself. It occurred during the 1949 Billy Graham Crusade in Los Angeles. And the conversion was trumpeted across the pages of the newspaper, since Vaus was a fairly notorious individual.

When Jim's allegiance to Christ was declared, naturally the Mafia heard about it. The new convert was then faced with a decision. I will never forget his words, which went something like this: "I was in my home shortly after I had given my testimony at a Billy Graham Crusade. I'd turned the lights out in one room after another. Suddenly, I stopped and looked out in my driveway as two long, black limousines pulled up—very familiar cars." Knowing full well that the mission of those inside the cars was to kill him, Jim prayed, "Lord, my life is in Your hands. I trust You right now." He opened the front door and walked right out in the driveway—no doubt a surprise to the occupants of the limousines. Immediately the doors on both vehicles swung open and several men in three-piece suits stepped out. They stood in a group around Jim as he told them calmly yet directly, "I have trusted Jesus Christ and Him only as my Lord and my Savior. And I can no longer work with you." God marvelously protected him from harm and preserved his life. Jim stood alone, and he stood firm. He didn't hide his faith or deny his Lord. When he declared his allegiance at that threatening moment, God changed the gang's plan to kill him. As his heart pounded in his throat, Jim watched the men return to the limousines and drive away.

This reminds me of one of the greatest promises in all the Proverbs: "When a man's ways are pleasing to the Lord, He makes even his enemies to be at peace with him" (Prov. 16:7).

I have seen that happen in a Marine Corps barracks. I've seen it happen on a college campus. I've seen it happen in a business office. I've seen it happen in a medical group. I've seen it happen in a neighborhood. When you declare your allegiance to Him, God does something wonderful in the lives of others around you.

The story of Gideon continues with an intriguing plot. Read it carefully so that you don't miss the way God whittles down the number of people who will fight with Gideon. It's amazing!

> And the Lord said to Gideon, "The people who are with you are too many for Me to give Midian into their hands, lest Israel become boastful, saying, 'My own power has delivered me.' Now therefore come, proclaim in the hearing of the people, saying, 'Whoever is afraid and trembling, let him return and depart from Mount Gilead.'" So 22,000 people returned, but 10,000 remained (Judg. 7:2–3).

That tells you how thrilled most of the Israelites were about fighting. As soon as they had a chance, they split—22,000 of them! It also tells you how many people had begun to follow Gideon, at least 32,000. He originally had 32,000 people on his heels following him, but now it's down to 10,000. But God isn't through. He always works out a way to keep us trusting Him, doesn't He?

> Then the Lord said to Gideon, "The people are still too many; bring them down to the water and I will test them for you there. Therefore it shall be that he of whom I say to you, 'This one shall

go with you,' he shall go with you; but everyone of whom I say to you, 'This one shall not go with you,' he shall not go." So he brought the people down to the water. And the Lord said to Gideon, "You shall separate everyone who laps the water with his tongue, as a dog laps, as well as everyone who kneels to drink." Now the number of those who lapped, putting their hand to their mouth, was 300 men; but all the rest of the people kneeled to drink water. And the Lord said to Gideon, "I will deliver you with the 300 men who lapped and will give the Midianites into your hands; so let all the other people go, each man to his home" (vv. 4–7).

4. Remember that God prefers to work through a remnant. God does His best work, it seems, when those who serve Him are fewer than those against Him. The twelve disciples who walked with Christ, for instance, formed a remnant. People who change a campus are invariably not the majority, but a remnant. Those on the ball team who stand firm in their testimony are fewer than those who don't. The same is true in God's world mission program. The missionaries are always fewer in number than those being reached. God prefers to work in that unusual circumstance, and that is exactly what happened in Gideon's case.

These few fighting eagle types became courageous, devoted to God, and absolutely invincible. It was only a matter of time before the Midianites fell into their hands.

Now the Midianites and the Amalekites and all the sons of the east were lying in the valley as numerous as locusts; and their camels were without number, as numerous as the sand on the sea-shore. When Gideon came, behold, a man was relating a dream to his friend. And he said, "Behold, I had a dream; a loaf of barley bread was tumbling into the camp of Midian, and it came to the tent and struck it so that it fell, and turned it upside down so that the tent lay flat." And his friend answered and said, "This is nothing less than the sword of Gideon the son of Joash, a man of Israel; God has given Midian and all the camp into his hand" (vv. 12–14).

Gideon was simply listening to a fellow tell his dream, but look what happened:

> And it came about when Gideon heard the account of the dream and its interpretation, that he bowed in worship . . . (v. 15).

Suddenly Gideon realized, "God *is* working!" And at that moment, he paused to worship. He communed with his God. He "practiced the presence of God," as the old Puritans would say.

As a result of this strange strategy, God used Gideon to turn the tide. He won the battle. He led God's people to victory. Now, for the first time since many could remember, they had homes, they had crops, they had camels and horses. Finally, the Israelites had begun to walk in prosperity. Unlike before, when they had not fought for victory, the Israelites were now humble and grateful. In fact, they invited Gideon to be their leader.

> Then the men of Israel said to Gideon, "Rule over us, both you and your son, also your son's son, for you have delivered us from the hand of Midian." But Gideon said to them, "I will not rule over you, nor shall my son rule over you; the Lord shall rule over you" (Judg. 8:22–23).

5. <u>Do not accept the glory after God uses your life.</u> Our most vulnerable moment, as you may have heard before, is immediately after a great victory. With masterful restraint, Gideon models godly (and rare) humility.

It is exciting for me to imagine how some who read this chapter will put these guidelines to use. You will discover that you can declare your allegiance and you will begin to stand alone. You will give it a try. God will change the hearts of those who were once enemies. He may even give you a large following. He may use you in the lives of those in the office or on the campus or in the neighborhood as you have never been used before.

Those who appreciate your stand will say, "Wow! What a great person you are!" *Wait* a minute. *Watch* yourself at that vulnerable moment. Continually think of yourself as a mirror, reflecting the light of Jesus Christ to them, or as a servant, honoring the Master. Don't let the crowd get their eyes on you and make an idol out of you. Keep giving God the glory.

Isn't it interesting that when God uses our lives and we truly begin to soar as an eagle, it is easy to gravitate to one of two erroneous extremes? Either we embrace a false humility, failing to recognize and exercise our gifts as fully as we could; or we fall into the clutches of pride and arrogance so totally that God no longer uses us in mighty ways.

Gideon guards against the latter by saying, "Look, I won't rule over you." In fact, if you study the latter part of his life, you'll find that he continued to live in his own home and he ultimately died a very quiet death. I am truly impressed with the strength of the man's life and the humility with which he wore it. Gideon was used of God to break the people free from the grip of discouragement, but he refused to prance around like a peacock when everyone sang his praises. God is still looking for such people!

THE INFLUENCE OF JUST ONE

Periodically, I return to a single verse of Scripture from the pen of the prophet Ezekiel because it never fails to challenge me.

"And I searched for a man among them who should build up the wall and stand in the gap before Me for the land, that I should not destroy it; but I found no one" (Ezek. 22:30).

Same God, same need, different era. Here God admits His pursuit for one person who would stand in the gap. He's not looking for a flock; just one eagle will do. Today God is still looking for Gideons. But there is one major problem: They are scarce.

You may be that one person God wants to use in your sphere of influence. And if it is discouragement that is keeping you from being totally available to Him, come to terms with whatever brought it on. Get rid of it so that God can launch you and use you greatly.

I remember an evening several years ago when my family and I did something we had never done before. It was about eight o'clock, and we were finishing supper after a very big day. I was tired and weary. And everyone else seemed fairly low, too. I said, "Okay, let's hear two things from everybody at the table tonight: your *lowest moment* in the day and your *highest moment* in the day." It was a little tough getting going, but once we did, everybody participated. From the youngest to me, the dad—all the way around the table. You know what I discovered? I discovered hurts that I had not even known were there in that one day. We listened. We cared. We wept. We comforted. We encouraged. And I discovered heights that I didn't know were there because until then we'd never given a chance for them to be shared. We took our time. We rejoiced. We even applauded! For all I know, we may have hatched a few eagle eggs. Hopefully, we all began to soar a little higher. You might want to try that same project tonight.

Yes, eagle types can have down days. Sometimes the cold, gray slush can get pretty thick. In fact, some eagles get so weighed down with discouragement that they can't get airborne again. Why? Because there is no one with whom to share their burden. Maybe this is the place for you to begin. Cultivate one friend with whom you can share your discouragement. That could free you and get you back in the air as a modern-day "Gideon eagle." The Lord knows, we can always use a few more! Not only does He know it, but He is forever on a search for one who will be courageous enough to "stand in the gap."

Are you available?

Standing
Strong When
Tempted

16

Throughout these chapters I have been addressing the things
that lead to excellence. I have also been exposing the things
that hinder us from achieving it. From start to finish, my favorite
word picture has been the eagle—soaring high and free, thousands of feet above the distractions of earth, virtually impervious
to the turbulence and temperatures of its habitat. I have chosen
the eagle because no other creature better exemplifies my theme:
living above the level of mediocrity. Eagles represent independence, responsibility, strength, freedom, keenness of vision, rarity,
and a dozen other admirable traits that we wish to emulate.

But, though strong of heart and awesome on wing, eagles are
not superbirds incapable of being captured or immune to acci-
dent or disease. Like all other creatures, they have weaknesses.
They can make mistakes, misjudge distances, and miscalculate
dives. Falling victim to such perils can leave them with broken
bones, earthbound and defenseless, soon to be devoured by much
slower and less elegant yet more powerful beasts of prey.

We seldom think of eagles in such vulnerable conditions. Can you remember the last time you saw a photograph or drawing of a helpless eagle? I never have seen one. The eagle is always portrayed in graceful flight or diving for the kill, never in the claws or mouth of its captor. And for that reason, it is easy to become so convinced of the eagle's magnitude, solitude, and fortitude that we cannot imagine its ever falling prey to a mightier creature. But just remember I am using the eagle only as a symbol. To think of the eagle (really, ourselves) as invincible is to immortalize the analogy and to carry it to the point of fantasy. The pages of history are strewn with the litter of "eagle skeletons," each one a mute reminder of how the mighty have fallen.

FOUR POWERFUL PERILS

May I remind you of four of the more powerful perils that can level even the mightiest of eagle types? They are fortune, fame, power, and pleasure. Each works overtime to win a hearing, to gain a foothold, to woo us in. With relentless persistence, each message bombards the eagle's nest with missilelike pleadings for acceptance. Whether subliminal, subtle, strong, or supreme, these messages search for chinks in our armor as they appeal to our natural appetites. "Get rich!" (fortune). "Become known!" (fame). "Gain control!" (power). "Be satisfied!" (pleasure). Each of these attractive snares invites our attention, holds out a juicy carrot, makes beautiful promises; yet each is an enemy always crouching and ready to plunge. Being masters of deceit, these messages employ one favorite method throughout our lives— *temptation.* And why not? It's worked for centuries. All it takes to be effective is our nod of acceptance—it doesn't even need to be visible—and the once-strong, high-flying eagle is reduced to mediocrity, like the majority. My concern is that we stay riveted to reality. Let all who soar take heed lest they take a fatal dive!

A ONCE-MIGHTY EAGLE WHO BIT THE DUST

Rather than leaving everything in the theoretical realm, let's put a flesh-and-blood example before us. I find that it's much easier to build a case with a real person than with a nice-sounding theory that looks good on paper but allows no room for identification. The person I have in mind is a biblical character that you have probably heard of but may not have studied very closely. Just the mention of his name will tell you why I have chosen him as the example: Samson. He's the one I often think of as a he-man with a she-weakness. Few eagle types ever had the potential to fly higher or fall harder than Samson.

Favorable Circumstances

Contrary to popular opinion, the man had a godly heritage and was born into a tremendously secure, solid home.

> Now the sons of Israel again did evil in the sight of the Lord, so that the Lord gave them into the hands of the Philistines forty years. And there was a certain man of Zorah, of the family of the Danites, whose name was Manoah; and his wife was barren and had borne no children (Judg. 13:1–2).

Samson's mother is never named in Scripture; she is simply called the wife of Manoah. Manoah and his wife were waiting before the Lord for God to answer and provide for them a child. That's exactly what happened. The long-awaited promise was finally heard.

> Then the angel of the Lord appeared to the woman, and said to her, "Behold now, you are barren and have borne no children, but you shall conceive and give birth to a son" (v. 3).

Ancient Hebrew women lived with no greater stigma than barrenness. Manoah's wife was no exception. She must have been elated when God visited her and said words that brought music to her ears. Her son-to-be was in rare company. Most births were not preceded by angelic visits. But like John the Baptizer and Jesus of Nazareth, Samson's birth was divinely announced.

In addition to heralding the birth of Samson, the angel also clearly revealed the purpose for Samson's life. ". . . He shall begin to deliver Israel from the hands of the Philistines" (v. 5).

Not only were these parents thrilled to hear that they would have a baby, but they were also informed of the direction his life would take. Wouldn't that be great to know, moms and dads? We wouldn't have to wrestle with career guessing games. Right off the bat we could help our kids make the right choices in life that would prepare them for that particular God-given calling.

Let's look a little closer at what Manoah and his wife heard. They were told that their son would "*begin* to deliver Israel from . . . the Philistines." He was not to be the only deliverer; he was to *begin* to deliver his people from Philistine oppression. I take it that God had a plan, sort of a one-two punch. Samson was the "one." Someone else, later on, would be the "two." Samson would *begin* to drive the initial wedge, locally, among the Danites and then there would come another who would finish the job, nationally.

Samson was also fortunate to have been born to parents who were deeply spiritual. Look at the words in verse 8, "Then Manoah entreated the Lord. . . ." Manoah was a godly Jew surrounded by godless Jews in the tribe of Dan, most of whom had begun to live like the Philistines. Not this man! He still sought the Lord, still waited before God in prayer. And this godly father-to-be says:

. . . "O Lord, please let the man of God whom Thou hast sent come to us again that he may teach us what to do for the boy who is to be born" (v. 8).

In other words, "Lord, we want to hear all we can from Your angel because we want to know exactly how to direct our boy's life." What father hasn't felt that urgency at times? "Lord, reveal to me how to rear my son. Help me know the right steps to take." He realized the spiritual indifference of those around him, so he requested help in knowing God's clear direction. He also knew the impact young Samson's environment could have on him. He wanted to do all he could to train his son correctly.

And God listened to the voice of Manoah; and the angel of God came again to the woman as she was sitting in the field, but Manoah her husband was not with her. So the woman ran quickly and told her husband, "Behold, the man who came the other day has appeared to me." Then Manoah arose and followed his wife, and when he came to the man he said to him, "Are you the man who spoke to the woman?" And he said, "I am." And Manoah said, "Now when your words come to pass, what shall be the boy's mode of life and his vocation?" (vv. 9–12).

That's just like a father, isn't it? That is the way dads think: *Now, what's going to be his vocation? I know he's going to deliver Israel, but how is he going to make a living? What will be his work? What will be his style of living?* So we find both Manoah and his wife genuinely seeking God's mind for the rearing of their son.

This is an ideal moment for me to put in a plug for godly parents. Were you raised by spiritually minded, eagle-type parents? You may have to say, "Well, *one* of them was." Or, "Well, later on in life they were." Whatever, have you ever stopped to thank them? Ever stopped to spell out specific reasons for your gratitude? Let me encourage you to do that soon. Don't wait. Your interest in soaring like an eagle is probably strong because your parents first set the pace. Though imperfect, they wanted what was best for you. Few blessings are greater than being influenced by good parents.

But there's another factor I must mention: Being godly parents is no absolute guarantee you'll have godly kids. Doing a good job of training children and teens provides no airtight promise that they're going to turn out exactly right. You and your mate might walk very close to God today. You might have begun to walk with Him soon after your child was born. You may have had the highest hopes for your child, but you're not experiencing the delight of your heart. At least, not yet. Nothing thrills us more than to know that our children are walking in the truth and nothing hurts us more than to realize they're not. There is an ache that cannot be described in the heart of a mother or father whose child deliberately departs from good training. I mention that because it is precisely what happened in Samson's life. All these favorable circumstances were not sufficient to guarantee Samson's spirituality. He had all the makings of a powerful eagle, an impressive, high-flying model of excellence, but his refusal to heed his parents' counsel and to stand strong when tempted led to a tragic downfall, as tragic as any on biblical record.

Unfavorable Characteristics

As Samson grew, his story doesn't get better, it gets worse. Little by little the boy's character was being chipped away. The erosion was silent but steady. By the way, I should point out before we get into his life any further that Samson was set apart to be a Nazarite. According to the Law of God, whoever took such a vow maintained a strict adherence to three disciplines. First, he watched his diet very closely. He neither drank alcoholic beverages nor ate certain foods. Second, he never went near the dead. Whether a cadaver or carcass, he never went near a dead animal or a dead human. Third, he never cut his hair. Since God revealed to his parents that Samson was to be a Nazarite from the womb, those three requirements applied to their son. Surely, throughout his early years, they must have drilled these disciplines into his head.

The next time we read of Samson, we find him fully grown. We're never told what happened during his childhood. But we do know that both his parents were with him through those formative years and watched with keen interest as he reached adulthood. As Samson shows up on this next scene, he may be grown physically, but he's not emotionally or spiritually mature. When the man makes his first appearance on the scriptural scene, we immediately detect a character flaw. He possesses a lustful, passionate drive that he does not attempt to restrain—neither now nor later.

> Then Samson went down to Timnah and saw a woman in Timnah, one of the daughters of the Philistines. So he came back and told his father and mother, "I saw a woman . . ." (Judg. 14:1–2).

I think it is highly significant that the first four recorded words from Samson's lips are, "I saw a woman." That is the story of his life. *He focused on the wrong objective.*

> . . . "I saw a woman in Timnah, one of the daughters of the Philistines; now therefore, get her for me as a wife." Then his father and his mother said to him, "Is there no woman among the daughters of your relatives, or among all our people, that you go to take a wife from the uncircumcised Philistines?" But Samson said to his father, "Get her for me, for she looks good to me." . . . So he went down and talked to the woman; and she looked good to Samson (vv. 2–3, 7).

Right off the bat, we see that lust becomes Samson's foremost unfavorable characteristic, something that would haunt him all his days.

Samson's focusing on the wrong objectives proved to be his downfall. First, he focused on physical appearance and little else. Second, he focused on pleasing himself and no one else. Twice we read in this account that the Philistine woman "looked good" to the young Israelite. Let me get painfully specific. As he looked at the daughter of Timnah, Samson liked the way she was built. Today he would come right out and say she had sex appeal. He liked her body. Frankly, it turned him on. There is not a word in this passage regarding her character. Why? Well, first of all, he didn't bother to notice. Second, since she was a Philistine, there was no spiritual character there to appeal to a Jew. But he could not care less. She "looked good" and that was all that mattered to him.

This is a good time to be very candid regarding the issue of physical attraction as seen through the eyes of males. There is an incredible difference between the sexual appetite of a man and the sexual appetite of a woman. Dr. James Dobson, my longtime friend and a much-respected professional psychologist heard by many of you on his radio program, "Focus on the Family," writes helpful words regarding two major differences between what excites men in contrast to what excites women.

First, men are primarily excited by *visual* stimulation. They are turned on by feminine nudity or peek-a-boo glimpses of semi-nudity. (Phyllis Diller said she had the first peek-a-boo dress: men would "peek" at her, and then they would "boo"!) Women, by contrast, are much less visually oriented than men. Sure, they are interested in attractive masculine bodies, but the physiological mechanism of sex is not triggered typically by what they see; woman are stimulated primarily by the sense of touch. Thus, we encounter the first source of disagreement in the bedroom: he wants her to appear unclothed in a lighted room, and she wants him to caress her in the dark.

Second (and much more important), men are not very discriminating in regard to the person living within an exciting body. A man can walk down a street and be stimulated by a scantily clad female who shimmies past him, even though he knows nothing about her personality or values or mental capabilities. He is attracted by her body itself. Likewise, he can become almost as excited over a photograph of an unknown nude model as he can in a face-to-face encounter with someone he loves. In essence, the sheer biological power of sexual desire in a male is largely focused on the physical body of an attractive female. Hence, there is some validity to the complaint by women that they have been used as "sex objects" by men. This explains why female prostitutes outnumber males by a wide margin and why few women try to "rape" men. It explains why a roomful of toothless old men can get a large charge from watching a burlesque dancer "take it all off." It reflects the fact that masculine self-esteem is more motivated by a desire to "conquer" a woman than in becoming the object of her romantic love. These are not very flattering characteristics of male sexuality, but they are well documented in the professional literature. All of these factors stem from a basic difference in sexual appetites of males and females.

Women are much more discriminating in their sexual interests. They less commonly become excited by observing a good-looking charmer, or by the photograph of a hairy model; rather, their desire is usually focused on a *particular* individual whom they respect or admire. A woman is stimulated by the romantic aura which surrounds her man, and by his character and personality. She yields to the man who appeals to her emotionally as well as physically. Obviously, there are exceptions to these characteristic desires, but the fact remains: sex for men is a more physical thing; sex for women is a deeply emotional experience.[1]

Samson's opening line is a classic example of Dr. Dobson's observations. But for Samson, the *only* thing that mattered was satisfying his lust. The man was driven by one of the most natural and powerful drives in the human male. I find it interesting that the young Philistine woman is never called by name. Why? Again, all Samson saw was a body, and he wanted that body for his own sexual gratification. He focused completely on the physical and nothing more.

I can imagine a man's reading this chapter and thinking, *Does this mean that I am lustful even to consider physical beauty? Am I wrong to look at a woman's beauty and be attracted by it?* Of course not! My point here is that Samson's focus was physical attraction *only.* That four-letter word *only* is all-important when it comes to understanding why Samson yielded to the alluring charms of temptation.

Now there is a second characteristic of Samson that was also unfavorable. *He handled his leisure carelessly.* Do you remember what the angel said about the purpose of his life? He was to "begin to deliver Israel." Seems to me he is getting sidetracked. So far he has spent very little time delivering Israel. The man is mainly into pleasing himself.

You need to know that when Samson made one of his trips to visit this girl, he killed a lion. Then on a later trip, he found the remains and observed something strange: the lion's carcass had a beehive built within it. He paused long enough on his way to see his woman to eat a little honey out of the hive. By the way, that little sidetrack broke his Nazarite vow, since he had to touch the dead lion to get the honey. How careless he was! But that was only the beginning.

In customary fashion, when Samson finally arrived with his father to marry the Philistine, a number of her friends were invited to a big feast.

> Then his father went down to the woman; and Samson made a feast there, for the young men customarily did this. And it came about when they saw him that they brought thirty companions to be with him. Then Samson said to them, "Let me now propound a riddle to you; if you will indeed tell it to me within the seven days of the feast, and find it out, then I will give you thirty linen wraps and thirty changes of clothes. But if you are unable to tell me, then you shall give me thirty linen wraps and thirty changes of clothes." And they said to him, "Propound your riddle, that we may hear it." So he said to them, "Out of the eater came something to eat, and out of the strong came something sweet" . . . (Judg. 14:10–14).

Hold it! Here's a guy who should have been soaring, beginning to deliver Israel, as God had commanded. But what is he doing? Posing riddles to these ding-a-lings from Philistia!

They scratched their heads and yanked their beards for three days and couldn't come up with the answer. Well, certainly not. Who could? What in the world did it matter, anyway? What's a God-given eagle doing sitting around with the mediocre rabble making up poetry? What's he doing leisurely hanging around a Philistine camp cultivating friendships? The man was so off target it was almost humorous.

Well, the Philistines couldn't figure out the riddle, and it ticked them off. Embarrassed and perturbed, they moved in on the woman with this threat:

... "Entice your husband, that he may tell us the riddle, lest we burn you and your father's house with fire. Have you invited us to impoverish us? Is this not so?" (v. 15).

Camp on that word *entice* for a moment. The original Hebrew term used in this passage literally means "to be wide open." It can also mean "to seduce, to persuade." They must have realized that Samson was open-minded, even gullible. A lustful eye isn't difficult to detect. Determined not to be narrow like his "rigid" mother and father, Samson shoved the pendulum to the opposite extreme.

So they said, in effect, "Look, toots, seduce this man or we'll burn your place down!" Great group of guys to have at your wedding, huh?

So Samson's wife turned on woman's most powerful weapon, TEARS. Did she ever!

And Samson's wife wept before him and said, "You only hate me, and you do not love me; you have propounded a riddle to the sons of my people, and have not told it to me." And he said to her, "Behold, I have not told it to my father or mother; so should I tell you?" However she wept before him seven days . . . (vv. 16–17).

Try to imagine that scene. Seven days of "You don't love me . . . you hate me . . . ," plus sobs and tears. Seven days! That's a long, torturous time. No man can withstand seven days, day in, day out, no appetite, no kisses, just crrryyying. She nagged him and nagged him and cried in front of him until finally he would have told her anything to quiet the crying. Finally, she pressed him so hard he told her the riddle.

And it came about on the seventh day that he told her because she pressed him so hard. She then told the riddle to the sons of her people (v. 17).

I confess I'm getting pretty impatient about now. What in the world is this Israelite eagle doing scratching around in enemy territory with a pen full of Philistine turkeys, making up riddles and spending his time with a gobbler like this? What a waste! Mediocrity on display. No wonder temptation won the first round. The man does not know how to handle his leisure.

Let's hurry on—maybe things will change, right? As much as I hate to disappoint you: The answer is *Wrong!* Let's put two verses together to emphasize a contrast:

So he judged Israel twenty years in the days of the Philistines.
Now Samson went to Gaza and saw a harlot there, . . . (15:20–16:1).

After twenty years of judging Israel (whether it was spectacular or spotted, we're not told), the eagle with limitless potential is right back at the same old stuff. In his leisure he's hustling an unnamed prostitute down in Gaza. And if that is not enough, he turns right around and locates yet another woman down in the valley of Sorek.

After this it came about that he loved a woman in the valley of Sorek, whose name was Delilah (16:4).

Again, I remind you, he isn't interested in delivering Israel—he's on the prowl for another female. To Samson, leisure was synonymous with lust. It was bad enough that he fanned the flame of lust, but in addition to that, he continued to run with a bad bunch. We've learned by now that this combination inevitably spells disaster.

Now we come to Samson's third unfavorable characteristic: *He developed a close alliance with the wrong crowd.* Complete corruption was just around the corner, thanks to the bad company Samson kept. All that time spent with the Philistines was the catalyst—the major force—that caused him to fall prey to Delilah's advances.

After this it came about that he loved a woman in the valley of Sorek, whose name was Delilah. And the lords of the Philistines came up to her, and said to her, "Entice him, and see where his great strength lies and how we may overpower him that we may bind him to afflict him. Then we will each give you eleven hundred pieces of silver" (16:4–5).

Sound a little familiar? "The guy's a pushover. *Seduce* him, Delilah. Find out where his strength lies; he's a mystery to us. He can whip a thousand of us without even breaking into a sweat.

Find out how come he is able to fight like that." Apparently, Samson didn't look like Arnold Schwartzenegger but just like any other Jewish male of that day. "Find out how he can be so strong and yet look like everybody else? Get at it, Delilah. Do your thing. *Entice him.*"

Running with the wrong crowd, Samson is heading straight for trouble. The man is dancing to temptation's addicting tune, so he plays right into Delilah's hands. Every time I read this story, I wonder how the man could have been so stupid.

> So Delilah said to Samson, "Please tell me where your great strength is and how you may be bound to afflict you" (v. 6).

Honestly, you've got to be pretty thick to miss their plot. In so many words, Delilah says, "Samson, honey, would you tell us why you are strong? You see, we plan to trap you. And if you will simply tell us your secret, we'll just finish you off!" Playboy Samson must have thought, *Well, that'll be a lot of fun. I'll play their game.* So he gives her a few clever possibilities. For starters he says:

> . . . "If they bind me with seven fresh cords that have not been dried, then I shall become weak and be like any other man" (v. 7).

So she did that—she whipped up the fresh cords and wrapped them around him and yelled, "The Philistines are upon you, Samson." Pop! He snaps all the cords and moves out. And the Philistines whine, "Aw, we've been deceived" because Samson's strength was not discovered. But don't think they're about to quit. Samson may be playing around, but they're not.

Delilah goes right back.

> . . . "Behold, you have deceived me and told me lies; now please, tell me how you may be bound." And he said to her, "If they bind me tightly with new ropes which have not been used, then I shall become weak and be like any other man" (vv. 10–11).

Hey, here's the Israelite eagle who ought to be delivering Israel from the hand of the Philistines, still messing around with the mediocre mob. Ridiculous! Same song, third verse:

> Then Delilah said to Samson, "Up to now you have deceived me and told me lies; tell me how you may be bound." And he said to her, "If you weave the seven locks of my hair with the web [and fasten it with a pin, then I shall become weak and be like any other man." So while he slept, Delilah took the seven locks of his hair and wove them into the web.] And she fastened it with the pin, and said to him, "The Philistines are upon you, Samson!" But he awoke from his sleep and pulled out the pin of the loom and the web (vv. 13–14).

Notice what is happening? In the fun 'n' games of the moment the eagle gets perilously close to danger in his dive near the craggy rocks. He starts to play with his hair, the sacred secret of his life. Now you and I know that Samson's strength wasn't actually in his hair, but his hair was a *sign* of his strength. It was a *reminder* of his vow. Nevertheless, while he was playing around, he blurted out, "Well, why don't you just weave my hair into this web?" And so she did.

Samson is beginning to presume upon sacred things. And that's his fourth major flaw: *He didn't take his vow seriously.* Let's just change the word *vow* to *God.* Samson didn't take his God seriously. I wonder if he remembered something about mom and dad's setting him aside, back when he was just a child, for the Nazarite vow. Maybe he reminisced for a moment, but thought, *Aw, I can handle it; I'm bigger than that now.* So he impulsively says, "Why don't you just mess around with my hair?" And so she did. But once again Samson's strength was not diminished.

> . . . "How can you say, 'I love you,' when your heart is not with me? You have deceived me these three times and have not told me where your great strength is" (v. 15).

Can't you just picture it? "Samsey baby . . . how could you?"

Finally, Samson poured it all out; he told her *everything.* "A razor has never come on my head. . . . If I am shaved, then my strength will leave me and I shall become weak and be like any other man" (v. 17). All of a sudden, he was in so deep he couldn't back out. The old eagle miscalculated his final, fateful dive. This time he struck the ledge! How could he? Why hadn't he realized the peril of his situation? What was it that had drawn him closer, closer, closer to that ledge?

What was the secret of Samson's defeat? Simply this: He didn't choose to say NO to temptation. The following words from Dietrich Bonhoeffer provide the most plausible explanation of temptation I've ever read.

In our members there is a slumbering inclination towards desire which is both sudden and fierce. With irresistible power desire seizes mastery over the flesh. All at once a secret, smouldering fire is kindled. The flesh burns and is in flames. It makes no difference whether it is sexual desire, or ambition, or vanity, or desire for revenge, or love of fame and power, or greed for money, or, finally, that strange desire for the beauty of the world, of nature. Joy in God is in course of being extinguished in us and we seek all our joy in the creature. At this moment God is quite unreal to us, he loses all reality, and only desire for the creature is real; the only reality is the devil. Satan does not here fill us with hatred of God, but with forgetfulness of God. And now his falsehood is added to this proof of strength. The lust thus aroused envelops the mind and will of man in deepest darkness. The power of clear discrimination and of decision are taken from us. . . .

It is here that everything within me rises up against the Word of God. Powers of the body, the mind and the will, which were held in obedience under the discipline of the Word of which I believed that I was the master, make it clear to me that I am by no means master of them. "All my powers forsake me," laments the psalmist. They have all gone over to the adversary. The adversary deploys my powers against me. In this situation I can no longer act as a hero; I am a defenseless, powerless man. God himself has forsaken me. Who can conquer, who can gain the victory?[2]

Heroes, listen up! Spiritual leaders, pay attention! My fellow eagle, take heed! "[Every man] is tempted when he is carried away and enticed by his own lust" (James 1:14). The Greek word translated "enticed" means "to lure by a bait." The bait is dropped, and the fish, seeing the bait, is lured away from its safe hiding place. Likewise, we move closer to grab the bait of pleasure, and as we do so God becomes quite unreal. In fact, He's momentarily *forgotten*. The bait is real; God is not. And for that brief moment we are thinking of one thing—how pleasurable it will be to grab that morsel.

Let me mention another very practical thing about temptation.

I have found that if I can stop the process fairly early, I'm safe. But if I leave my hiding place and venture toward the bait, there is a point of no return. I cannot turn around. If I go that far, I'm sunk.

That's the way it is with us, and that's the way it was with Samson. He pandered with leisure and played with the wrong crowd and messed around with the bait so much he could not turn around. At that point God had become totally unreal to him. With God blocked out, "He told her all that was in his heart." No wonder we read that he didn't even know the Spirit of God had departed from him. I think how great it would have been if Samson had suddenly stopped, dashed out of that place and into the street, and lifted up his arms and screamed, "O God, I am so weak—so near the ledge. Give me the strength I need right now. Help me to soar again!" If only the man had called for help. If only—

The Inevitable Consequences

Within a matter of seconds, "The Philistines seized him." The very first action they took against him was to gouge out both his eyes. Why, of course—his EYES, the gateway to lust! Those Philistines knew him better than he knew himself. They didn't want any further trouble in Philistia from this weak shell of a man who could not resist temptation. So they blinded the eagle; he never flew again, not like before.

J. Oswald Sanders, in his book *Robust in Faith,* titles his chapter on Samson, "The Champion Who Became a Clown."[3] The Philistines dumped Samson in a prison—". . . and bound him with bronze chains, and he was a grinder in the prison" (v. 21).

Many years ago I read something by someone who summed up the wages of temptation in six tragic words: "sin blinds, sin binds, sin grinds." That is so true—so tragically true. The Israelite champion was now reduced to nothing more than a clown in a Philistine house of horrors.

Two inevitable consequences follow in the wake of those who play the fool and yield to temptation's alluring bait. Both expose lies from the world system.

First: *We are weakened, not strengthened.* The world says that a playboy lifestyle will make you strong. Ever heard words like this? "By being exposed to temptations, by getting up close to lust, you learn you can handle those temptations." No, Samson shows us that such a lifestyle really weakens us. If we don't break away, it isn't long before the weakness becomes an addiction, leading to a tragic end.

Radio personality Paul Harvey tells the story of how an Eskimo kills a wolf. The account is grisly, yet it offers fresh insight into the consuming, self-destructive nature of sin.

"First the Eskimo coats his knife blade with animal blood and allows it to freeze. Then he adds another layer of blood, and another, until the blade is completely concealed by frozen blood.

"Next, the hunter fixes his knife in the ground with the blade up. When a wolf follows his sensitive nose to the source of the scent and discovers the bait he licks it, tasting the fresh-frozen blood. He begins to lick faster, more and more vigorously, lapping the blade until the keen edge is bare. Feverishly now, harder and harder the wolf licks the blade in the Arctic night. So great becomes his craving for blood that the wolf does not notice the razor sharp sting of the naked blade on his tongue nor does he recognize the instant at which his insatiable thirst is being satisfied by his *own* warm blood. His carnivorous appetite just craves more—until the dawn finds him dead in the snow!"[4]

Second: *We become enslaved, not freed.* The system says, "Free love frees you up." Well, that's a lie. It actually puts you into bondage. Samson became a victim of the very ones he was supposed to conquer.

When I was stationed in the Orient with the Marines, I lived in a Quonset hut with forty-seven other guys. The whole unit was shot through with an illicit lifestyle. A large percentage of them had either previously had or at that time had some kind of venereal disease. Those guys could withstand anything but temptation!

One young man—I'll call him Bobby (not his real name)—lived regularly in open sin. He had come from a fairly strict home and had never known what it was like to be free of parental guidance. But once he was on his own, the guy went wild. One weekend he went into the village and shacked up with a prostitute. By the time he returned to the base, late Sunday night, he was terribly afraid he had contracted a disease. He stumbled half drunk down to the bunk where I was. He was talking with another guy and then turned and grabbed hold of me and said, "Hey, Swindoll, I want you to talk to me. I'm scared to death."

We took a walk that night down by the mess hall and then over toward the only place that was lit through the night—the chapel. The farther we walked and the longer we talked, the more he sobered up. That very night Bobby got down on his knees and openly confessed his bondage to lust. I will never forget his simple words: "I ask Jesus Christ to come into my life. How I need Him!" And I also remember his saying, "Lord, I have a habit that You've got to help me break." I'll never forget his praying that. For the next seven months we worked closely together. The battle was a long, tough one. But finally, he began to soar above and beyond his bondage. Another eagle was in the sky by means of a power other than his own—the power of Christ.

AN EAGLELIKE STRATEGY FOR FLIGHT

This chapter is plenty long already. No need to lengthen it with numerous words. So let me close with a straightforward, succinct strategy for a soaring flight.

First: *Our natural focus must be counteracted.* The natural focus for some is homosexuality, a subtle, gnawing temptation. The natural focus for others is a continuation of illicit affairs outside the marriage bond. The habit for others is some kind of hidden, more shameful sensuality.

That natural focus must be counteracted. Openly confess your weakness. Hide nothing. One of the best ways to get back in the air and soar as you once did is through consistent, systematic Scripture memory. I detailed this at length in the first chapter of this book. Scripture memory replaces sensual thoughts with spiritual thoughts.

Another essential technique is to learn how to handle the eye gate. "I made a covenant with my eyes," said Job. "I will not stare at a girl." And guys, you and I have to make that kind of covenant or we will stare. No problem with the first glance. Our problems occur with the second look, which leads to the long stare. A casual glance is no big deal. But what we need is a covenant, a vow before God, and a regular accountability before others. Develop a disciplined technique to counteract your natural focus.

Second: *Our leisure time must be guarded.* Students, you can't tolerate an aw-so-what? flippant attitude when you face the summer. Business men and women who travel, your leisure can lead to your downfall. Cultivate a plan, perhaps an exercise program, an intensive reading program, a hobby, a series of practical projects which occupy your time. Watch out for those video movies piped into your room! If necessary, keep the television off. And stay away from the magazine rack. Lust can no more be trusted than a snake. Don't mess with it!

LeRoy Eims offers superb counsel in his book *Be the Leader You Were Meant to Be:*

> Rattlesnakes are fairly common where I live. I encounter one almost every summer. It is a frightening experience to see a rattlesnake coiled, looking at you, ready to strike. He's lightning quick and accurate. I have a two-point program for rattlesnakes: shun and avoid. You don't need much insight to figure out what to do with something as dangerous as an old diamondback rattler. You don't mess around.[5]

Third: *Our close companions must be screened.* Take a good look at your circle of friends. Do an honest evaluation of those with whom you spend personal time. I can offer you a principle you can bank on: Until you clean up your companionships, you'll never clean up your life. You may want to. You may have sincere desires and the highest of ambitions, but if you plan to soar, pick your partners with great care. Remember, eagles fly with only a few other eagles—never in flocks.

Fourth: *Our vow to God must be upheld.* Just as jealously as we would guard the marriage vows, we're to guard our promises to God and our commitment to purity. May I remind you of your primary vow?

> I urge you therefore, brethren, by the mercies of God, to present your bodies a living and holy sacrifice, acceptable to God, which is your spiritual service of worship. And do not be conformed to this world, but be transformed by the renewing of your mind, that you may prove what the will of God is, that which is good and acceptable and perfect (Rom. 12:1–2).

When we personalize those words, we understand them to contain the warning, "Don't let the world around you squeeze you into its mold." Need a place to start? Start with these words. Read them before the Lord and say something like this: "Father, this is where I want to start. Before facing any kind of temptation today, I want to declare my allegiance to You. Give me strength to stand all alone, to stand strong in Your power. Renew my mind. This is my vow, and I take it seriously before You."

Isn't it time you got serious about soaring? You know it is! I don't care if you've begun a hundred other times, don't let anyone try to tell you that it is useless to begin again. It is never too late to start doing what is right.

Excellence—moral, ethical, personal excellence—is worth whatever it costs. Pay the price. Start today! You are made for one great purpose—soaring! Nothing less will ever satisfy you or glorify God.

Conclusion

Who's Appraising Your Excellence?

Badness you can get easily, in quantity: the road is smooth, and it lies close by. But in front of excellence the immortal gods have put sweat, and long and steep is the way to it, and rough at first. But when you come to the top, then it is easy, even though it is hard.

—Hesiod, 700 B.C.

When I embarked on this literary journey many moons ago, I entertained one major concern: "Can I communicate the importance of excellence without leaving the impression that it is a synonym of success?" I mean success as the world uses the word. In my opinion we have more than enough books on that subject already. Motivational material, sales techniques, and self-help success-oriented volumes are all about us. Some are helpful, others little more than hype. But all too little is written about a commitment to excellence—true excellence, the kind of excellence that conveys superior quality, attention to significant detail, care about that which really matters.

Excellence is a difficult concept to communicate because it can easily be misread as neurotic perfectionism or snooty sophistication. But it is neither. On the contrary, it is the stuff of which greatness is made. It is the difference between just getting by and soaring—that which sets apart the significant from the superficial, the lasting from the temporary. Those who pursue it do so because of what pulsates within them, not because of what others think or say or do. Authentic excellence is not a performance. It is there whether anyone ever notices or tries to find out.

When the Statue of Liberty received her much-needed facelift back in 1985–86, she was examined with a fine-tooth comb. The craftsmen and artists who did the repairs had ample opportunity to study the original workmanship. They were impressed—perhaps a better word is *amazed*—with the design of her sculptor,

275

the noted Frenchman, Frederic Bartholdi, and his crew who applied their artistic skills over one hundred years ago. Nothing had been overlooked. One example is the beautiful work that was done high atop Liberty's spiked crown and head. The superb attention to detail was carried out so thoroughly, one would have thought that this section would have been viewed by everyone. But the fact is, no one would see her from above. Once she was raised to her full height, 151 feet, only a few seagulls would ever notice her coiffure. Little did those French artisans even imagine a day when helicopters would hover, giving time for the human eye to observe and enjoy such exquisite beauty. But you see, excellence characterized the design of Liberty's head whether or not anyone would ever stop to notice or admire.

Mediocrity is fast becoming the by-word of our times. Every imaginable excuse is now used to make it acceptable, hopefully preferred. Budget cuts, time deadlines, majority opinion, and hard-nosed practicality are outshouting and outrunning excellence. Those forces seem to be winning the race. Incompetence and status quo averages are held up as all we can now expect, and the tragedy is that more and more people have virtually agreed. Why worry over the small stuff? Why concern yourself with soaring when so few even glide anymore? Why bother with the genuine now that the artificial looks so real? If the public buys it, why sweat it?

To make it painfully plain, why think clearly since most folks want someone else to think for them? Why live differently in a society where it's so much easier to look the same and swim downstream? Why fight fiercely when so few seem to care? Why stand courageously if it means risking ridicule, misunderstanding, or being considered a dreamer by some and a fool by others?

Why, indeed? To quote young David just before he took on that Philistine behemoth in the Valley of Elah, "Is there not a cause?" Must we wait for someone else to establish our standard or to set our pace? Not on your life! There is too much eagle in some of us to be comfortable taking our cues from the majority. It is my firm conviction that those who impact and reshape the world are the ones committed to living above the level of mediocrity. There are still too many opportunities for excellence, too much demand for distinctiveness, to be satisfied with just getting by. As Isaac

D'Israeli once wrote, ". . . it is a wretched taste to be gratified with mediocrity when the excellent lies before us."[1]

Although I never knew him, the late Albert Schweitzer seemed to be a model of remarkable excellence. Norman Cousins, having spent considerable time with Dr. Schweitzer at his little hospital at Lambaréné in French Equatorial Africa, wrote of those days long after they had passed. His recollections are well worth repeating.

> The biggest impression I had in leaving Lambaréné was of the enormous reach of a single human being. Yet such a life was not without the punishment of fatigue. Albert Schweitzer was supposed to be severe in his demands on the people who worked with him. Yet any demands he made on others were as nothing compared to the demands he made on himself. He was not concerned about the attainability of perfection; he was concerned, however, about the pursuit of perfection. He considered the desire to seek the best and work for the best as a vital part of the nature of man. When he sat down to play the piano or organ, and he was alone, he might stay with it for hours at a time. He might practice a single phrase for two hours or more. The difference between the phrase when he first played it and when he himself was satisfied with it might have been imperceptible even to a trained musical ear. But he had a stern idea of his own capacity for interpreting Bach, for example, and he felt he must stretch himself to whatever extent was necessary to achieve it. This was no mere obsession. He sought his own outermost limits as a natural part of purposeful living. . . .

> History is willing to overlook almost anything—errors, paradoxes, personal weaknesses or faults—if only a man will give enough of himself to others. . . .

> . . . If sacrifice is required, we shall have to sacrifice. If we are to lead, what we say and what we do must become more important in our own minds than what we sell or what we use. . . .[2]

As I have emphasized throughout this book, a commitment to excellence is neither popular nor easy. But it is essential. Excellence in integrity and morality as well as ethics and scholarship. Excellence in physical fitness and spiritual fervor just as much as excellence in relationships and craftsmanship. A commitment to excellence touches the externals of appearance, communication, and products just as much as the internals of attitude, vision, taste, humor, compassion, determination, and zest for life. It means not being different for difference' sake but for God's sake. After all, He is the One in whose Book we read, "if there be any excellence . . . set your mind on these things" (Phil. 4:8).

That's it in a nutshell: A setting of our minds on these things—even if no one else on earth cares or dares.

It matters not, I repeat, what others may think or say or do. We must seek our own "outermost limits"—not merely drift along with the tide or half-heartedly catch a wave and wash ashore. No, *we must soar.* Since it is the living Lord in the final analysis who appraises our excellence, it is He whom we must please and serve, honor and adore. For His eyes only we commit ourselves to living above the level of mediocrity. He deserves our very best; nothing more, nothing less, nothing else.

That alone is excellence.

Notes

Chapter 1. It Starts in Your Mind

1. Earl D. Radmacher, *You & Your Thoughts* (Carol Stream, IL: Tyndale House Publishers Inc., 1977), 51–52.
2. Roger von Oech, *A Whack on the Side of the Head* (New York: Warner Books, Inc., 1983), 9.

Chapter 2. It Involves Another Kingdom

1. From *Who Switched the Price Tags?* (pp. 25–26) by Anthony Campolo, copyright © 1986; used by permission of Word Books, Publisher, Waco, TX.
2. Richard J. Foster, *Money, Sex & Power* (San Francisco: Harper & Row, Publishers, 1985 [© 1985 by Richard J. Foster]), 13.
3. Ibid., 176.
4. From *Christ and the Media* (p. 30) by Malcolm Muggeridge. Copyright © 1977 by Wm. B. Eerdmans Publishing Co., Grand Rapids, MI.
5. *Money, Sex & Power,* 218–219.
6. From *Tell Me Again Lord, I Forget* (p. 23) by Ruth Harms Calkin, published by Tyndale House Publishers, Inc. © 1974. Used by permission.
7. John R. W. Stott, *Christian Counter-Culture* (Downers Grove, IL: InterVarsity Press, 1978), 53.
8. Used by permission of the author.

Chapter 3. It Costs Your Commitment

1. Thomas Paine, *The American Crisis,* no. I [December 23, 1776].

2.   Douglas Southall Freeman, *Lee, Abridgment in One Volume* by Richard Harwell of the four-volume *R. E. Lee* by Douglas Southall Freeman (New York: Charles Scribner's Sons, 1961), 587–588.

3.   Hal Lindsey, *Combat Faith* (New York: Bantam Books, 1986), 1–2.

Chapter 4.   It Calls for Extravagant Love

1.   G. Campbell Morgan, *The Gospel According to Mark* (Westwood, NJ: Fleming H. Revell Company, 1957), 284.

2.   From *Rabboni* (pp. 222–223) by W. Phillip Keller. Copyright © 1977 by W. Phillip Keller. Published by Fleming H. Revell Company. Used by permission.

3.   From *Life Without Limits* (pp. 248–249) by Lloyd J. Ogilvie, copyright © 1975; used by permission of Word Books, Publisher, Waco, TX.

4.   From *Up with Worship* (pp. 22–24) by Anne Ortlund. Copyright © 1975, Regal Books, Ventura, CA 93006. Used by permission.

Chapter 5.   Vision: Seeing beyond the Majority

1.   Eugene H. Petersen, *A Long Obedience in the Same Direction* (Downers Grove, IL: InterVarsity Press, 1980), 11.

2.   Isaac Watts, "Am I a Soldier of the Cross?" (1709).

3.   Aleksandr I. Solzhenitsyn, "A World Split Apart," commencement address delivered at Harvard University, June 8, 1978. Copyright © 1978 by Aleksandr I. Solzhenitsyn. English language translation copyright © 1979 Harper & Row, Publishers, Inc. Published in *East and West* (New York: Harper & Row, Publishers, 1980), 45.

4.   Reprinted by permission from *Bringing Out the Best in People* (p. 35) by Alan Loy McGinnis, copyright © 1985 Augsburg Publishing House.

5.   Ibid., 38.

6.   From *Life Is Tremendous* (pp. 62–64) by Charles E. Jones. Published by Tyndale House Publishers, Inc. © 1968. Used by permission.

Chapter 6.   Determination: Deciding to Hang Tough

1.   Author unknown.

2.   Don B. Owens, Jr., *Quote Unquote,* ed. Lloyd Cory (Wheaton, IL: Victor Books, a division of SP Publications, 1977), 236.

3.   From *Think and Grow Rich* (p. 164) by Napoleon Hill. Published by E. P. Dutton, Inc., © 1958. Used by permission.

4.   "It's What You Do, Not When You Do It" (Hartford, CT: United Technologies, 1979). Used by permission.

5. Taken from *The Making of a Christian Leader* (p. 120) by Ted W. Engstrom. Copyright © 1976 by The Zondervan Corporation. Used by permission. Ted Engstrom retells this story from *What a Day This Can Be,* ed. John Catoir (New York: The Christophers).

Chapter 7.   Priorities: Determining What Comes First

1.   From "I Wish I'd Been There," *A Sense of History* (New York: American Heritage Press, 1985), 1–37.
2.   From *When I Relax I Feel Guilty* (p. 89) by Tim Hansel, © 1979. Used with permission by David C. Cook Publishing Co.
3.   Robert Goldman, "Getting Stuck on the Way Up the Corporate Ladder," *Wall Street Journal,* January 6, 1986. Used by permission.
4.   Jon Johnston, "Growing Me-ism and Materialism," *Christianity Today* (p. 16–I), January 17, 1986. Copyright © 1986 by Christianity Today, Inc., Carol Stream, IL. Used by permission.
5.   William Barclay, *The Gospel of Luke, The Daily Study Bible* (p. 203). Reproduced by kind permission of The Saint Andrew Press, Edinburgh, Scotland.

Chapter 8.   Accountability: Answering the Hard Questions

1.   From *There's a Lot More to Health Than Not Being Sick* (p. 74) by Bruce Larson, copyright © 1981, 1984; used by permission of Word Books, Publisher, Waco, TX.
2.   Ibid., 61.
3.   Ibid., 67–68.

Chapter 9.   Winning the Battle over Greed

1.   William Barclay, *The Gospel of Luke, The Daily Study Bible* (p. 168). Reproduced by kind permission of The Saint Andrew Press, Edinburgh, Scotland.
2.   Martha Snell Nicholson, "Treasures," *Ivory Palaces* (Chicago: Moody Press, 1949).

Chapter 10.   Slaying the Dragon of Traditionalism

1.   e. e. cummings, in a letter written in 1955, as cited in *You Bring the Confetti* by Luci Swindoll (Waco, TX: Word Books, 1986), 35–36.
2.   Robert M. Brown, *Quote Unquote,* ed. Lloyd Cory (Wheaton, IL: Victor Books, a division of SP Publications, 1977), 341.
3.   Jaroslav Pelikan, *The Vindication of Tradition* (New Haven, CT: Yale University Press, 1984), 65.

4. From *The Problem of Wine Skins* (pp. 189–190) by Howard A. Snyder. Copyright 1975. Used by permission of InterVarsity Press, Downers Grove, IL.

Chapter 11.   Removing the Blahs from Today

1. C. S. Lewis, *The Screwtape Letters* (London: Geoffrey Bles, 1942), 65, 143.
2. From *No One's Perfect* (pp. 21–22) by Betty Carlson, copyright © 1976. Used by permission of Good News Publishers/Crossway Books, Westchester, IL 60153.
3. Unpublished sermon by Dr. Ray Stedman, pastor of Peninsula Bible Church, Palo Alto, CA. Used by permission.
4. From *Tell Me Again, Lord, I Forget* (p. 83) by Ruth Harms Calkin. Published by Tyndale House Publishers, Inc. © 1974. Used by permission.

Chapter 12.   Becoming a Model of Joyful Generosity

1. Sir Winston Churchill, as cited in *Familiar Quotations* (New York: Little, Brown and Company, 1955), 746, 743, 745.
2. Ron Blue, *Master Your Money* (Nashville, TN: Thomas Nelson Publishers, 1986).

Chapter 13.   Standing Alone When Outnumbered

1. Taken from *Rebirth of America* (p. 77). Copyright © 1986 by The Arthur S. DeMoss Foundation, Saint David's Center, Saint David, PA 19087. Edited by Robert Flood. All rights reserved. Used by permission.
2. Donald Grey Barnhouse, *Romans, Vol IX, God's Discipline* (Grand Rapids, MI: Wm. B. Eerdmans Publishing Co., 1964), 8.
3. From *The Log,* published by The Navigators, Colorado Springs, CO (date unknown).

Chapter 14.   Standing Tall When Tested

1. From *Hide or Seek* (pp. 126–127, revised edition) by James Dobson, copyright © 1974, 1979 by Fleming H. Revell Company, Old Tappan, NJ. Used by permission.
2. Merrill F. Unger, *Unger's Bible Dictionary* (Chicago: Moody Press, 1966), 172.
3. Billy Graham, *Faithful Witness, Urbana '84* (Downers Grove, IL: InterVarsity Press, 1985), 139.

Chapter 15.   Standing Firm When Discouraged

1.   From *Psalms of My Life* (p.29) by Joseph Bayly. Published by Tyndale House Publishers, Inc. © 1969. Used by permission.

2.   F. B. Meyer, *Christ in Isaiah* (Grand Rapids, MI: Zondervan Publishing House, 1950), 9–10.

Chapter 16.   Standing Strong When Tempted

1.   From *What Wives Wish Their Husbands Knew about Women* (pp. 114–116) by James Dobson. Published by Tyndale House Publishers, Inc., Copyright © 1975. Used by permission.

2.   Dietrich Bonhoeffer, *Temptation* (London: SCM Press, 1955), 33–34.

3.   J. Oswald Sanders, *Robust in Faith* (Chicago: Moody Press, 1965), 102.

4.   Chris T. Zwingelberg, "Sin's Peril," *Leadership* 8 (Winter 1987): 41. Used by permission.

5.   LeRoy Eims, *Be the Leader You Were Meant to Be* (Wheaton, IL: Victor Books, a division of SP Publications, 1975), 105.

Conclusion.   Who's Appraising Your Excellence?

1.   Isaac D'Israeli, *Curiosities of Literature* [1834] "On Quotation," as cited in *Familiar Quotations,* ed. John Bartlett (Boston: Little, Brown and Company, 1980), 417.

2.   Norman Cousins, *Albert Schweitzer's Mission* (New York: W. W. Norton & Company, 1985), 135, 138, 140. Used by permission.

Other Word Products
by Charles R. Swindoll

BIBLE STUDY GUIDES

Christ's Agony and Ecstasy
Coming to Terms with Sin
Contagious Christianity
Daniel
Dropping Your Guard
Excellence in Ministry
Galatians: Letter of Liberation
Hebrews, Volume 1
Hebrews, Volume 2
Improving Your Serve
Jesus, Our Lord
Joseph: From Pit to Pinnacle
Koinonia
Learning to Walk by Grace
Letters to Churches
Living on the Ragged Edge
Moses
Living Above the Level of Mediocrity
Old Testament Characters
Prophecy
Proverbs
Relating to Others in Love

BOOKTRAX (Books on Cassette)

Improving Your Serve. 201–0503–007
Living on the Ragged Edge. 201–0508–009
Living Above the Level of Mediocrity. 201–0514–009
Strengthening Your Grip. 201–0509–005

FILMS

People of Refuge. This single film provides practical examples for the individual and for the church to become genuinely compassionate and friendly to the lonely and distressed. (also available on video cassette)

Strengthening Your Grip. Six powerful films that speak to all Christians about making the right choices, living adventurously as the years advance, enjoying leisure without guilt, taking true godliness seriously, overcoming negative thinking, and establishing a biblical attitude toward authority.

MULTIPLE AUDIO CASSETTE PACKAGES

Dropping Your Guard. This 13-week curriculum resource is designed to help build relationships. Based on Chuck Swindoll's bestselling book, it investigates what it takes for Christians to drop their masks and relate openly and lovingly to each other in order for the church to provide the strong mutual support Christ intended. Includes twelve addresses by the author, tape transcript, member's study guide, and the hardcover book, *Dropping Your Guard.* 201–0733–002

Growing Pains. In this four-cassette package, Chuck Swindoll addresses eight of the most difficult and frustrating tests in life: failure, misunderstanding, loss, mistakes, weakness, fear, monotony, waiting. 201–0711–009

Improving Your Serve. This biblical concept of servanthood, as modeled by Jesus Christ, is discussed in relation to today's "look out for number one" world. Includes twelve audio cassettes in a vinyl binder, complete printed transcripts, discussion guide. 201–0691–008

Koinonia: Authentic Fellowship. In this four-cassette package, Chuck Swindoll addresses the issue of "fellowship," the authentic display of love and acceptance, care and compassion, support and forgiveness. 201–0785–002

Living on the Ragged Edge. This series of 24 addresses (on 12 audio cassettes) draws a striking parallel between Solomon's story in the Book of Ecclesiastes and today's overworked, aggressive, success-oriented executive who attempts to find satisfaction in his or her achievement alone. 201–0780–000

Strengthening Your Grip. Sixteen hard-hitting addresses on the essentials of life: priorities, involvement, purity, integrity, prayer, godliness, money, discipleship, the family, and more. Twelve cassettes in a vinyl binder with complete transcripts and discussion/study questions. 201–0707–001

Strengthening Your Grip. The sure foothold and firm grip on biblical essentials in an aimless world, described in the author's film series and bestselling book, are now available in this challenging four-cassette album. 201-0732-006

SINGLE CASSETTES

Adolescents in Adult Bodies. Swindoll analyzes three biblical characters who reflected the "Peter Pan Syndrome" then illustrates the relevance of this problem in today's society. He equips us to recognize and confront this syndrome. 201-0222-733

Attitudes: Choosing the Food You Serve Your Mind. Swindoll's outstanding address on "Attitudes" from the film series *Strengthening Your Grip* is excerpted here on cassette. With warm wit, he addresses our tendency to worry about things over which we have no control, and helps us focus on the positive. 201-0190-734

Dropping Your Guard. With material from the power-packed opening chapter of his bestselling book, Chuck Swindoll challenges us to drop the masks and break the bonds of fear which keep us from relating to others. 201-0181-735

Improving Your Serve. The meaning, challenge, and rewards of true servanthood are discussed by Charles R. Swindoll in this audio cassette based on Mark 10:45. 201-0146-735

Influence That Inspires. Chuck Swindoll speaks to business and professional people, as well as everyone who is in a position of responsibility, about the practical dimension of leadership. Chuck explains how leadership that is loving, sensitive, and affirming of people can exercise an inspiring influence. 201-0209-737

Kingdom Authority. On this Life Lifter cassette, Chuck Swindoll emphasizes the importance of God as ruler of all things in life—in our becoming the kind of Christian who wants to embrace the simple purpose of God. 201-0232-739

Knowing God: Life's Major Pursuit. In this Life-Lifter cassette, Chuck Swindoll points out that more so than ever before people are seeking more possessions, more desires, more success. But why, even when these goals are realized, does an ache, an empty voice remain? With powerful biblical insight, Chuck answers: Because none of those goals were designed to be our major pursuit. Then, he again turns to Scripture to reveal that which is life's most significant and satisfying pursuit. 201-0216-733

People of Refuge. Using many practical examples, Chuck Swindoll helps us become a supportive fellowship of compassionate human beings by showing how we can provide genuine friendship to the lonely and comfort to those in distress. *People of Refuge* is a powerful reminder of our responsibility to communicate a love that convicts without condemning and heals without scolding. 201-0198-735

Strategic Use of the Mind. A discussion of capturing your mind for Christ by replacing carnal thoughts with scriptural truths, with emphasis on the importance of Scripture memory. 201-0156-730

Strengthening Your Grip on Money. On this timely single audio cassette, Charles Swindoll points out the lack of contentment among successful people today and urges Christians to learn to be content with what they have. 201-0176-715

Success: A Godly Perspective. On this Life Lifter cassette Chuck explores the marks of authentic Christianity in ministry and servanthood. 201-0237-730

VIDEO

Godliness. (Film 4 of the *Strengthening Your Grip* Film Series) Ever wonder if you can get too much religion? Dr. Swindoll believes so, stating that zealousness is not godliness. Tapping the source of true godliness is his goal for us, as he explains how to regain and maintain our "delight in the Lord." (52 minutes) 801-0102-792

People of Refuge. With many practical examples, Charles Swindoll tells how you and your church can become a supportive fellowship of compassionate human beings who provide genuine friendship to the lonely and comfort to those in distress. (60 minutes) 801-2800-799